Figurative Thinking and Foreign Language Learning

Figurative Thinking and Foreign Language Learning

Jeannette Littlemore
University of Birmingham

and

Graham Low
University of York

First published in 2006 by
PALGRAVE MACMILLAN
Houndmills, Basingstoke, Hampshire RG21 6XS and
175 Fifth Avenue, New York, N.Y. 10010
Companies and representatives throughout the world.

PALGRAVE MACMILLAN is the global academic imprint of the Palgrave Macmillan division of St. Martin's Press, LLC and of Palgrave Macmillan Ltd. Macmillan® is a registered trademark in the United States, United Kingdom and other countries. Palgrave is a registered trademark in the European Union and other countries.

ISBN-13: 978–1–4039–9602–2 hardback
ISBN-10: 1–4039–9602–4 hardback

This book is printed on paper suitable for recycling and made from fully managed and sustained forest sources.

A catalogue record for this book is available from the British Library.

Library of Congress Cataloging-in-Publication Data

Littlemore, Jeannette.
    Figurative thinking and foreign language learning / Jeannette Littlemore and Graham Low.
        p. cm.
    Includes bibliographical references and index.
    ISBN 1–4039–9602–4
        1. Figures of speech – Study and teaching. 2. Metaphor – Study and teaching. 3. Languages, Modern – Study and teaching. 4. Thought and thinking. I. Low, Graham. II. Title.

P301.5.F53L58 2006
808.0071—dc22   2005057508

10 9 8 7 6 5 4 3 2 1
15 14 13 12 11 10 09 08 07 06

Printed and bound in Great Britain by
Antony Rowe Ltd, Chippenham and Eastbourne

For Dan, Joe, Oscar, Ros, Chris and Paul, with love

Contents

Part I   Figurative Thinking

Part II   Figurative Thinking and Communicative Language Ability

Part III   Conclusions

List of Tables

List of Figures

List of Boxes

Acknowledgements

It is our pleasure to thank the many people who have helped in the preparation of this book. First we would like to thank Jill Lake for her constant encouragement, and the anonymous reviewers whose comments have been very valuable. On a personal level, we owe a great deal to Dan Malt and Ros Low, who have read through countless versions of the various chapters, and with whom we have engaged in many insightful discussions.

We would also like to thank the following colleagues for all their helpful suggestions: John Barnden, Maureen Bell, Frank Boers, Lynne Cameron, Alice Deignan, Martin Hewings, Susan Hunston, Philip King, Almut Koester, Fiona MacArthur, Emma Marsden, Rosamund Moon, David Oakey, Elena Semino, Sophia Skoufaki, Malcolm Wren and Zazie Todd.

We are also grateful to the following language informants, who provided us with valuable information about the ways in which their languages work: Rafael Alejo, Didier Apelbaum, Andy Arleo, Zoltan Dörnyei, Valerie Leick, Amornrat Luangsaengthong, Oru Mohiuddin, Yasuo Nakatani, Makiko Okazaki, Ana Roldan Rejos, Ayumi Takahashi, Mika Tatsumoto and Wang Weiqun.

We would like to express our gratitude to all the students who participated in the studies at the University of Birmingham and the Université Libre de Bruxelles.

The authors and publisher are grateful to the following for permission to reproduce extracts from copyright material:

Brian Patten (c/o Rogers, Coleridge and White, 20 Powis Mews, London, W11 1JN) for permission to reproduce his poem *Hair today: no her tomorrow.*

Celia Roberts of Kings College London and Director of the Patients with Limited English and Doctors in General Practice (PLEDGE) project, who kindly gave permission to use the data from the project.

Equinox publishing, for permission to reprint an extract from Cameron, L. and Stelma, J. (2005) 'Metaphor Clusters in Discourse: Methodological Issues', *Journal of Applied Linguistics*, 1 (2), 107–136.

Lawrence Erlbaum Associates for permission to reprint an extract from Corts, D.P. and Pollio, H.R. (1999) 'Spontaneous Production of

Figurative Language and Gesture in College Lectures', *Metaphor and Symbol*, 14 (2), 81–100 (p. 91), and an extract from Cameron, L. and Deignan, A. (2003) 'Using Large and Small Corpora to Investigate Tuning Devices Around Metaphor in Spoken Discourse', *Metaphor and Symbol*, 18 (3), 149–160.

Lee McIntyre, for permission to reprint an extract from McIntyre, L. (2004) Review of 'Making Social Science Matter: Why Social Inquiry Fails and How It can Succeed Again', *Philosophy of Science*, 71, 418–421.

Oxford University Press, for permission to develop a number of ideas that were originally presented in Littlemore, J. and Low, G. (forthcoming). 'Metaphoric competence, second language learning and communicative language ability. *Applied Linguistics;* and for permission to reprint Bachman's (1990) model of Communicative Language Ability, from Oxford Applied Linguistics: *Fundamental Considerations in Language Testing* by Lyle F. Bachman © Lyle F. Bachman, 1990.

The Economist, for permission to reprint an extract from 'What the Squid Did' (11 June 1988), p. 129.

The New Scientist, for permission to reprint an extract from Walker, G. 'Ice magic' (12 April 2003), pp. 30–34.

Introduction

We hope you will actively enjoy reading this book and that it will stimulate you to carry out research into the learning and teaching of figurative language and/or to design and test out better instructional materials.

Why have we written the book?

In recent years there has been a growing interest in the problems that figurative language poses for foreign language learners, how learners cope with figurative language, how they learn it, and what sort of instruction facilitates the ability to communicate in the short term, and learn in the long term. In order to address some of these issues, applied linguistic researchers have begun to explore some of the *linguistic* aspects of figurative language. They have developed reliable research methods that make use of naturalistic settings and data, including the use of corpora and authentic texts. Other researchers have taken a more *cognitive* approach, resulting in a number of new theories, many of which follow on from Lakoff and colleagues' work in the 1980s on conceptual metaphor and metonymy. These two areas of interest are not necessarily mutually supportive, as much of the theorising at a conceptual level does not rely on naturally occurring data, whereas much of the linguistic work has focused on non-conceptual aspects of figurative language. It is therefore a good time to put together the findings from both areas of interest, review the resulting applied research base, and argue for an approach to teaching that is consistent with it.

What is the aim of the book?

Our aim is to consider what foreign language learners for the most part need to learn, to review the empirical evidence concerning teaching and/or learning figurative language, and to develop a set of instructional and self-help ideas, which we group under the umbrella term 'figurative thinking' and which we try at various points to illustrate with real-life examples. At a secondary level, our aim is to present ideas and research in language that is as jargon free as we can make it and to be honest in cases where we can find no research studies, where theory and research do not match up, or where research findings disagree. Given the abstractness and relative opacity of some recent theorising about metaphor and metonymy, we hope readers will find our approach refreshing rather than simplistic! The opening sentence about enjoyment was meant seriously.

Who do we hope will read the book?

While we are able to suggest some 'answers' to language learning problems, the research base for figurative language remains minimal compared with that for other areas of foreign language acquisition. Indeed in some areas, particularly connected with the issue of learning how to control figurative language in discourse, it is almost non-existent. The ideal reader is therefore someone who needs to be informed about the current state of relevant research, but also someone who is not trying to find a set of ready-made answers. Rather, he or she is someone who can pick up the ideas and run with them, either carrying out more and better research, or else developing better teaching materials, reference materials and classroom procedures. We would therefore hope that the book is read and used by teachers, materials designers and language testers, as well as applied linguists and postgraduate students.

What is the scope of the book?

When we started, we believed that we could cover all the main figures of speech and thought. However, it became increasingly clear that (a) there was far too much linguistic and conceptual data to fit into a short book and (b) there was virtually no foreign language instruction (or learning) research involving figures other than metaphor. The result is that the book focuses primarily on metaphor and (very much) secondarily on metonymy. Given the exciting theoretical work that has appeared recently on metonymy by authors like Barcelona (2001), Radden (2005), Otal Campo *et al.* (2005) and Ruiz de Mendoza and Otal Campo (2003), we feel badly about the relative backgrounding of metonymy – but it remains the case that research into the role of metonymy in foreign language teaching is almost non-existent.

A word is also needed on the theoretical position taken. The field of metaphor in particular is currently characterised by warring territorial groups who take few prisoners. We have tried to maintain the role of educationalists and, as such, to steer a middle course between conceptual theorists, corpus analysts, discourse analysts and psychologists. Our concern is with foreign language learners, not the desirability of adhering to a single theory.

How is it organised?

The book is in three parts. Part 1 (Chapters 1–4) sets the scene and explores the main concepts and processes we want to use. Part 2 (Chapters 5 to 9) shows how figurative language plays an important part in all aspects of communicative competence. Part 3 (Chapter 10) pulls together the main pedagogical ideas and examines a number of areas that impact directly and concretely on the learner.

In Part 1, Chapter 1 offers a rapid overview of relevant aspects of metaphor and metonymy and outlines what we mean by 'figurative thinking'. In Chapter 2, we try and connect figurative language with foreign language learning, using the context of vocabulary development, as this is the area that most of the recent intervention research has focused on. We argue that even though much of the research evidence is based, perhaps inevitably, on fairly restricted forms of teaching, it broadly supports the usefulness of figurative thinking as a teaching–learning tool. In Chapter 3 the argument is expanded to examine psychological processes like *noticing, schema activation, associative fluency, analogical reasoning,* and *image formation* that language learners need to employ in the production and interpretation of figurative language, and we look at these processes 'in action' in language teaching settings. In Chapter 4, we assess how far figurative thinking can be used without a teacher to develop learner autonomy. The discussion includes an examination of barriers to comprehension or learning such as the cultural nature of encyclopaedic knowledge, semantic opaqueness, the student's own vocabulary limitations, learning style, and the investment that is required in terms of mental effort and time.

Part 2 of the book, the discussion about the contribution that figurative language makes to communicative competence and the need for teachers and learners to come to terms with it, is loosely structured around Bachman's (1990) model of communicative competence. We are well aware that this model suffers from being a classificatory rather than a process-based account (Skehan, 1998) and that the categories are not always as distinct as they might be, but it is well known to educationalists and, most importantly, it was designed for teachers and testers to check that they had not omitted any major topics. Chapter 5 briefly introduces the model and then extends Bachman's view by discussing the relationship between figurative language and culture, dialect and register. We suggest ways in which foreign language learners might be helped to employ figurative language to enter new speech and discourse communities, and consider the often-overlooked mismatch between 'culture' as reflected in language and 'culture' as something relevant to the learner. In Chapter 6, we move on to illocutionary competence, and look at the ways in which figurative language can be used to convey opinions, build relationships, manipulate one's audience, control the behaviour of others, and create and extend one's environment for humorous or aesthetic purposes. We also suggest how foreign language learners might be helped to use figurative language to perform these functions. Chapter 7 examines patterns of figurative language use in discourse. We select three key topics: figurative clusters or bursts, topic transition, and overarching metaphors. We attempt to draw a number of educational conclusions at regular points through the chapter, and we consider some potentially useful teaching procedures. Chapter 8 focuses on grammatical competence. Again, we select a small set of key areas from the many that have been proposed in the literature (demonstratives, prepositions, phrasal verbs, aspect, modality and grammatical 'patterning') and try to balance the conceptual and linguistic considerations – the opposition between the two schools of thought is perhaps at its starkest here. Chapter 9 examines strategic competence. This chapter is somewhat shorter than the others simply because the more interactive aspects of strategic competence have already been discussed. Discussion is therefore limited to compensation strategies, and we look in particular at questions of word coinage, circumlocution and creative transfer. The position we take is close to that of Dörnyei (2005) who emphasises the role of focussed effort and active engagement by the learner.

In Part 3 (Chapter 10), we assess how a focus on figurative language can be incorporated into mainstream language teaching methodologies, and evaluate the coverage that is given to metaphor and metonymy in published language teaching materials.

Throughout the book, we will use the term 'L1' to refer to a learner's first language (i.e. their mother tongue), and the term 'L2' to refer to the language that they are learning.

Part I
Figurative Thinking

1
What is 'Figurative Thinking'?

1.1 Introductory comments

This book has three aims. The first is to demonstrate that metaphor and metonymy are central to language and language use and that foreign language learners really do need to engage with them. The second aim is to explore *how* learners might usefully engage with them, in order to understand, produce and learn a foreign language. As there is much less systematic empirical research into learning figurative language than learning other aspects of a foreign language, our third aim is to identify what teachers, textbook writers and researchers need to focus on in the coming years.

Part of the book accordingly involves a review of relevant empirical research, where this exists. We draw on linguistic, psychological and educational research to develop a flexible approach to thinking about or querying figurative language, which we call 'figurative thinking' and which can be used by teachers and learners to deal with language which is potentially, as well as clearly, figurative. Our basic thesis is that since learners do not have native speaker competence in the target language, they are not always able to process figurative language in the same way as native speakers do. At times, they may benefit from taking a more analytical, 'enquiring' approach, which we label 'figurative thinking'. Figurative thinking is thus quite intentionally a pedagogic construct.

To show what we are talking about, we begin with a short extract from an article in an academic (*Applied Linguistics*) journal:

I have anchored this survey on two generally accepted observations about formulaic language. The first originates with Saussure ... *Fighting the tide of Chomskyan linguistics*, the same idea was expressed by Becker (1975) who spoke of 'ready-made frameworks on which to hang the expression of our ideas'. (Wray, 2000: p. 32; underlining ours)

Most native speakers of English will already have encountered the expression 'fighting the tide' or a similar-sounding expression (such as 'holding back the tide') before, and will therefore process it fairly automatically, understand what Wray means more or less straight away, and move on. On the other hand, readers who have not encountered 'fighting the tide' before, or non-native speakers of English who do not have an equivalent expression in their own language, may need to analyse it a little more deeply, as its meaning may not be entirely transparent to them. Indeed, as we might expect, research has shown that language learners do tend to slow down for longer periods of time than native speakers when reading prefabricated chunks such as this (Underwood *et al.*, 2004). One reason for this, particularly where *figurative* multiword items are concerned, might be that the language learners are attempting to analyse their individual components, or engage in some sort of querying routine.

So what form might such a querying routine take when a learner is faced with the expression 'fighting the tide'? If they are already familiar with the words 'fighting' and 'tide', a simple solution would be just to think more about 'fighting'. In a physical fight you try to stop an opponent hurting or killing you, and where the fighting is figurative, the opponent is often negative or undesirable, like cancer. So 'Chomskyan linguistics' is probably being evaluated as something undesirable and possibly something destructive.

It is of course perfectly possible (but less necessary) for a native speaker to adopt such an enquiring approach, if they want to. They might for instance spend a moment thinking about the features of a tide: it is a characteristic of something bigger with some substance, namely a sea or ocean, it comes in and then goes out, it is regular and predictable, it is unstoppable, it is caused by the moon, it is dangerous if you are on the beach. Is the author saying Chomskyan Linguistics is popular? That the popularity is predictable? That the fashion cannot be stopped? That the fashion may be swamping other theories now, but it will go away in time? The reader may not be sure, but he or she can make an ad hoc working decision.

Some readers might also wonder whether they were supposed to make a connection with a literary reference ('a tide in the affairs of men', or 'fighting the good fight'), or even with King Canute, the English monarch who vainly ordered the tide to stop. Is the clause then a sarcastic aside, or a cry of philosophical despair? And if the latter, is it by Becker or Wray? We are not saying that all readers of this text, or even all readers who are unfamiliar with the expression, will necessarily analyse it in such a detailed manner as this. We are simply saying that it is *possible* to analyse the expression in such a way, and that this type of analysis may aid comprehension, particularly for the foreign language learner.

Alison Wray, as the writer, also had choices to make at both the editing and drafting stage. Should she be explicit about whether the negativity is hers or Becker's? How negative can one be in an academic paper? How many words was the aside/evaluation worth? When would it start to deflect the reader's focus from the main message? Should she use a complex image (fight + tide) rather than a simple one (e.g., combat)? Would it actually be preferable to avoid such a visualisable image? Should she use words that evoke other events (like Canute, who is most definitely evoked for us by the choice of 'fighting the tide')? Having already used 'anchored', should she use or avoid another marine image?

This example suggests several important points:

- Figurative language occurs in even the most serious of academic texts.
- The full meaning of an expression may not always be transparent from the context.
- The context may rule out some possible meanings, but essentially both reader and writer still have to decide (whether consciously or subconsciously) which of the remaining ones are most pertinent.
- Much of the decision making will be subconscious and hard for an analyst to access. Even so, we would predict variation in nature and length depending on previous knowledge and experience, and readers will definitely vary when deciding how much effort to expend and when to stop processing.
- It is reasonably easy for an analyst to construct a range of explicit verbal query routines designed to suggest likely meanings or possible links to different degrees of detail. The routines may involve establishing how words like 'fight' are generally used in English, what a 'tide' tends to consist of and what other notions it is associated with, what other expressions or events 'tide' evokes' and what exactly is intended by the abstract cover label 'linguistics'. They may also involve wondering whether there is any significance to the clustering of two marine images.
- Examining what a marine tide involves in order to establish what 'tide' means in the text essentially invokes *metaphor*, while asking

whether Canute is relevant to the discussion invokes *metonymy*. We explain both terms later, but for now we simply note how both figures of speech work closely together.

Foreign language learners have the advantage over monolingual native speakers that they can call on knowledge and experience of other languages or language-use situations, but in other respects, they tend to face a more complex set of difficulties when it comes to figurative language. This is because:

(a) They may be unaware of conventions governing when and how to use it (Low, 1988; 1999a).
(b) They may be unaware of cultural connotations that need to be invoked in order to understand it.
(c) They may not have access to a repertoire of prefabricated, and readily understood, figurative multiword items. They may therefore try and understand each word separately (e.g., Bortfeld, 2003).

Learners might thus need to query the intended meaning more consciously and more often than native speakers. Indeed, the notion of a query routine as an aid to decision making seems eminently suited to foreign language learners. Moreover, the ability to control relatively easily for length, explicitness and degree of detail suggests that teachers can intervene helpfully when learners get stuck. We wish to explore in this book whether learners are able to cope with exploratory and decision-making routines when dealing with figurative language. If they *are* able to do so, we would like to know which routines work best and which aid learning rather than (or in addition to) simply facilitating communication.[1] We are also interested in whether these routines are facilitated by trainable psychological skills such as associative fluency and how far learners can successfully apply them on their own, without a teacher.

We coin the term 'figurative thinking' to denote the use of a query routine which assumes that an unknown expression might be figurative, or which asks what the implications of using a figurative expression might be. The term is adapted from Gibbs (1994) who was primarily interested in psychological processes employed by native speakers. We try to approach the concepts of figurative language, figurative thinking and learning in an unbiased way; we will describe different theories about them, but we do not adhere *a priori* to any particular one. This may be felt to be a weakness by some readers, but we would argue that it is more of an advantage, in that it allows us freedom to take a more

---

Box 1.1 Japanese teachers' discussion of the expression 'skirt around' (Littlemore 2004a)

Teacher	When we're teaching grammar at lower levels, we sometimes skirt around the hardest topics.
Student A	What is 'to skirt'?
Teacher	What do you think it means?
Student B	Hiding them? [Stands up. Mimes a skirt shape i.e., starts off moving hands down from waist to knees and gradually moving outward, then moves hands round knees about 20 centimetres away from knees, in a circular motion, following the hem of an imaginary skirt.]
Student C	[Looking at Student B's mime] Go round?
Student D	[Also looking at Student B's mime] Avoid?

---

objective stand and to only promote theoretical notions where there is empirical evidence to support them.

It may be wondered at this point whether the conceptualisation of figurative thinking as some sort of routine is too narrow or artificial to be useful. We argue that it is not, as long as it is allowed to encompass examples like the following (from Littlemore, 2004a: p. 64), where gesture is used in place of words and not all the inferences, or connections with prior learning, are made explicit. Box 1.1 is part of a discussion between one of us (Littlemore) and a group of Japanese language teachers on an in-service training course in the United Kingdom (May 2003). In a collaborative attempt at identifying meaning, two of the students (C and D) made figurative interpretations of a visual clue that was provided inadvertently by one of their classmates (student B). By doing so, they were able to ascertain the meaning of the expression. Student B appears to have picked up on one of the salient features of a skirt: that it serves to hide, or cover, what is underneath. He then uses mime in an attempt to work out the meaning. This strategy does not appear to help him, but it does seem to help the student sitting opposite (student C), who suggests 'go round'. Student C appears to bring together, possibly subconsciously, the idea from the mime that a skirt is an outer-garment which goes round the knees, and the original word 'around'. This triggers the suggestion of 'avoid' by student D. Student D either knows one of the figurative meanings of 'go around', in which case C's verbalisation allows him to use a semantic analogy, or else he computes the likely sense of the expression directly. Although the student performing the mime is not able to work out the meaning of the expression for himself, his mime provides a valuable clue for the other students in the group, illustrating the powerful learning effect that collaboration can have in the language classroom. The students did not identify the true etymology of 'skirt', but this is unimportant; the point is that they persisted in querying 'skirt' by using their prior understanding of the word (and concept) and reached a contextually adequate understanding. A teacher could develop this more explicitly, but there is enough systematicity to see it as a routine.

Having stated the aims of the book, this first chapter continues with a short discussion about restricting figurative language to metaphor and metonymy, followed by more detailed overviews of the two figures. We use these to create educationally relevant constructs for metaphoric thinking and metonymic thinking.

1.2   Figure and figurative

Greek and Roman philosophers were generally agreed on the importance of appropriate figurative language to drama, poetry, courtroom speeches and other formal speech events. The aims were to dignify, clarify, intensify and persuade. The Roman philosopher Quintilian famously defined a *figura* in the first century AD as an artful deviation from normal spoken usage.[2] Deviations involved changes of form or word order ('schemes'), or changes of meaning or thought ('tropes'), where the intended or disguised meaning had to be worked out by the receiver (Corbett, 1990: p. 425). The ten or so tropes included over- and understatement (litotes and hyperbole), irony, puns, metaphor and metonymy. Despite the recognition as time passed of more and more figures, metaphor and metonymy maintained a position of key importance, 'cluster[ing] at the centre of the figurative space' (Levin, 1977: p. 80).

Recent research by authors like Lakoff (1993), Kövecses (1995) and Radden (2005) has shown that metaphor and metonymy are not restricted to formal speech events or poetic style; they are heavily involved in everyday language that few people other than linguists would see as figurative. They also occur at most levels of language, from phonology to discourse, they involve the construction of basic frameworks whereby cultures and individuals conceptualise and describe the world (Kimmel, 2004), and they are a central factor in language change (Sweetser, 1990). These findings reinforce the importance of metaphor and metonymy, but they rather destroy the 'artful deviation' argument for treating the different 'figures of speech/thought' as a coherent rhetorical group.

Language learning research has also focused on metaphor (and, to a lesser extent, metonymy), with the result that almost nothing is known about the problems of teaching, say, irony or hyperbole in a foreign language.

Because of the importance of metaphor and metonymy to language and thought, because they are, as we will show, so closely intertwined and because more is known about their pedagogical implications, we have chosen to restrict this book to them. Other figures, particularly hyperbole, will be mentioned at times, but in a secondary way. This inevitably causes some problems with the words 'figure' and 'figurative'. In most cases, and particularly when we talk about 'figurative thinking', we are referring to working with aspects of metaphor or metonymy, or (as with 'fighting the tide') both. Thus figurative implies a degree of semantic or conceptual reorganisation. At times, however, 'figure' and 'figurative' are broadened; hopefully these cases should be clear from context.

1.3 Metaphor

Metaphor involves treating (or describing) one entity in terms of another, apparently different entity. It often serves some sort of evaluative function. For example, when Margaret Atwood (2003: p. xxii) wrote 'Writing has to do with darkness and the desire ... to enter it ... and to bring something back out to the light' or 'writing is motivated ... by a desire to make the risky trip to the Underworld, and to bring something or someone back from the dead' (ibid., p. 140), the two entities are in each case clearly specified: writing and either a journey through darkness or a journey to the land of the dead. Both images carry ideas of the unknown and for many people a sense of fear. Such clear specification tends to occur more in literary or educational texts than in 'everyday' writing or talk. Thus if a journalistic text suggests that the Japanese Government is putting taxes on car imports in order to create *a level playing field* for Japanese car manufacturers, the reader is presented with just one entity, the playing field, and is forced to guess that, if the topic is commerce not sport, the other entity must relate to something like 'the Japanese car market'. This ad hoc or hypothesised entity 'car market' is then temporarily understood as a level playing field. If you are aware that a football, cricket or bowls team can be at a disadvantage if the playing field slopes at their end, then you can easily understand that the focus is on competitive fairness and that there is an implicit evaluation that things are currently not fair. But of course you need a degree of cultural knowledge about sports and about expected behaviour to add this interpretation.

Some expressions are more obviously metaphoric than others. If someone says 'You *gave* me the idea; I *took* your conceptualisation of the car and then *had* a *revelation*', 'revelation' is highly likely to be metaphoric unless the designer really did believe he had been divinely inspired. Giving and taking ideas is somewhat less obviously metaphoric, though clearly one cannot transfer them like a spanner or a Christmas present. 'Having' a revelation is even less obvious, though one could argue that turning ideas and revelations into objects that one can possess and transfer represents a way to cope linguistically with vague abstract notions; without such a reformulation, it would be hard to talk at length about anything. Non-salient metaphor can often be brought to life without great difficulty, say in a joke or ironic comment like 'You took my idea as if it was a free gift!', so it can sometimes be useful to think about words that are potentially metaphoric.

Intuitively, one tends to think of metaphors with Grice (1975) as the identification of literal untruths from which the listener tries to construct statements (or 'implicatures') that fit the 'be truthful' maxim. This immediately encounters obstacles, however, as negative metaphors ('He's no oil painting!') are hardly 'untrue'. It also leads to problems with Wray's 'fighting the tide' (see before), as there is no way of telling precisely which 'overtones' are or are not 'true', or even which were intended. 'Is there really a tide (in the world as I know it, or in the world of the text)?' will thus prove a useful question to ask as part of an exploratory routine, but will often not prove sufficient.

If you are trying to decide if a word like 'tide' is metaphoric in a text, then a more useful approach is to see whether the word has one or two basic meanings which differ markedly from the contextual sense (the text concerns language, not seas or oceans). At times people will differ about whether a meaning is more basic and it is hard to establish a universal definition (Steen, 2005), but basic meanings tend to be more concrete and more closely connected with familiar human experience, in the sense of actual bodily experiences, interactions with physical objects, or culturally mediated events like making a fire and cooking (Gibbs, 2005). The basic meaning of tide is clearly related to the sea and bears little obvious relationship with fashion or trend.

A further point about metaphor when used in discourse (rather than as an isolated vocabulary item) is that not only can the boundary between metaphoric and non-metaphoric be unclear, but people frequently operate on both levels at the same time. Numerous advertisements rely on multiple levels, and indeed on the progressive recognition of them, but so do novels. For instance, 'My wedding day, I remember, was stormy' (Alina Reyes, 1993: p. 3), could be a comment about the weather or about the relationships between the people present at the wedding, or given the frequent symbolic linking of weather and events in novels, both.

Metaphoric thinking

Metaphoric thinking thus involves trying to determine whether, in a given context, two entities are to be treated as incongruous (or the relationship between the two needs some reorganisation), and if they are, deciding which aspects of the one are relevant to the other. This may require knowledge of the world, or specific cultural knowledge. The metaphoric thinking associated with these decisions is designed to help the listener understand what the speaker is trying to say about (here) linguistics, writing or car sales, and in many cases, how that speaker evaluates them. The result may not be as clear-cut as one hoped, but one can tailor the amount of effort to the perceived importance of the task.

Linguistic and conceptual metaphor

At this point, it is important to distinguish between 'linguistic metaphor' and 'conceptual metaphor'. It has to be said as a sort of advance warning that many researchers approach metaphor very much from one angle or the other. They thus emphasise their particular approach and tend to ignore the other. The result is that we can give a reasonably clear idea of both types of metaphor, but the precise relation between the two is unknown and at the time of writing is beginning to be seen as a major area of research.

The phrase *level playing field* is a linguistic metaphor, because it consists of three words concerning sport, in an utterance concerning a different topic, commerce. In this expression, the 'Japanese car market' is the *Topic*, the 'level playing field' is the *Vehicle*, and the reason for connecting the entities, such as 'games need a flat terrain to be fair' is called the *Ground* (Richards, 1936; Brown, 1958).

In short, linguistic metaphors are words or expressions that are uttered or written. As such, they can be represented by any part of speech, not just nouns. You may immediately ask what you do if there is no overt Topic, as in the 'level playing field' example? We *hypothesised* 'car market' (see before) as a Topic, but by doing so we effectively moved beyond the realm of actual words into unclear territory. One recent well-known study of linguistic metaphor (Cameron, 2003) accepted the Topic/Vehicle distinction, but got round the problem of an unclear or absent Topic by treating Vehicle terms (e.g., 'level playing field') as the 'linguistic metaphors'. Thus in order to identify a linguistic metaphor, you just need a Vehicle term, plus a degree of incongruity with the surrounding text (ibid., pp. 10–11).

Our glib 'just need a Vehicle term' hides at least three problems which we will touch on here. First, it can prove difficult to identify the boundaries of a Vehicle in a precise way. In 'they discussed the topic in some depth', is the noun 'depth' the linguistic metaphor, or do we isolate the phrase 'in some depth'? Again, in 'He took a deep breath and resigned', is 'deep' a separate linguistic metaphor, or is it inside, and dependent on, a larger metaphor 'took a breath'? It is hard to find a principled way of deciding.

Second, the Vehicle can be just as indirect as the Topic. Perrine (1971) cites the line '*Sheathe* thy impatience' and notes that this only makes sense if the inferred Vehicle is a dagger or sword.

Third, in some cases, the metaphoric sense is more common than the literal sense (e.g., buttress) (Deignan, 1999a). In such cases, becomes hard to identify the metaphoric sense as being incongruous or not.

Despite these unresolved problems with the linguistic approach to metaphor, we will continue to draw on it in this book as it usefully allows us to focus on situations where a known word appears in a new context, with a slightly different or unexpected meaning. We are interested in discovering what second language learners do in situations such as these, as they are likely to occur on a regular basis as exposure to the target language increases (e.g., the Japanese teachers in Box 1.1 dealing with 'skirt'). We are particularly interested in looking at how learners are able to restructure their existing knowledge of the senses of the words and expressions to fit the new contexts, and in assessing the extent to which their efforts to do this contribute to their language learning.

Conceptual metaphors are different from linguistic metaphors. They are not linguistic expressions, but rather relationships like PEOPLE ARE PLANTS that underlie expressions, such as 'she's blooming' or 'he's a budding journalist'. The conceptual metaphor THEORIES ARE STRUCTURES is reflected in expressions, such as those in Box 1.2 from the *Bank of English* corpus.

Another common conceptual metaphor, PROGRESS THROUGH TIME IS FORWARD MOTION, leads to numerous expressions such as 'to move on', 'to plan ahead', 'back in the '60s' and 'reach a crossroads'. Here the expressions derive either from the static concept of a person facing a desired goal, or from the culturally elaborated dynamic concept of a journey towards the goal.

The two main components of a conceptual metaphor are by convention written in capital letters (e.g., THEORIES ARE STRUCTURES), and

---

Box 1.2   Linguistic expressions reflecting THEORIES ARE STRUCTURES

You have to *construct* your argument carefully.
But they now have *a solid weight of* scientific evidence.
The pecking order theory *rests on* sticky dividend policy.
This theory is *totally without foundation*.
In which case, the entire theory would have no *support*.
He has done his best to *undermine* the theory.
In an attempt *to build a formal theory of* underdevelopment the value of a scholarly theory should *stand or fall* on the character of the evidence.

---

constitute separate *domains*. The thing being described (e.g., THEORIES) constitutes the *target domain*, and the thing that is being used to describe it (e.g., STRUCTURES) constitutes the *source domain*. Lakoff (1993) describes the relationship between the two domains of a conceptual metaphor as a 'function', where specific features of the source domain are transferred to (or 'mapped onto') the target domain. So in the conceptual metaphor THEORIES ARE STRUCTURES, features of the source domain, STRUCTURES, such as needing a foundation or being built from component parts, are mapped onto the target domain of THEORIES, allowing us to talk about theories being *built* on assumptions and axioms, or *put together* by connecting smaller ideas. The relationship is thus one way; theories are treated as structures, but structures are not treated as theories – which would be a very different metaphor. Domains are thus broad, often complex, cluster-like categories that can provide a rich source of mappings. It is also reasonably easy to create a mental image of domains, leading Lakoff and others to talk, at times, of 'image schemas'. We return to image schemas in Chapter 3.

It is important to note that the precise words used to describe the two domains in a conceptual metaphor (like 'TIME' and 'MONEY') are not important, or at least not crucial. This is very different from the situation with linguistic metaphors, where it is the exact words that constitute the metaphor. Indeed, the whole point of a conceptual metaphor is that it stands apart from actual exemplars.

An important point to note about conceptual metaphors is that we can never be certain about our formulations. Essentially, we have to guess. We may sometimes dignify guessing with a label like 'generalising across examples', but the fact remains that it is still informed guesswork. It is very easy to invent conceptual metaphors to explain almost any behaviour; proving they represent anything more than the analyst's individual interpretation is quite another matter (Low, 1999b; 2003). For this reason, conceptual metaphor theory is considered to be somewhat controversial in some circles.

Despite the controversy surrounding conceptual metaphor theory, we will draw on it periodically throughout this book. One reason for this is that conceptual metaphors involve rich, complex domains, which are likely to vary across languages, in terms of the ways in which they are elaborated, and the linguistic expressions that they 'produce'. For example, although the conceptual metaphor THE BODY IS A CONTAINER FOR THE EMOTIONS appears to be universal, some cultures show a preference for 'locating' particular emotions in specific parts of the body. In Hungarian culture, for example, the emotion of anger is commonly 'located' in the head, whereas in Japanese culture anger can rise from the stomach via the chest to the head (Kovecses, 1995). One would expect these sorts of differences to have significant implications for foreign language learners, which we address in Chapter 5.

Finally, in this section, we need to rethink briefly the notion of 'literal meaning'. Four findings in particular destroy the idea that language is essentially non-figurative and that a literal account of a situation or event is perfectly feasible. These are (a) that numerous conventional 'everyday' words and expressions have one or more conceptual metaphors buried in them, (b) that a smallish set of conceptual metaphors concerning everyday human life and experience accounts for a very large number of expressions in many (probably all) languages, (c) that the metaphors often have discernable structure, in terms of transferred relationships and correspondences, and (d) that, as we show later, there is often a principled metaphoric connection between 'everyday' and poetic or literary utterances.

As 'literal meaning' tends to imply a total absence of metaphor (or metonymy), we will either avoid the word (preferring 'basic' in many cases) or, following Lakoff and Turner (1989: 119), just use it as shorthand to indicate cases where a particular metaphoric transfer has not taken place.

The relationship between linguistic and conceptual metaphor

It is difficult to identify the exact nature of the relationship between linguistic and conceptual metaphor. When faced with a linguistic metaphor in oral or written discourse, we may look for an underlying conceptual metaphor as a means of understanding it and/or working out connections with other parts of the discourse. The conceptual metaphor is unlikely, however, to have much connection with the part of speech used in the utterance, the syntactic structure or phraseology, the location of the expression (e.g., the end of a paragraph), or aspects of pronunciation like alliteration. Nor does it relate closely in many cases to the function which the metaphor is serving, such as an evaluation, toning down an extreme position, or flagging the irony in a statement. To take a simple example, when trying to interpret *'slavery was well on the road to extinction'* it may be helpful to think in terms of the conceptual metaphors PROGRESS IS FORWARD MOTION and PROGRESS IS A JOURNEY. But this by itself does not indicate why the author preferred 'road' to the less imagistic, but more alliterative, 'way', the less important 'path' or the more abstract 'route'. 'On the road' appears to suggest greater definiteness or momentum than the other words, and to have culturally positive overtones; taken together, these imply progress which would be harder to stop. Collocation and phraseology are therefore important components of linguistic metaphor.

At a more subtle level, linguistic metaphors often need to be matched to specific features of the local context, rather than to the more general, prototypical (or stereotypical) features that conceptual metaphors tend to employ. So someone might say *'my teacher's a bit of a witch'* simply to reflect the fact that she has a hooked nose. If the utterance had no context, however, the listener would be likely to employ stereotypical conceptual notions of vindictiveness, old age, ugliness, or hatred of children.

Once coined, linguistic metaphors have a distinct tendency to fossilise, or at least to be used in a relatively fixed form and with the same parts of speech. They also tend to collocate repeatedly with the same set of words (Deignan, 2005). This frequently aids interpretation by native speakers of a language, as it tends to keep metaphorical and non-metaphoric forms distinct. Thus while 'a hare' is an animal, 'he hared off' is unlikely to be describing a hare. The fixedness, part of speech and the collocates are, on the other hand, of very little concern to the creation of the conceptual metaphor A FAST PERSON IS A HARE.

The point is that isolating a conceptual metaphor does not exhaust the meaning of a linguistic metaphor, just as discussing the features of a linguistic metaphor may fail to establish the point of the metaphor and the complex conceptual structure underlying it. Metaphoric thinking may therefore at times involve the conscious activation of a conceptual metaphor, but additional mental processing will also be required.

Conventional and novel metaphoric expressions

With the major differences between linguistic and conceptual metaphor clarified, we now need to make a broad distinction between two types of metaphoric expression: *conventional* and *novel*. The conceptual metaphors underlying expressions such as 'to have an idea' (A MENTAL EVENT IS AN OBJECT) or 'the top of the profession' (UP IS GOOD/IMPORTANT) are highly conventional and generally overlooked in discussions of poetic metaphor. On the other hand, Lakoff and Turner (1989) have emphasised that large numbers of powerful metaphoric phrases in literary texts simply extend existing conceptual metaphors in innovative ways. Thus where Charlotte Brontë (1853, p. 373) suggests that there was silence because 'the storm had roared itself hoarse' she takes the conventional metaphor A STORM IS AN ANGRY PERSON/ANIMAL, or even EXTREME THREATENING NATURAL FORCE IS ANGER, and extends it to a fact that is *not* conventionally exploited, namely that shouting loudly for a long time can leave you exhausted and unable to speak. Even conventional expressions like 'have an idea' can be creatively extended by appealing to a corresponding conceptual metaphor, allowing us to talk, for example, about 'playing with an idea, twisting it in different directions, before throwing it in front of possible critics'.

We would also like to add an important point that will be developed at various points in the rest of the book. When writers use metaphoric expressions deliberately, they are likely to employ reasonably novel metaphor (or creatively extended conceptual metaphors), but there is no hard and fast connection between deliberateness and novelty (Cameron, 2003). A writer may write 'Jean was *in* love' simply because that is how you express things in English – we do not say 'on love', 'at love', 'within love' or 'under love'. However, the idea of being inside a closed container, or being surrounded by fluid, and feeling repressed *may* equally be an important part of the message. People may thus deliberately employ conventional metaphor. The main point that we would like to make is that conventional and novel metaphors may pose slightly different problems of production and interpretation, but they are essentially interconnected and overlap, and we will therefore deal with both in this book.

Questions of terminology regarding metaphor

We noted earlier that the expression 'a metaphor' can mean different things depending on whether you are talking linguistically or conceptually. As we will be drawing on both linguistic and conceptual perspectives, we will seek to avoid confusion by employing the term 'metaphoric expression' to talk about linguistic metaphor. However, on rare occasions we will use 'noun/verb metaphor' as shorthand for linguistic expressions. We also have a problem deciding when to use the linguistic labels 'Topic/Vehicle' and the conceptual labels 'Target/Source'. The terms 'target domain' and 'source domain' have the advantage of high-lighting the complexity and richness of the two entities that are being brought together, and allow us to explore the mistakes that language learners might make when transferring from one domain to another. On the other hand, we are also interested, in line with the linguistic approach to metaphor, in the precise words that are used. We will therefore talk of 'source domain terms' and 'target domain terms' when we refer to words or expressions that trigger a complex domain. Unfortunately, this still leads to problems and when, in later chapters, we distinguish 'a dog' (meaning a disaster), for example, from 'to dog' (meaning to follow ceaselessly), we will talk inconsistently about 'noun metaphors' and 'verb metaphors'. Our defence is that it will make reading easier.

1.4 Metonymy

If a bookseller says 'Atwood's in the corner', 'Atwood' means books written by Margaret Atwood, or possibly books written about her or her work. The bookseller could easily have used a more precise expression, to make it clear that she was (a) talking about books and (b) which sort of books. Metonymy is traditionally this sort of lexical substitution, whereby one word substitutes for, or stands for, another word or phrase. The word spoken generally involves a salient or important aspect of the intended entity, so 'hoovering' is vacuum cleaning, 'keeping an *eye* on' means actively watching and 'giving a *hand*' means helping. Metonymy does not show the sort of discrepancy between what is spoken and intended that metaphor does; indeed, both are somehow part of the same 'thing'. The idea of linguistic metonymy is that it acts as a short-hand means of referring to something, either to save time and space, or to create a technical (or slang) term. Thus when transistor radios appeared in the 1960s, everyone had to have a 'trannie'.

The Atwood example illustrates a very important point; the intended 'thing' is never explicit and has to be inferred. Although many examples can be inferred with a high degree of accuracy, because the links are conventional (hoover = PRODUCER FOR PRODUCT and INSTRUMENT FOR ACTIVITY; eye = PART FOR WHOLE), many others cannot and context is needed to help decide. Thus 'The White House refused to comment' could refer specifically to the president, or more generally to the political staff, the administrative staff, a mixture, or even to the American government. Such vagueness can of course be used as a deliberate rhetorical device. Indeed the book buyer might have felt patronised if the bookseller had actually specified that she was talking about books.

It is already clear, even from two or three examples, that there is often not an exact word or phrase that underlies what is actually said; what is important is the general idea or concept. Even formulations like PRODUCER FOR PRODUCT are emphasising a conceptual dimension. It is therefore possible to talk of 'conceptual metonymy', and, like conceptual metaphor, allow it to apply beyond language. It is sometimes argued that while conceptual metaphor is a transfer between two different domains, conceptual metonymy is a relationship within the same domain (eye and human body; White House and politics), but Radden and Kövecses (1999) have argued that this is too restrictive. If you say 'Lets go to bed', this either refers to a frequent first step in going to sleep, or a conventional first step in having sex. There may be no actual bed in either case; the point is that we are selecting one aspect of a process or 'scenario' of sleeping or sex (hopefully context makes it clear which – though again the vagueness can be deliberately exploited). This idea of selecting one part of a process or 'scenario' has been applied to a range of activities, such as shopping (Radden and Seto, 2003) or requesting a drink, and it has been noted that languages vary with respect to which aspect can conventionally be referred to. Thus in English one can focus on the result, 'I'll have a beer', but in German one cannot (Radden, 2005: p. 23).

Conceptual metonymy theorists tend to follow Langacker (1993) in treating metonymy as a reference point device; 'Atwood' or 'eye' give 'mental access' to a broader concept. The notion of mental access justifies the inclusion by Radden and Köveceses of the somewhat controversial notion of *evoking* as an aspect of metonymy. An actor saying 'to be or not to be' metonymically evokes all other performances of it that you have heard or read about. A postcard of an English landscape metonymically evokes stereotyped visions of traditional life, or personal memories of childhood. Conceptual metonymy has recently become very broad (e.g., FORM FOR CONTENT covers the relationship between *any* word, or even sign, and its meaning), to the point that it is not clear to us whether it remains a unified phenomenon. Even so, it is undeniable that metonymy underlies numerous expressions and utterances, that it can occur when broadly construed, at any level of language (Radden, 2005), that it varies across languages and that it can account for why learners have problems with details that native speakers may well treat as self-evident.

Metonymic thinking

We will interpret metonymic thinking as an attempt to work out how a word or expression is being used to refer to a related process or scenario, and second, how this fits into the overall message. This message can include evaluations and attempts to identify, or distance oneself from, concepts, individuals or social groups: what LePage and Tabouret Keller (1985) called 'Acts of Identity'. This may mean trying to decide what scenario is intended, and what the other contents of it might be. It may also involve trying to establish whether a well-known A FOR B relationship (i.e., a conceptual metonymy) is being referred to and deciding for instance whether a particular course of action is definitely implied or simply hinted at.

1.5 The relationship between metaphor and metonymy

There are several different relations between metonymy and metaphor. One particularly common relation is that one or more metonymies are buried deep in, or to put it differently, contribute to, a metaphor. Indeed there is increasing evidence that this is the case for a large number of conventional conceptual metaphors (Kövecses, 2002; Grady 1998). For example, the conceptual metaphor ANGER IS HEAT may well have originated in the metonymic association between anger and body heat. In other words, when people are angry, they often actually become hot, so heat can be used as a kind of shorthand for anger. Even when there is no actual heat involved, the idea remains, but becomes metaphoric. Kövecses lists other examples of conceptual metaphors that may have had metonymic beginnings, for example, the conceptual metaphor SEEING IS KNOWING may once have been a metonymic concept due to the fact that, in many cases, we have to see something in order to be aware of it (Kövecses, 2002: pp. 157–158), evaluate it, or draw conclusions about what to do next.

Grady and Johnson (2002) view 'primary metaphor' as a more fundamental way of envisaging how metonymy is embedded in metaphor. Primary metaphors are more basic than conceptual metaphors and one primary metaphor can often underlie several conceptual metaphors. For example, the primary metaphor EXPERIENCE IS A VALUED POSSESSION is held to underlie the conceptual metaphors DEATH IS A THIEF, A LOVED ONE IS A POSSESSION and OPPORTUNITIES ARE VALUABLE OBJECTS. Primary metaphors like this seem largely or entirely metonymic, making the distinction between metaphor and metonymy less clear than ever!

A different relation between metonymy and metaphor, that of working together rather than embedding or motivating, can be seen in expressions such as 'We need a bit of new blood in this company!' Here we have a part-whole metonymy BLOOD FOR A WHOLE PERSON and a metaphor CREATIVITY IS BLOOD. The two are quite separate and need to be combined to get to the meaning of 'we need some people with new ideas'. Even here, however, we may note, if we dig deeper, that CREATIVITY IS BLOOD appears to have a series of metonymies embedded in it. BLOOD symbolises LIFE (as it flows in the body when you are alive) and LIFE IS A FORCE, so BLOOD can be used to represent bodily energy. The focus on mental innovation may evoke the conceptual metaphor PSYCHOLOGICAL ENTITIES ARE PHYSICAL ENTITIES, but it still has a metonymic component as the mind relates to the brain, which is a part of the body.

How far language learners need to engage with the complexities of metonymy to understand the above expressions remains unclear. If they already know ANGER IS HEAT, then 'hot under the collar' can be interpreted with no extra evidence. If not, then metonymic thinking ('When does your neck feel hot?') is likely to be useful. However, in the case of 'new blood', a reasonable guess as to the sense can be made simply by focusing on 'new' and either 'blood is a life force' or 'blood is part of a person'; either way, using metonymy helps one to understand most of the phrase.

How then do we distinguish metaphor and metonymy? Analytically, we may note that the 'distance' between source and target domains can vary between zero and 'a great deal', so there is a cline from conceptual metonymy to conceptual metaphor (Radden, 2003). Radden (2005) develops this as a cline from literal to metaphoric, with metonymic in the middle. 'A high building' is clearly 'literal' (although for reasons mentioned previously, we would prefer to talk in terms of 'basic' rather than 'literal' meaning) and 'high quality' is clearly metaphoric. ' A high tide' is a bit metonymical because tides involve quantity as well as vertical height, but 'high prices' could be either metonymy or metaphor (the commonly associated display of a rising line on a graph might suggest metonymy, while recognition that verticality and cost are different domains would suggest metaphor). Psychological studies of children's interpretations also suggest that, at a very general level, children tend to interpret metaphor by initially using context literally, then using metonymy and finally by using metaphor, though Piquer Piriz (2004) notes that there is no clear cut-off point. Even so, this does suggest a rough psychological cline that parallels Radden's, in terms of ease of understanding, or at least of preferred interpretive strategies.

Given the current focus on metonymy as a purely conceptual phenomenon (Radden, 2005: p. 15), our final question in this section is to ask whether there remain any areas where the linguistic aspects are relevant, especially for learners. The answer would seem to be yes. To master 'keep an eye out for', the learner has to know that only one eye can be referred to ('keep both eyes open' has a different meaning), that few verbs other than 'keep' would be acceptable, but that 'open' can often be substituted for 'out'. Mastering collocations and recognising their limits are thus as important in learning to deal with metonymy as they are in learning to deal with metaphor.

1.6 Conclusion

While there are traditionally a large number of different figures of speech, all potentially relevant to mastering a foreign language, metaphor and metonymy have increasingly come to be regarded as two of the most important, if not as the most important. They pervade all aspects of language, accounting not just for poetic uses, but for large amounts of conventional, everyday language that now seem connected in systematic, if sometimes complex, ways. Metaphor and metonymy have also been found to be the most frequent figures in non-literal language (e.g. Deignan and Potter, 2004). They thus account in large measure for Gibbs's (1993: p. 253) comment that,

> Speakers can't help but employ tropes in everyday conversation because they conceptualise much of their experience through the figurative schemes of metaphor, metonymy, irony, and so on. Listeners find tropes easy to understand precisely because much of their thinking is constrained by figurative processes.

Unsurprisingly, metaphor and metonymy also account for a high proportion of precisely the aspects of a target language that learners find difficult, because they lack the necessary cultural knowledge that allows a native speaker to say 'right I've understood that expression, I can now stop processing and move on'. This is why we will be looking, in this book, at the cognitive processes that language learners employ when faced with metaphor and metonymy, and at the ways in which these processes contribute to language learning and communication. Although systematic empirical research into the educational aspects of metaphor and metonymy is only just beginning to appear, we decided that there were already enough implications to restrict the book to just these two.

We have given a very brief overview of recent research into both phenomena and tried to indicate where controversy remains, such as the connection between linguistic and conceptual metaphor, the boundary between metaphor and metonymy, or limiting the scope of metonymy. Though we have tried to make our argument fairly easy to understand, it important to recognise from the start that the relationship between the two 'figures' is often complex, involving inclusion (metonymy inside metaphor), co-occurrence or a progressive shading of one category into the other.

We have at all points tried to make it clear that our aim is essentially educational. Our interest is not so much how native speakers mentally process either figure, but rather whether foreign language learners can improve their understanding, performance or learning. We are accordingly more interested in whether learners can be aided by routines which draw in various ways on research into figurative language, or by developing skills that appear to be connected with fluent production and interpretation of figurative language. We have therefore tried to characterise *figurative thinking*, and more specifically *metaphoric thinking* and *metonymic thinking*, in educationally relevant ways. As such, they are constructs which we can use to talk about classrooms and learning; thus we can validly suggest that learners might engage in figurative thinking without being open to the stricture, 'well that's not how a native speaker would do it'.

Chapters 2, 3 and 4 will examine figurative thinking in classroom contexts in rather more detail and will explore some of the psychological skills that seem potentially relevant to learning figurative language, or that have in fact been shown to be relevant. We will also consider the important question of how far our suggestions are compatible with recent ideas about learner autonomy and self-regulation.

2
Why is Figurative Thinking Important for Foreign Language Learners?

2.1 Introduction

In Chapter 2 we connect the theory in Chapter 1 with teaching and learning a foreign language. The primary aim is to establish how far research supports the usefulness of figurative thinking, and the types of query routine outlined in Chapter 1. The chapter focuses on vocabulary learning, because metaphor and metonymy have been found to underlie a great deal of vocabulary formation (Sweetser, 1990; Yu, 2004), and because most of the empirical research into learning figurative aspects of a foreign language has focused on vocabulary, as 'the greatest stumbling block in language acquisition' (Verspoor and Lowie, 2003: p. 547). We begin with a brief discussion of comprehension, production and recall, and then evaluate research relating to four instructional contexts. We end with a look at the specific topics of synaesthesia, idioms and simile.

2.2 Comprehension, production and recall

A learner faced with an unknown expression in the foreign language can ignore it, guess it, or try and work out a likely sense. As we noted in Chapter 1, learners, even at advanced levels, do not have the same tools for resolving this problem as a native speaker; they know fewer words, they have a smaller network of semantic or conceptual links and, if reading a text, the cumulative effect of previous guesses means they are likely to have a less well-defined idea of the 'context thus far' from which to reason.

On the other hand, foreign language learners will frequently encounter figurative extensions of words whose more basic senses they are already familiar with. The reason for this is that figurative processes underlie a great deal of vocabulary formation, semantic extension and polysemy (Sweetser, 1990). For example, expressions such as the *key* issue, a local *branch*, the *outskirts* of the city, *breaking* a promise or to *run through* an exercise are commonplace inside, as well as outside, the classroom. Learners will also meet numerous common expressions based on the human body, such as the *mouth* of a river, the *eye* of a needle, the *long arm* of the law. As the vast majority of these expressions represent metaphoric or metonymic extensions of more basic 'original' senses of the words, there would seem to be some logic to learners asking themselves a reasonably principled set of questions about the meaning of such items in their new context (Walter, 2004).

The key question is whether simple questions can be developed and whether asking them will lead to an accurate prediction. Our preliminary answer to this is yes. A very large number of noun-based figurative expressions involve relatively simple transfers of similarity of shape or function: 'the *foot* of the bed', 'the *head* of a family', the *body* of the text', 'the *eye* of a storm'. The learner simply needs to ask 'What does a foot do?' (supports the main body) or 'What does an eye look like? (round). Such querying will also disentangle metonymies like 'keep an eye on him' (*eyes* are used for looking and *keep* means don't stop) or 'the head of the bed' (the important end/where your head goes). There are limits to this; for instance in order to understand which end of a queue is the 'head', you need to think of an animal and appreciate that 'head is the opposite of tail' and that 'the head is at the front'. However, a small amount of experience (or instruction) will suggest the primacy in English of head as top, head as front or head as main part.

Many figuratively extended verbs also relate to familiar human activities ('I didn't catch what you said', 'Can you just run through the main points', 'Shut up'). A question like 'What does catching involve?' can be answered by 'Not dropping or missing an object' or 'Holding what someone throws at you'. The final comprehension step is eased considerably if you know (for 'catch' = hear) that English tends to conceptualise communication as transferring objects full of meaning between speaker and listener, or (for 'run through' = summarise) as a journey. If you think of bodies as containers and you know that 'up' tends to imply stopping, finishing or completion, you can easily arrive at 'shut up'. Again, there are limits, but a few basic ideas about the ways in which the target language (or 'L2') makes figurative use of containers, journeys and transfer will get the learners a long way with minimal effort.

Some expressions will probably always remain obscure. This may be because the learner does not know the basic meaning of the word(s), or because the source concept is archaic or recondite; pig kicking the bucket when it has been beheaded, or the use of a (red) herring to create a scent for hounds. 'False friends' can also create confusion; 'ears of corn' do not derive from human ears (Skeat, 1993). However, querying the shape of ears or the function of kicking buckets will let you reach a rough approximation of the meaning, as long as you have some context. Simple figurative thinking can therefore be useful even with 'false friends' and dead metaphor – both dead in the sense of an inaccessible original reference (Goatly, 1997) or dead as in having few related connections (the 'leg of a table') (Lakoff, 1987).

In short, querying routines involving straightforward questions about basic senses can get the learner a considerable way towards appropriate comprehension. They are also likely to promote what Craik and Lockhart (1982) call 'deeper processing'. Deeper processing occurs where someone actively engages with a topic, queries it and makes meaningful connections with other topics. Making connections with other words and concepts is needed if the learner is to go beyond establishing a form-meaning link and wants to consolidate and integrate a word into his or her existing knowledge (Verspoor and Lowie, 2003). Hulstijn (2003) notes that learning appears to be facilitated where such processing takes place.

On the other hand, the usefulness of querying routines may be more limited when it comes to figurative language production. Producing figurative language requires considerably more than just understanding it. At the very least, you need to remember the form of the expression, check that its meaning is appropriate to the topic, the audience and the type of discourse and check that the grammar and collocation are appropriate.

2.3   Figurative thinking

Our basic suggestion for figurative thinking is straightforward, but allows for complex activities, as when a teacher guides an extended negotiated querying session with a learner. In order to work out, and remember, the meaning of an unknown item we suggest:

- Identify familiar or basic senses of the words.
- Ask about the shape, components, structure and function of the entities.
- Use the context to establish whether the answers suggest an appropriate meaning.
- If it does not, ask about peripheral detail, associations, and concepts known to be involved in metaphor and metonymy in the L2 (journeys, containers etc.).
- Use the context (again).

Metaphor analysts recognise that basic senses are not necessarily straightforward or easy to identify (Steen, 2005).[1] At a technical level, there are for example concerns about what to do when a particular form, like 'to hare', which, as we saw in Chapter 1, has only a figurative meaning, and whose basic sense is found in a different part of speech (the noun 'a hare'). Conversely, some words seem to have more than one basic sense: a year may be 365 days or simply a cycle of say autumn to autumn. There are also difficulties deciding where the cut-off lies between semantic extension and metaphoric transfer. Again, can one validly talk of basic meanings with 'delexicalised' verbs like 'have (a laugh)' or 'make (a mistake)' which collocate with thousands of nouns and seem to have little independent meaning? Despite these problems, we will see in Section 2.4 that focussing on a word's basic sense and thinking figuratively can at times facilitate understanding and retention.

The focus on basic senses has implications for teaching. Whereas some corpus analysts (e.g., Sinclair, 1990) have proposed presenting the most frequent forms of the target language first, we would balance this with the suggestion that it is beneficial, at times, for a student to consider the relationship that a figuratively used word or phrase has with its more basic sense, as this involves deeper processing, which can aid retention. We discuss this idea in more depth in Section 2.4, where we look at modes of teaching and learning. We would also suggest teaching something about the big cognitive models early (like communication as transfer, thinking as a linear journey, or the body as a container for thoughts and emotions), so that learners have some chance of adding conceptualisation ideas to their querying. We recognise that not every figurative expression is worth teaching like this. Some can indeed be translated from the learner's first language (or 'L1') – we look more at intercultural and cross-linguistic questions in Chapter 5. Others need to be used figuratively at an early stage of teaching (classroom management phrases: 'write it down', 'go through it', etc.). Others again one may want to teach as a formula so that they can act as reference points for later expressions. Yet others may have a basic sense that most learners will never need ('buttress (an argument)'). However, the default recommendation remains: where feasible, teach basic senses first and balance this against teaching the most frequent forms first.

Routines like these do take time and are of limited usefulness during 'online' speaking or listening. They are likely to be most useful when preparing or reflecting on a text or an activity, or actively engaging in 'deep' learning of a word or expression. The fact that words like 'head' have several possibly conflicting figurative senses suggests that figurative thinking with the help of a teacher might be more useful than completely autonomous querying. One might also expect this sort of active engagement with the language to have positive spin off effects in terms of language production, however, more research is needed in this area.

2.4   Modes of teaching and learning

In this section we review research that has investigated the potential of figurative thinking to promote vocabulary comprehension and retention. The research has focussed on four different types of learning situation: where students work without a teacher intervening; where a teacher offers initial guidance and explanation; where teachers and learners collaborate; and the less personal computer-learning situation.

Learner-led learning

Several recent studies have focused on learners guessing without prior training – a procedure which Hulstijn (2003) and Verspoor and Lowie (2003) found generally to have a low success rate. Boers and Demecheleer (2001) found that when 78 French-speaking advanced-level students of English were asked to guess at the meaning of imagistic idioms without any help, 35 per cent of their guesses pointed to what the researchers considered were the appropriate metaphors. Success was, however, variable; idioms were more easily 'guessable' when they related to metaphoric themes that were salient in French. On the other hand, Skoufaki (2005a), working with 40 advanced level Greek learners of English, each guessing at the meaning of twelve multiword metaphoric idioms, like 'too hot to handle' or 'kick the bucket', found that only 6.5 per cent of the answers appeared to involve use of a conceptual metaphor when the expressions had no context and 8 per cent when they did. Moreover, establishing meanings when the expressions were used in a text, rather than when they were just listed, significantly *reduced* the degree to which the learners spontaneously used imagery, their first language, a word-by-word figuring-out procedure, or possible extensions of the individual words. Thus a learner-led situation involved little use of conceptual metaphor, and the presence of contextual clues context suppressed figurative thinking.

Both the above experiments appear to have involved primarily individual work rather than collaboration between individuals. However, classroom learning is known to be often more effective where learners engage actively in small group collaborative work (Oxford, 1997). While we know of no published experimental studies specifically testing the relative effectiveness of collaboration with respect to figurative thinking, it seems likely that collaboration might in many cases work well.

Anecdotally, at least, we have found situations where it does work. One example concerns a group of East Asian graduate students of English for Academic Purposes in the United Kingdom (January, 2002) who came across the word 'rooted', in the following written context (bold ours):

> '[These] problems are **rooted** in the technological uncertainties, ambiguous customer signals and immature competitive structures'. (*The Financial Times*, 13 January, 2001)

The members of the group were already familiar with the basic sense of the word 'roots' and its entailments: that roots are usually in the ground, that they generally lie below the plant, that they attach it to the ground, and that they feed the plant. They used the context to establish that 'problems' was part of the target domain (though they did not themselves use the term). By making explicit their knowledge about structure and function of roots, and in some cases perhaps using their L1 knowledge, they were able to work out by themselves the meaning of 'rooted' in the abstract sense in which it was being used (namely: be based on; have their foundations in; be fed by). The teacher was not involved in the figuring out discussion.

More research is needed to establish the extent to which foreign language learners spontaneously approach unknown vocabulary by exploring attributes or appealing to underlying conceptual structures. Initial findings suggest that collaboration may facilitate such thinking, but that immediate contextualisation appears to suppress it. Moreover, there seem to be limits to what learners can do on their own. We will return to this in Chapter 4, where we look in a little more detail at learner autonomy.

Teacher-led intervention

Teacher-led intervention is where a teacher (or a worksheet) gives an example and or a definition, thereby guiding and constraining guessing by the learner. There is little or no extended negotiation between teacher and learner. Several studies suggest that this approach can contribute significantly to the learning of figurative language by foreign language learners.

For example, a series of research studies by Boers and colleagues (Boers, 2000a; 2000b; Boers, Demecheleer and Eyckmans, 2004a) showed that when teachers systematically drew the attention of language learners to the source domains of words whose senses had been figuratively extended, then the students' depth of knowledge of those words, and their ability to retain them improved significantly. There is some suggestion from the Boers *et al.* studies that this explanatory technique also led learners to understand connotations, and to inductively detect what made the words differ from their near-synonyms. The studies all involved university undergraduates with a fairly advanced level of English and focused on immediate learning and short-term retention periods of up to five weeks.

Similar findings were made by Li (2002), who conducted five experiments concerning metaphoric words, idioms and proverbs on a total of 394 Chinese undergraduates of intermediate to advanced levels of English. The first four experiments tested the effect of presenting conceptual metaphor information in the context of (a) a ten-minute discussion with the teacher, (b) being told about conceptual metaphors and (c) actively engaging with the data. In experiments 3 and 4 experimental groups drew or looked at images. The worksheets also had querying routines, like the following:

Mind is a container; Anger is heat
Hit the ceiling
What image do you have in your mind when you read hit the ceiling?
Where does this force come from?
What's the result after the ceiling was hit?
Who hits the ceiling?

The participants were asked to explore these questions with their peers, then learn and memorise the expressions concerned. Li found that the students in the experimental groups who had carried out these activities recalled the form and meaning of the idioms significantly better than those in the control groups, who had been given memory-based tasks. One shortcoming in Li's work is that the students in the control groups were not always asked to engage with the material to quite the same extent as those in the experimental groups. It could simply be that deeper engagement led to better retention, and the actual nature of the engagement may not be important.

A conceptual metaphor approach was also employed by Skoufaki (2005b), who had three groups of to who presented sets of idioms in their conceptual metaphoric groups to three groups of ten advanced Greek learners of English. The first group was shown examples and definitions of metaphoric idioms and given a brief explanation of the key underlying metaphors, such as UNDERSTANDING IS SEEING. The second group was also given these examples and definitions, but the participants were asked to guess at their meaning before being shown the example/definition sheet. Both groups were given meaning-focused practice activities. The third group was presented with the idioms in same way as the first group, but participants were encouraged to engage in more form-focused practice activities. All groups of participants were then tested for their retention of both form and meaning. Skoufaki's first finding was that the second group, who had been encouraged to guess at the meaning of the idioms with the help of the Conceptual Metaphoric clues, had the highest scores. Her second finding was that the first and third groups did not differ significantly in terms of form and meaning retention, despite the fact that they had been given different types of practice task. The first finding indicates that when learners are given unambiguous meaning clues, the use of guessing strategies leads to better retention than mere exposure input in metaphorical groups. The second finding suggests that Conceptual Metaphor approaches to the teaching of idioms do not necessarily need to be supplemented by form-focused activities for the form of the expressions to be retained.

Verspoor and Lowie (2003) tested the usefulness of providing learners with basic senses. They gave one group of learners a basic (concrete) sense of a word, and gave another group a more abstract (non-core) sense. They explored 18 words with 78 Dutch pre-university students (the actual level of English is unclear). The guided guessing phase was followed by a short memorisation worksheet where answers to the earlier guessing were given. The aim was to learn a reasonably figurative sense (intermediate between the two clues) of each word. The results showed that provision of basic senses had a significantly greater effect on both guessing correctly and retention after two weeks, though, predictably, if the learners were unable to work the meaning of the basic sense (e.g., 'watershed'), it did not help much.

On a slightly different note, MacArthur (2005) investigated the benefits of providing intermediate Spanish learners of English with pictures in order to help them learn L2 idioms. She was particularly interested in the nature of the pictures provided, hypothesising that more congruent pictures would lead to better retention. She gave her participants three types of pictures to help them learn the idioms. 'Type 1' pictures were congruent with the wording but incongruent in other ways. 'Type 2' pictures were congruent with the meaning but diverged in affect. 'Type 3' pictures were congruent with both the meaning and the evaluative stance. For example, in order to teach the idiom 'look down your nose at someone', the Type 1 picture had a woman examining her nasal passages, the Type 2 picture had someone with a prominent nose depicted in a higher position, smiling and observing someone in a lower position, and the Type 3 picture had a snooty-looking person in a higher position observing someone in a lower position. MacArthur found that all three types were equally helpful in prompting recall of the wording of an idiom if decontextualised, but that Types 2 and 3 were more successful in a gap-fill exercise where participants were restricted to typical cases (e.g., look down your nose at someone vs. something). More importantly, when asked to choose between a literal and a figurative expression to end a short passage, those exposed to Type 3 visuals showed greater awareness of the appropriate use of idioms in context. These findings indicate that it is important to have appropriate pictures as they can explain the motivation not only of the semantics but also the affect (e.g., whether an idiom positively/negatively/neutrally evaluates the situation in question).

To sum up this section, teacher-led activity can take different forms. It can involve: pointing out relevant conceptual metaphors; drawing students' attention to basic senses; and providing them with appropriate visuals. These activities appear to promote understanding and retention of meaning, and sometimes form, but to varying extents. We can tentatively conclude that they also aid production but only in very controlled environments. More research is needed into the effect that these different approaches have on the free production of idioms.

There is some evidence to suggest that once students have been introduced to a conceptual metaphor, they can then go on to use that metaphor to help them understand idioms that are completely new to them. For example, Kövecses and Szabo (1996) found that students who had been introduced to a set of conceptual metaphors to explain one set of phrasal verbs were then able to use these metaphors to work out the meaning of a totally new set of phrasal verbs. They went on to claim that the cognitive semantic approach is thus transferable to new information. However, Kövecses and Szabo only tested their participants on the particles. When Boers (2000b) replicated their study, testing his participants on their ability to understand *both* parts of the phrasal verb, he found that participants who had received relevant conceptual metaphor training did not significantly outperform those who had received no such training. On a more encouraging note, Picken (2002), examining how Japanese university students could be helped to understand vocabulary in a short literary text, does report that once a conceptual metaphor has been taught, students can use it to make sense of other literary texts that exploit the metaphor. We revisit the subject of phrasal verbs in Chapter 8.

Combining student- and teacher-led activity

Student-led activity involves inferencing, guessing and matching answers: the sort of self-monitored effort that characterised aspects of Carton's (1971) or Bialystok's (1983) inferencing and the good language learner profiles of Naiman *et al.* (1978).[2] Teacher-led intervention generates groupings and links and creates networks. It also builds student confidence, since if a student does not understand, he or she can negotiate with the teacher until things are clarified. Teacher-led activity also generates data that could be used in student-led inferencing strategies, either as an integral part of a class activity, or as a 'language-related episode' where learners withdraw for a group discussion about a language point (Storch, 1998; Swain and Lapkin, 1998; Jackson, 2001). The combination of teacher and student engagement should guide and reassure learners, yet retain their active engagement with establishing meaning. Holme (2004: p. 52) goes one step further and suggests, citing a number of informal class experiences, that joint negotiation can lead learners beyond confidence in constructing metaphoric interpretations towards a confidence that they can interpret whole texts in a rich and viable way: that is, to what is often called critical literacy. We have found no research studies specifically testing the relative effectiveness of combining teacher-led and learner-led activity with respect to figurative language *learning*, but we are able, like Holme, to offer a number of examples where it has led to successful *interpretation*.

Littlemore (2002) reports the case of Esther, a student on an English for Specific Purposes course at a UK university. During a one-to-one tutorial on reading and vocabulary development, Esther came across the following in a text about advertising (italics ours):

> How does an organisation win out against its competitors? Segmenting the market correctly and *targeting the right customers* are vital to a company's success. (*The Financial Times*, 13 January, 2001)

Esther said she did not understand 'targeting'. The interaction went as follows:

1. The teacher asked Esther if she knew the basic sense of 'target'; she said she did.
2. The teacher then asked her to say what 'target' made her think of and what associations the word might have.

3. Esther responded with *focusing on the target, taking aim, firing some-thing at it*, and *hurting it*.
4. She was then asked which of these associations / concepts she felt related best to the context of advertising.
5. She decided that only the first three were really appropriate.
6. She was then asked to form an interactive image of the metaphor (e.g., a firm firing a product at a particular customer, who is standing in a group).
7. When she did this, she was able to make further interpretations includ-ing, *the fact that it is important to identify the right customer, to see what that customer looks like, to find an appropriate arrow to hit that particular customer,* and *that there are difficulties inherent in the whole process.*

With the aid of the guided questioning by the teacher, Esther was able to establish not just the figurative sense of 'targeting', but also several of the entailments or connotations: that is to say, a very rich understand-ing of the word.

A second example (from Littlemore, 2004a) involves the same teacher and a group of four Japanese advanced learners of English. They were looking at an extract from McDonough and Shaw (1993: p. 160), in order to discuss the characteristics of spoken English. In this extract, the term 'cradle work' is used. 'Cradle work, involves window cleaners being hoisted up the sides of buildings in cradle-like boxes, in order to clean the windows. One of the students queried the meaning of this expression, and the following discussion took place (Box 2.1).

The approach adopted by the students to working out the meaning of 'cradle work' appears to have involved a measure of collaborative figura-tive thinking. Student B makes the initial connection between cradle and a tightly enveloping and swinging place for a baby to sleep – which has nothing to do with the context of buildings. The connection is, however, with a mother's arms rather than a wooden bed, which might be why he then focuses on the negative entailment of instability rather than the positive advantage of a supportive object which allows controlled access to the outside. It is student C who makes the more productive connection with safety, enveloping and painting. Interestingly, there is a lot of miming during this discussion, which suggests that the learners might have been actively employing some kind of imagery or physical experience as a search strategy. The physical activity also appears to have retained the active engagement of student D. The role of psychological processes, such as imagery, in metaphor interpretation is

Box 2.1	Class discussion of the meaning of 'cradle work'

Student A	What's cradle work?
Teacher	Well that's what I was going to ask you. Do you know what a cradle is?
Student B	[Mimes a rocking motion with her arms].
Teacher	Why do you think you would talk about cradle work on tower blocks? Do you know what a tower block is?
Student A	[Mimes a tall, thin shape] Tower blocks. Birmingham.
Teacher	If you look a bit further down you've got outside cradles, on the outside of tower blocks.
Student B	Oh, but maybe, I'm not sure but er how can I say [mimes up and down motion] Outside the high building in a cradle [mimes rocking motion].
Teacher	So why do you think it's called a cradle?
Student B	It's unstable.
Teacher	Any other reasons?
Student C	[Stands up holding his chair under his legs, mimes painting and rocking, then mimes the high sides of a cradle].
Students A, B and D	[Nod].

discussed further in Chapter 3. The teacher does not stress the need to think in an exploratory way, but she does need to inject images into the discussion and act as gatekeeper, indicating when a conclusion is not appropriate.

Finally, Littlemore (2004b) attempted to train a group of 43 upper-intermediate language learners to use the basic senses of ten words to work out their metaphorical senses in context. Participants were encouraged to use strategies involving mental imagery and contextual clues. Littlemore found that the strategies employed by the participants varied significantly according to the items. Highly concrete (or image-able) items provoked the use of mental imagery, but interestingly the use of such imagery did not necessarily lead to successful interpretation. In contrast, the presence of contextual clues did not necessarily lead participants to use these clues, but when they did use them, they were more likely to be successful. From this, we can conclude that different types of items provoke different types of strategies, and that different strategies are *appropriate* for determining the meanings of different types of items.

To sum up this section, combined teacher and student-led activity does appear to lead to depth of understanding for some items, but we do not yet have any data on retention.

Computer-aided activity

Computer-assisted contexts can vary markedly, from a single learner communicating with the computer, a learner communicating with a teacher, other learners, or a third party via the computer and the internet, and a group of learners collaborating on a non-computerised task and simply interacting with the computer when necessary. Research on learning a language using a computer currently recognises the importance of active engagement with meaning, working collaboratively, reflecting as a group and with a teacher, having a recognisable and 'authentic' task and obtaining helpful feedback (Tomlinson, 2003; Doughty and Long, 2003). Very little of this research has yet focused on understanding, using or learning figurative language.

In an attempt to fill this gap, Littlemore *et al.* (in preparation) presented a number of expressions in their original sentential contexts on computer to a group of 18 advanced students of English for Academic Purposes. Hypertext links were provided for each of the problematic words to corresponding images from 'clipart' (http://www.clipart.com/). A sample item was given on the screen, in which the word 'entrenched' was linked to an image of a First World War trench, and various properties of a trench were listed, such as the fact that it is deep, depressing, difficult to get out of, and one is likely to be there a long time. The learners were then presented with 13 further items, such as 'rooted' with an image of tree roots, 'spawned' with an image of a frog producing spawn, and 'anchored' with a picture of a ship's anchor, and so on. The learners were asked to read the text, access the image, think about 'ideas associated with the image', and then decide which associations might apply to the context. Having made a decision, they typed in the contextual meaning of the word. For each item, they were asked to indicate, by ticking a box on the screen, if they already knew the word, and these cases were eliminated from the analysis.

Many of the learners were able to come up with plausible and insightful interpretations without direct input from the teacher. For example, '*spawned* by the internet' generated 'spread'; 'published'; and 'put available'. 'Birmingham University has *embraced* all of these ideas' generated 'held'; 'incorporated'; and 'made as own'. 'The controversy surrounding lecturers' salaries was *re-ignited* recently' generated 'reactivated', 'made public again' and 'come again at the centre of the discussion'. However, not all the items were equally successful. The quality of the images for 'pitfall', 'spawned', 'bandwagon' and 'afloat' was not particularly clear, and the ability of the students to guess the meaning of the expressions from these images was correspondingly low. The study suggests that figurative thinking using images plus a worksheet-led task in a computer environment can lead to successful interpretation of meaning in a short context. On the other hand, it does not establish whether learning took place.

Long-term retention effects have been explored by Boers and his team in Belgium, using *Imagelex*, a battery of 1200 online exercises on 400 English idioms. The tool includes three stages of online exercises (see Boers *et al.*, 2004a). At stage 1, learners hypothesise about an idiom's origin by means of a multiple-choice test. When the correct source domain is identified, a short explanation about the origin or literal use of the expression appears on the screen as feedback. At stage 2, the learners do a more conventional type of multiple-choice exercise where they try and guess the meaning of the idiom. They keep trying until they click the correct response. At stage 3, the learners are asked to complete a gap-fill exercise in which they have to (re)produce the keyword of the idiom. This stage is intended to serve as consolidation in context. Learners are guided through these three stages by the program.

Boers and colleagues examined the responses of approximately 200 intermediate and advanced Dutch-speaking learners of English (Boers, 2001; Boers *et al.*, 2004a; 2004b; Boers *et al.*, forthcoming). Learners who had been made aware of the source domain (at stage 1) were significantly more likely to remember the idiom both in the short and long term (more than four weeks later) than learners who had only guessed using the multiple-choice exercises. Moreover, this advantage held for learners with both visual and verbal learning styles. Making learners aware of the source domain helped them later guess the formality level of some idioms, but the situation was complex and the overall gain was not substantial.

Boers and his team (personal communication) are beginning to explore the effects of presenting students with a combination of images and source domain information. Their initial findings indicate that the use of images facilitates comprehension. Interestingly however, when students use the version of *Imagelex* that contains the images, they are less able to recall the form of the idioms. One explanation for this could be that when Boers' students were presented with an accompanying image, they spent less time reading the etymological explanation (in which the target vocabulary was reiterated) because they were distracted by the image. The image thus helped them to recognise the meaning of the idiom in the subsequent tasks but did not help them to remember the exact form of the idiom. In other words, the use of images appears to facilitate reception but not production. In future task design, Boers recommends that one should avoid presenting the verbal information and the image together on the screen. If the verbal information and the image are presented separately, the students will have more time to process the verbal information and may process it more thoroughly. The team will explore this question in the next stage of their project.

More research is therefore required to establish whether a combination of images and source domain activities can increase both receptive and productive knowledge of idioms. Similarly, we do not yet know the impact of collaborative tasks, involving either on-screen or off-screen negotiation. Again, the Littlemore and Boers *et al.* studies have examined metaphor, but we do not know how far the same results would be obtained with metonymy. Nevertheless, we may conclude positively that a computerised environment using worksheet-led figurative thinking activities can aid the interpretation and recall of metaphoric expressions.

Conclusions

The studies all show, to varying extents, that learning occurs where there is some guided, explanatory input about basic meanings and/or about underlying conceptual metaphor, *and* the learners interact actively with the language (by thinking of examples, discussing, or querying). Visual images, whether imagined or drawn, involving basic senses or schematic entities like containers also seemed to aid recognition and recall. Only Li (2002) and Boers *et al.* (forthcoming) used overt querying, but the Skoufaki (2005a; 2005b) and Littlemore *et al.* (in preparation) studies both seem to logically require a measure of internal querying (jumping from a picture of a tree trunk and a root to predicting how a problem can be rooted would seem to imply the need for queries such as 'what does it do?' and 'how do the bits fit together?').

To sum up, the findings mentioned in this section appear to suggest that focussing on basic senses can aid the learning of metaphor. The field would, however, benefit from more empirically based classroom research, focussed on both retention and production. Such research could usefully compare, for example, the effectiveness of explicit versus implicit teaching approaches, and the effectiveness of intentional versus implicit learning. Finally, we are aware of no research that addresses the teaching of metonymy. Given the extensive role played by metonymy in vocabulary development, such research would be very useful. We will now briefly consider the relevance of figurative thinking to three specific areas of vocabulary learning: synaesthesia, idioms and similes.

2.5   Figurative thinking and synaesthesia

Synaesthesia is a psychological phenomenon, where a mental impression of one sense is generated by stimulation of another; a red room or the taste of chilli evokes hotness. The particular reaction that chillies taste 'hot' (English) or 'stabbing' ('piquante' in Spanish) appears to relate to responses by pain-detecting mechanisms in the body and have, in part at least, a physiological basis (Rakova, 1999). Languages also make extensive use of 'cross-modal transfer', like 'a sharp taste', 'a loud colour', 'a bright sound' or 'a soft edge'. Perceptions, mental categories and linguistic phrases – many conventional and thus part of vocabulary – are involved, but the precise connection between the three remains highly controversial (Rakova, 1999). The cognitive linguistic view, which Rakova rejects, tends to be that the senses are more or less discrete, certain concepts (like loudness, or softness) are primarily associated with one particular sense (hearing and touch), and the use of loudness with, say, colour represents transfer and thus metaphor (Sweetser, 1990; Shen, 1997). The connection of redness and heat would presumably be metonymy rather than metaphor.

Envisaging hot curries and hot colours as figurative is nevertheless a useful assumption for foreign language learning. Figurative thinking routines based on embodiment will get learners a reasonable distance: 'What happens when you are hot? You sweat, you go red and if very hot, you burn. Burning hurts'. 'What happens if you get hit by a hot object? You feel a short sharp pain, then a longer one'. Embodiment will not work for 'hard or soft edges', however, as the key factor is not the perception of smoothness, but rather a line where each side does or does not mix with/fade into the other. One needs to ask rather more broadly 'What happens when two hard/soft things meet?'. This questioning will also get you to 'hard light' and 'soft light'. 'Dark' or 'heavy' music involves low notes and minor keys, while 'lighter' or 'brighter' music is more likely to involve more high notes and major keys. Again, much of the meaning can be reached by querying what happens when things are heavy (they fall), or by accessing common conceptualisations of 'dark' (unknown, worrying, mysterious).

Problems will occur where languages conceptualise 'dark' or 'heavy' differently, and where phrases within a language develop fixed collocations (you can have 'bright sunlight' and 'a dull light', but not 'dull sunlight'). But on balance it would seem worth asking learners to think figuratively about synaesthesic expressions.

2.6   Figurative thinking and idioms

Idioms are multiword units whose meaning cannot be established simply by adding the basic meanings of the component words. They vary markedly in terms of the extent to which the words can be substituted or modified, and the extent to which the meaning can be related to the component meanings. A high proportion are also figurative. Grant and Bauer (2004) restrict 'idioms' to the small class of fully fixed and opaque (non-metaphoric) expressions, like 'red herring', 'swinging the lead (prevaricating)' and 'shooting the breeze', but even here, it is not difficult, as we noted, for teachers to reactivate 'red herring', so we prefer to stick with the broader, more gradable sense of the term.

Idioms are central to learning a foreign language because there are a lot of them, they frequently involve cultural references (Lazar, 2003), they have differing usage restrictions and they can look confusingly similar, especially where particles and prepositions are involved ('look up', 'look out', 'look into').

In this last case, cognitive linguists would treat 'up', 'out' and 'into' as clearly figurative, whereas other analysts see them more as relatively meaningless markers. This impacts on pedagogic techniques and on whether learners should be encouraged to decompose idioms. We will defer discussion of this to Chapter 8.

Where idioms relate to 'richer' source domains such as boating, or cricket, the situation seems less controversial. Given the restricted decomposability of an idiom, learners would seem to need to apply more information than shape and function of single words (as in Verspoor and Lowie, 2003). Boers *et al.* (2004a; 2004b) and Boers *et al.* (forthcoming) offered etymological guidance about the whole expression ('it comes from sailing ...') to overcome this, and also to allow for the fact that many idioms might already have been figurative when used in sailing, gardening or other such activities. The findings were summarised in Section 2.4: brief initial etymological help plus short contexts frequently aided guessing as well as short-term recall and not all items were equally susceptible to such help, but the researchers offered no explanation why. The average success rate was considered high enough for the researchers to suggest a querying routine which encouraged teacher–learner collaboration (Boers *et al.*, forthcoming: p. 20): (i) ask the students to hypothesise about the origin of the expression; (ii) refine or rectify their hypothesis; (iii) ask the students to interpret the figurative meaning of the idiom by combining etymology and context; (iv) refine or rectify their interpretation.

This technique is clearly useful for one-off idioms with a clear cultural source domain (like baseball). It is less suited to expressions like 'hit the roof', '(smoke) came out of her ears' or '(he) flipped his lid' which seem better cued by reference to the main underlying metaphor(s) ANGER IS A HOT LIQUID IN A CONTAINER which expands and rises, leading to an explosion. In these cases, our earlier suggestion for using a mixture of basic sense data (about, say, how you hit a roof) and reference to common conceptual metaphors seems preferable.

Proverbs ('In for a penny, in for a pound'; 'A stitch in time saves nine'; 'Don't put all your eggs in one basket') are a special class of idiom in the sense that the wording is fairly fixed, they are short moral comments, the literal reference is frequently to an activity no longer common in Britain or America, and their use in modern discourse is highly restricted. Most importantly, understanding them requires you to establish two sets of meanings (Lakoff and Turner, 1989): a general scenario like 'a single solution can be dangerous', then its application to the specific contextual situation, like 'we need to advertise in more countries'. Li's (2002) fifth experiment (see Section 2.4 for a discussion of the first four) involved 16 proverbs, and he encouraged his participants to work in pairs with a worksheet containing the following collaborative querying routine:

> *Don't put all your eggs in one basket: don't invest all your resources into a single objective*
> **Life is a container; Beliefs are possessions**
> What image do you have in your mind when you read 'Don't put all your eggs in one basket'?
> What are the eggs?
> Why does he put all his eggs in one basket?
> What might happen to those eggs in that basket?

Li found that the participants who had followed such routines were significantly better at retaining the meanings of the proverbs than those who had simply been asked to learn and memorise them. This is an encouraging result, although there are issues to do with engagement in all of Li's experiments, which do need to be addressed (see Section 2.4). Routines do not always need to refer quite so explicitly to conceptual metaphors. Giving Boers-type information about origins (e.g. the expression 'don't pull all your eggs in one basket' comes from the days before egg storage boxes) can also be effective. If you simply ask what problematic things happen to eggs in a basket, the answer is that, if you move, they break and are ruined. Sometimes quite minimal querying will provide adequate comprehension (though possibly not recall). Thus, if you know that being 'in time' or even 'on time' is culturally 'a good thing' in English, you can get the gist of 'a stitch in time ...' with no knowledge of sewing. Multiple types of guidance or querying would seem useful, but the fact that proverbs (and many sayings) are often used in abbreviated form ('a stitch in time, you know!') means that recall tests should probably include 'whole from part' recognition.

A learner's ability to guess and predict the meaning of an idiom is likely to be affected by their L1. Sakuragi and Fuller (2003), for example, building on work by Kellerman (1987a; 1987b), found that learners were more likely to predict that an L1 idiom could be translated into L2 if the figurative concept was similar in appearance (rather than function) to the literal one (e.g., 'eye' in a bulls eye is round). Adult learners thus acted like children, who learn (in their L1) to compare appearance before function (Gentner, 1988). This would seem to be another argument for teaching more concrete senses of a word first. Li (2002: experiment 3) also found that recall was enhanced when the learners were given L1 equivalents and explanations.

Despite the lack of research on acquiring L2 metonymy, it should be noted that many idioms are motivated as much by metonymy as metaphor (Goosens, 1990). For example, 'bite the dust' (meaning to die), 'throw in the towel' (meaning to give up) and 'point your finger at someone' (meaning to blame them) all use a salient act to refer metonymically to a series of events (Gibbs, 1995). If you 'bite the dust' in, say, a Hollywood Western gun fight, your head hits the ground as you die. 'Dust' is a type of ground (linked to dryness and death) and biting is a metonymic reflection of grimacing with pain (or death). 'Throwing in the towel' is what the corner men in the boxing ring do to symbolise that a boxer is giving up, as well as being the conventional boxing phrase for 'giving in'. When someone is blamed for a mistake or accused of doing something wrong, fingers may literally be pointed at them to emphasise the accusation.

2.7 Figurative thinking and similes

Formally, similes seem simple and they are frequently treated as such by language course books. On the surface, there are always two explicit terms and they are connected by an adverbial such as 'as' or 'like', or by a verb such as 'resembles' or 'is similar to'. The learner only needs to find the connection and s/he can be absolutely certain that a comparison is needed. As if in answer to the learner's plight, many such utterances do actually contain the Ground directly ('Jean is like a rose *in that she has smooth pink skin*') or by implication and ironically ('it's as *clear as mud*'), so there can be little need to think much about why the terms are being connected.

If we define simile formally as a comparison with a linguistic marker, then not all similes are figurative; 'John is like Fred, in the sense that they both have red hair' is a straightforward non-figurative comparison. However, if we define simile rhetorically as an overt comparison between two disparate entities, then we start to enter the realm of figurative thinking. The standard conceptual metaphor view of similes is that the figurative ones are rather uninteresting, as they are simply weakened or hedged metaphors (Lakoff and Turner, 1989: p. 133). Remove the 'like' and you have the same meaning only stronger. There is also a psychological theory, the 'comparison theory', which argues much the same thing. Advocates of the comparison theory, such as Chiappe and Kennedy (2000) – not conceptual metaphor theorists as it happens – believe that metaphor comprehension and simile comprehension are similar. For comparison theorists, this means that listeners/readers need to find in each case relevant common properties between the two parts of the expression.

It is easy to demonstrate this view does not adequately explain all simile that learners are likely to come across, or the thinking learners must engage in. First, some figurative similes involve metonymy rather than metaphor. If we take the comment from teachers that 'Teaching is like organizing' (see Oxford *et al.*, 1998), we have to recognise that organising plays a large part in virtually all teaching. That is simply what teachers do. The 'like' here may be foregrounding the organisational aspects of teaching, or generalising to other types of organising. The reader may therefore need to think along two lines, one metonymic the other metaphoric, and decide which is more important in context.

A further type of difference between metaphor and simile can be shown from three short paired examples. The first involves the idiomatic 'X is a joke', the second is literary (from Adrien Henri's poem 'Love is ...'), the third is invented:

Life is a joke
Life is like a joke

Love is a fan club with only two fans
Love is like a fan club with only two fans

Love is a Catholic priest getting married
Love is like a Catholic priest getting married

'Life is like a joke' might actually imply that life has a dimension of humour to it. 'Life is a joke', on the other hand, implies exactly the opposite, namely that life is so grim that it is hard to believe the Deity was being serious. Humour, entertainment, amusement and pleasure are only relevant in the simile.

In the fan club example, it can be hard to even put a meaning on the simile, the more one thinks about it. Fan clubs consist of a celebrity who is the focus of interest, but not necessarily a member, and a set of fans who may not even know each other. The metaphor requires us to restructure our notion of a fan club, so that each fan becomes an object of intense interest to the other. The rhetorical power derives precisely from the need to restructure 'fan club'. The simile conveys no such need, and indeed love is *not* like such a fan club.

The difference is even clearer in the priest example. The simile suggests horror, awfulness, (or cynicism perhaps) as priests are morally sworn to celibacy: marriage is 'like' something awful. The metaphor, on the other hand, may suggest sympathy and warmth: extreme devotion to the point that you are prepared to break all other vows. To reach this interpretation, though, you need to background the immediate moral reaction to vow breaking.

All three pairs illustrate a common fact about similes; they tend to focus attention on typical, or central, characteristics of the Source (or Vehicle), while metaphors may, as we showed earlier, involve peripheral, or non-central, characteristics and require the interpreter to do more conceptual restructuring. This difference in types of attribute or relation may help account for the fact that metaphors often appear to be more open-ended than similes. This ought, on balance, to make figurative thinking routines more straightforward for similes.

We know of no experimental studies exploring the interpretation of simile by foreign language learners, especially where simile is more than just a relational analogy in, say, a Physics lesson. We therefore simply conclude, first, that instances of simile cannot always be treated as if they were direct instances of A IS B metaphor and, second, that figurative thinking would still seem to be necessary, especially if the Ground is not stated directly.

2.8   Conclusion

In this chapter, we have seen that figurative thinking can contribute to foreign language learning in at least two ways. First, by alerting learners to the figurative processes that underlie extended word meanings, it appears to be possible to promote deeper learning, longer retention and more flexible use of existing vocabulary, especially where teachers and learners work together, imagery is involved and learners have some understanding of how common conceptual patterns operate in the L2. Second, the research evidence strongly suggests that straightforward querying routines can be effective as a way of promoting both comprehension and recall. Evidence for aiding production is very limited and evidence about L2 metonymy appears non-existent.

In Chapter 3 we look in more depth at the nature of figurative thinking itself and try to make connections with specific psychological processes or skills, particularly trainable ones, that appear to underlie it or be closely associated with it. We will discuss how foreign language learners might be encouraged to employ these processes so as to increase their figurative thinking capacity in the context of their foreign language learning.

3
Psychological Processes Underlying Figurative Thinking

3.1 Introductory comments

In Chapters 1 and 2, we introduced the idea of figurative thinking and saw that the ability to engage in it is likely to be advantageous to foreign language learners in terms of vocabulary learning. In this chapter we look in more depth at the *nature* of figurative thinking, particularly as it applies to metaphor and metonymy. We begin by outlining several of the major theories that have been put forward to explain metaphor comprehension and production from a psychological processing perspective. Section 3.3 then outlines a set of psychological processes that foreign language learners might usefully employ to comprehend metaphor. In each case, the argument focuses initially on ways in which the process aids comprehension, but goes on to note whether it has also been shown to aid (foreign language) learning. In section 3.4, we look at the psychological processes involved in the processing of metonymy. After having suggested a range of psychological processes that language learners might use to help them think figuratively in the target language, the chapter closes, in section 3.5, with two concrete examples showing how language learners can be helped to use these psychological processes in order to understand metaphor and metonymy.

3.2 How do people understand and produce metaphors?

Before beginning this section, we would like to point out that, although there has been a great deal of research into the comprehension of metaphor, there has been very little research into how metaphors are produced. The main body of this section therefore focuses on metaphor comprehension. As a partial defence of this imbalance, one could argue that foreign language learners probably need to understand metaphor more often than they need to produce it.

There is very little across-the-board consensus on how metaphors are understood. Most theories of metaphor comprehension fall somewhere between two general views. The more traditional views of metaphor comprehension assume that in order to comprehend metaphors listeners and readers first need to analyse and reject their 'literal' meanings. On the other hand, adherents of the more recent 'direct access view' maintain that listeners and readers do not necessarily need to access the complete literal meaning of metaphors in order to understand their meaning, as adequate clues are provided in the context to point them in the right direction (Gibbs, 2001: p. 318). The timing of the role played by context is therefore debatable; does it come into play after all possible interpretations have been activated, enabling the listener to choose between them?; Or does it come into play right from the start, restricting all contextually inappropriate interpretations from being activated, or at least suppressing them very quickly (Gernsbacher, 1990; Rubio Fernandez, 2004)? Another controversial issue is the nature of the interaction between the source and target domains. Some authors argue that metaphor comprehension involves the identification of similarities between the domains, others argue that the target domain is used to structure information from the source domain, and yet others argue for the existence of a third domain that is not intrinsically part of either the source or target domain. The main models that are currently used to explain metaphor comprehension are *the direct access view, the graded salience hypothesis, interaction theory, blending theory, the career of metaphor theory*, and *the class-inclusion model*.

As we saw earlier, *the direct access view* (Gibbs, 1994) assigns a crucial role to context in the process of metaphor comprehension. Listeners use the context to guide them to a contextually appropriate interpretation of the metaphor. According to this view, one does not need to access the entire 'literal' meaning of a metaphor in order to identify its metaphorical sense in the context in which it appears.

According to the *graded salience hypothesis* (Giora, 1997; 2003), when we encounter a metaphorical expression, we automatically access the features of both the source and target domains that stand out as most prominent and easily accessible (or, in Giora's words, *salient*) in our minds, even if they are irrelevant to the sense of the expression, in the particular context in which it occurs. According to Giora, this process is carried out by a 'linguistic processor', which works independently, yet simultaneously, with a 'contextual processor'. The contextual processor uses contextual clues to ascertain the intended meaning. Both of these processors are required to identify the meaning of metaphorical expressions, regardless of whether they are conventional or novel. Whilst the graded salience hypothesis provides a useful account of the contribution made by a listener's or reader's existing domain knowledge to metaphor interpretation, it is difficult to see why so much emphasis is placed on the independence of the linguistic and contextual processor, as they must, at some point, combine their efforts in order to determine meaning.

According to the *interaction theory* (Black, 1962), people use the target domain of a metaphor as a filter to organise and highlight certain aspects of the source domain while hiding other aspects. According to this theory, there may not be any *a priori* similarity between the source and target domains, but new meanings appear as a result of their juxtaposition. For example, Gineste *et al.* (2000) point out that when asked to interpret the metaphor 'a kiss is a fruit', informants come up with concepts such as *paradise, adoration, need, a token,* and *coming back for more*. None of these concepts is particularly central to the meaning of either kiss or fruit, but they do represent metaphoric associations of those words. In many cases, they reflect a second metaphor, the conceptual SENSUAL PLEASURE IS EATING. So when 'a kiss is a fruit' is being interpreted, these 'non-literal' associations are activated and highlighted, whereas the more 'literal' senses of 'kiss' and 'fruit' tend to be somewhat downplayed.

Under *blending theory* (Fauconnier and Turner, 1998) metaphoric mapping alone cannot fully account for all the interpretations that people come up with when faced with a metaphoric expression. Some interpretations include elements that do not appear to be related to either the source or the target domain. In order to account for these interpretations, Fauconnier and Turner hypothesise that metaphor comprehension involves a process of 'blending' or 'conceptual integration' of so-called mental spaces. According to Fauconnier and Turner (ibid., p. 136), mental spaces are 'small conceptual packets constructed as we think and talk, for purposes of local understanding and action'. In the context of a metaphor, they consist of the sets of associations that the listener has for each of the two domains in the metaphor. The blending process results in the appearance of a third, new mental space or 'blend', which may contain elements that are not intrinsically part of either the source or the target domain. These elements are known as 'emergent features'. For example, when interpreting the proverbial expression *Vanity is the quicksand of reason,* one might come up with notions such as 'prison' and 'doom', which at first sight do not appear to have much to do with either vanity or quicksand. However, this example highlights a problem with the concept of 'emergent features': the features in the above example only appear to be truly 'emergent' (i.e., not connected with vanity or quicksand) if we take a purely denotative, decontextualised definition of both vanity and quicksand (e.g., by seeing quicksand in purely geographical terms). If we take a broader, more encyclopaedic *gestalt* view, based on contexts in which people will have met, say, 'quicksand' and the likely connotations that the word has for different people, then quicksand could quite easily be seen to connote imprisonment, death, and so on. On the other hand, blending theory does make an important contribution to the field of metaphor research in that it emphasises the fact that some features of the source or target domain may develop a new intensity or importance when they appear in a particular metaphoric expression. One interesting aspect of Blending Theory is that it can be iterative; you can create a range of different blends for the same word, which can operate concurrently, or conceivably sequentially. This is quite important for understanding advertisements, which often rely, as we will show in section 3.3 later, on concurrent or sequential layers of meaning.

The *career of metaphor theory* (Gentner and Bowdle, 2001) proposes that metaphoric mappings can be accomplished through either comparison or categorisation processes, and that there is a shift in an individual's preferred processing mechanism from comparison to categorisation as metaphors become more conventionalised. For example, when a metaphor such as 'the eye of the needle' is encountered for the first time, the listener may have to compare an eye to a needle in order to work out its meaning. However, a listener who is familiar with the expression will simply access the feature of the word 'eye' that refers to the hole in the end of a needle. So when it becomes a conventional metaphor, it has several meanings, and the listener simply needs to access the one that is most appropriate to the context. Only novel metaphors require comparisons to be made. This bipolar division can be seen as similar to, but a simplification of, Giora's, graded salience, as it takes account of a listener's previous exposure to the metaphoric expression, and to its components. The career of metaphor theory is of potential interest to language teachers as it may account for the differences in metaphor interpretation techniques employed by native and non-native speakers of a language. More research is needed in this area.

According to the *class-inclusion model* (Glucksberg *et al.*, 2001), the two parts of a metaphor are put into a single category containing the attributes that they both share. Glucksberg *et al.* illustrate this model by referring to the metaphoric expression *my lawyer is a shark*. They argue that in order to understand the expression, a listener needs to create a superordinate class consisting of 'different types of lawyers', and then use the word 'shark' to select from them. According to the authors, this explains why irrelevant features of a shark (e.g., that it swims in water) are not activated; these features are simply nothing to do with the superordinate class of lawyers.

Each of the above theories (except for Blending Theory) offers a slightly different perspective on the main underlying fact that, for native speakers, metaphor comprehension requires the listener to identify some kind of relationship between the source and target domain. More often than not, this relationship involves a mapping of non-central features, or connotations, of the source onto the target domain. The above theories also agree on the fact that metaphor interpretation is largely determined by context, but there is some disagreement over the exact point at which context intervenes. The most important conclusion that we can draw for language teaching purposes is that, according to the above theories, the successful comprehension of metaphor requires that the listener attend to the knowledge of the source and target domain that they share with the speaker. As we will see later, this knowledge may well involve less central features of the source domain. This means that, in order to comprehend a metaphor in the target language, a foreign language learner must be aware of a wide range of features of the source domain in order to identify those that are being transferred to the target domain in that particular context. This process is not usually difficult for native speakers, as context and shared knowledge are usually sufficient to help them hypothesise the intentions of the speaker. Nevertheless, when foreign language learners come to comprehend metaphors, the situation is complicated by the fact that they may have different sets of features from their native speaker interlocutors, and that even when they do have similar sets of features, they may transfer the wrong ones.

3.3 Psychological processes that foreign language learners use to understand metaphor

Foreign language learners encounter metaphor simply as something unknown. If they have never seen the word before, they may first use the context to hazard a guess (see Carton, 1971 on 'inferencing'; Goodman, 1967 on guessing), or look it up in a dictionary and hope to find a solution that fits. If they have met the word before, but with a different (related) sense, as with the 'skirt' example in Chapter 1, they are in a position to either try and extend it to match the new context, or to search for an equivalent in their first, or another foreign, language (Kellerman, 1987a; 1987b). Where there still seems to be little transparency, they may continue to assume that inductive operations will lead to a workable answer and employ interpretation processes that are normally reserved for novel metaphor (even if the expression is conventional for native speakers). Our contention is that by encouraging their students to think 'figuratively' in this way, teachers can aid learning.

Having decided to treat something as novel metaphor, you need

(1) to identify the source and target domain terms,
(2) use the target domain to single out those aspects of the source domain that seem relevant within the given context and
(3) decide between competing alternative solutions.

To illustrate, we will take a slogan that has been repeatedly used to advertise a brand of beer from the industrial heart of the United Kingdom, Boddingtons. Advertisements typically show the beer in a smooth pint glass, with well-dressed people doing something slightly vulgar or risqué in an industrial setting. The slogan is 'Boddingtons the Cream of Manchester'. We have a *source domain term* 'cream' and a *target domain term* 'Boddingtons'. We can use these terms, in combination with the visual context, to infer that the *source domain* is 'features that we associate with cream', and that the *target domain* is 'qualities that this beer might have, and to which advertisers would want to draw our attention'. As we can see in Figure 3.1, not all of the source domain features are necessarily mapped onto the target domain and some features remain very unclear. Whether or not certain features are ultimately mapped onto the target domain is determined by the *nature* of the target domain, which in turn, is largely determined by the *context*. At least one feature would appear to be determined by a mixture of visual information in the advertisement and cultural knowledge; traditionally (or stereotypically) northern beers have a creamy foam 'head' on the top, while southern beers do not. Cream in a UK bottle of non-homogenised milk rises to the top, to form a visual, as well as textural parallel.

In this case the slogan is also complicated visually by the tension between sophistication, vulgarity and the no-nonsense northern industrial setting. The visual tension is complemented by the existence of the metaphoric idiom 'the cream of', which frequently refers to people; thus

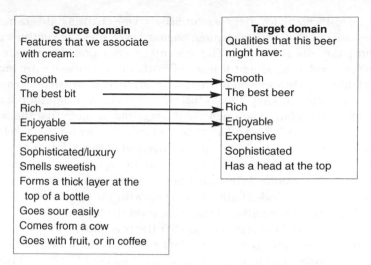

Figure 3.1 Mapping process that might take place when interpreting 'Boddingtons the cream of Manchester'

the focus moves (metonymically) from the beer to the drinkers – drinkers of Boddingons become the cream of society. The cleverness of the advertisement is that it offers two opposing messages about desirability: to prototypical southerners (who feel sophisticated, want to be chic and daring, but look down on industrial England) and protypical northerners (who are contemptuous of sophistication and see it as a hypocritical veneer, but see northern beer as the smoothest and best). Moreover, readers who do not identify with either position can treat the whole thing as irony – which in the United Kingdom is a reaction that advertisers often try to achieve.

What do foreign language learners do? If they have no knowledge of cultural stereotypes of northern and southern Britain or its beers, and/or little knowledge about advertisers' attempts to induce ironic interpretations, they will miss the subtle levels and simply focus (as per Figure 3.1) on what is creamlike about the beer. But even their reactions to 'cream' will depend on their previous cultural experience of it.

For example, when a group of four advanced Japanese learners of English was presented with this advertisement, they found it very difficult to understand, as they had no understanding of English cultural stereotypes, or advertising practices, and, moreover, fresh cream is not widely available in Japan (Littlemore, 2005). Further discussion revealed that typical 'cream' for them was artificial 'crème chantilly' that came in an aerosol container. The Japanese language even uses the English word 'cream' for this substance. The students' source domains for cream therefore contained salient features of froth and ephemeral substances. These salient features severely interfered with their ability to understand the advertisement. They argued that the advertisement did not put the beer in a particularly good light, as it suggested to them that the taste might be 'artificial', 'sugary' and 'short-lived'. In order for them to find an appropriate interpretation, it was therefore necessary to activate a more conscious search of the features of the source domain than a native speaker would. When they were encouraged to do so by the teacher, they were indeed able to come up with the fact that the cream is the best part of the milk and that it comes at the top, and that the beer is therefore good. However the idea that the beer should have a creamy texture did not occur to them, as in Japan, bitter is not widely available. Japanese people tend to drink lager, rather than bitter, and good lagers are more likely to be 'crisp' and 'refreshing' rather than 'creamy'. Therefore a gap in their *target domain* knowledge prevented them from accessing this interpretation. Moreover, while this approach definitely helped students understand the beer better, they were still unable to use the contextual clues correctly to infer that there were two target sub-domains involved, not one: the beer and the drinkers. Thus these learners had problems identifying the target as well as appropriately searching the source (see Cameron, 2003).

All of this means that successful metaphor comprehension by foreign language learners may involve psychological processes that are somewhat more conscious than those employed by native speakers. Below, we describe five psychological processes that foreign language learners can employ to improve their metaphor comprehension skills. These are *noticing, activation of source domain knowledge, associative fluency, analogical reasoning*, and *image formation*. We will present psycholinguistic and neurolinguistic evidence suggesting that these processes are employed by native speakers in metaphor comprehension and production, albeit at a subconscious level. We will argue that, by *consciously* engaging in these processes, language learners can improve their ability to understand metaphoric uses of the target language that are novel *to them*.

3.3.1 Noticing

In the field of Applied Linguistics, the last ten years or so have seen much debate over the issue of 'noticing' with some researchers (most notably Schmidt, 1990) arguing that aspects of language input need to be noticed before they can be processed, and others arguing that implicit (or subconscious) learning is equally likely (see for example, Ellis, 1994). Although we have no desire to get embroiled in this debate, we are interested in the role that noticing might play in the development of a language learner's metaphor interpretation skills. It is obvious that, in the majority of cases, a native speaker does not need to explicitly recognise an utterance as metaphorical in order to process it as such. And this is also true of language learners, most of the time. On the other hand, if a learner wants to improve their ability to deal with metaphor in the target language, they will need, at some point, to increase their awareness of how they process metaphorical expressions when they encounter them, and before they can actively process a particular expression as metaphorical, they need to notice the incongruity that signals it as such.

Student readiness for new metaphors may be enhanced by drawing attention to the various ways in which metaphors tend to be signalled verbally (Goatly, 1997; Cameron and Deignan, 2003), through use of auditory signals such as intonation (Vanlancker-Sidtis, 2003), and through the use of body language (Corts and Pollio, 1999). We discuss the nature of these signalling devices in more detail in Chapter 7. Another important factor is the extent to which language learners *expect* people to use metaphors. In our experience at least, many foreign language learners are not linguistically trained and view metaphor more as a poetic device; they do not expect to hear it used on a regular basis in more prosaic contexts.

It has been shown that, in written discourse, native speakers of English are most likely to notice metaphors that involve explicit comparisons; metaphors that act as special literary devices and metaphors that involve personification (Graesser *et al.*, 1988). They are also more likely to notice nominal metaphors than verb metaphors. Children are more likely to misinterpret verb metaphors than nominal metaphors (Cameron, 2003). This finding suggests that if language teachers want their students to be aware of metaphors, and the problems that they might cause, it is important to help identify less obvious ones, such as verbal metaphors. The only study of metaphor noticing in discourse by L2 learners, of which we are aware, was conducted by Steen (2004), who asked a group of 18 advanced Dutch learners of English to identify metaphors in the lyrics of *Hurricane*, by Bob Dylan. He found that metaphors were more likely to be noticed if they appeared in propositions containing more than one metaphorically used word, and if they appeared in propositions that form the main element of the sentence.

He also found that metaphors were more likely to be noticed if they appeared in postverbal position, and at the beginning or the end of the text. Steen's findings suggest that, when alerting language learners to the presence of metaphor, teachers may need to focus on metaphors that appear: on their own; in propositions that simply modify the main proposition; in preverbal position; or in the middle of a piece of text. On the other hand, it is important to bear in mind the fact that Steen's study focussed on song lyrics where line endings are emphasised, and further research is required in order to assess what kinds of metaphors learners notice in other, less literary, types of discourse.

If we want our students to focus explicitly on metaphor, the process of noticing must precede all the other psychological processes involved in metaphor comprehension. In contrast, the four psychological processes that are discussed in following sections are closely interlinked, and need to operate simultaneously. The order in which they are presented is therefore arbitrary.

3.3.2   Activation of source domain knowledge

In order to comprehend a metaphor appropriately, it is important, as we showed with the Boddingons slogan, to activate one's knowledge of the source domain. To take another example, to understand why Margaret Thatcher was often described as 'the iron lady', one needs to know that iron is hard, cold and inflexible. On hearing this expression, we know that these are the features of iron that we need to transfer to the target domain. When we see or hear a source domain term, it tends not to trigger a single sense, but a network of related and contextually relevant senses (or features) (Eco, 1979). In the 'iron lady' example, related notions such as 'steely' and 'iron-fisted' might also be triggered. In order to comprehend a metaphor, it is necessary for us to activate a network of features that corresponds roughly to those of our interlocutor, and then identify features within this network that relate to the target domain term.

When interpreting metaphors in their own language, native speakers are likely to activate a network of features that largely overlaps with that of their interlocutor (though the Boddingtons slogan indicates that overlap is not guaranteed). However, this process will be more difficult for foreign language learners because the networks of related features that surround certain source domain terms are sometimes culturally determined; within a network, some features are likely to be particularly salient for individuals from certain cultures (Giora, 2003). The network of features that is activated for them by a particular concept may therefore lack features that are present for native speakers (as we saw with 'cream' previously), or different features may be salient for them (again, the cream example; also Kecskes, 2000). It is therefore important for foreign language learners to be on the lookout for ways in which their networks of features might differ from those of native speakers.

3.3.3 Associative fluency

We have just seen that gaps in their salient source domain knowledge may mean that language learners are less likely than native speakers to come up with an appropriate interpretation of a metaphor first time round. One way in which they may be able to compensate for these gaps is by using *associative fluency*. Associative fluency refers to the ability to make a wide range of connections when presented with a given stimulus. It relies on the use of divergent search strategies for retrieval from memory. Divergent searches are broad and associational rather than logical, and they rely on vague search criteria (Miller, 1987). One would expect language learners to have a better chance of succeeding if they have several gos at understanding a metaphor before settling on a particular interpretation. The ability to identify a wide variety of source domain features may also help learners' productive skills, enabling them to think of a wider variety of metaphoric extensions of word meaning (a finding that Pitts *et al.*, 1982 made with native speakers).

Indeed, associative fluency is thought to underlie the ability to identify a wide variety of possible interpretations for a single given metaphor (Pollio and Smith, 1980). When applied to the comprehension of metaphor, associative fluency is usually termed 'metaphoric fluency' (Johnson and Rosano, 1993). Support for a relationship between associative fluency and metaphoric fluency comes from Carroll (1993) who, after factor analysing a number of tests designed to measure the ability to produce large numbers of 'related ideas', identified a highly specific 'associational fluency' factor. All the measures that loaded significantly on this factor had rubrics and scoring systems requiring that 'a series of associations are to be given, and the score is the number of associations produced (written) in a given time' (ibid.; p. 414). Specifically, Carroll found that a test in which participants were asked to think of several ways of completing unfinished similes loaded on this factor. This finding is relatively easy to explain; when asked to find multiple interpretations for a metaphor, people need to search the network of features surrounding the source domain in order to identify features that can be transferred to the target domain. Individuals with a divergent search strategy will make a broader search, accessing meanings that are not included by those with a convergent search strategy. This may mean that they are more likely to access the less central metaphoric meanings that are often necessary for appropriate metaphor comprehension.

In short, associative fluency is a potentially useful skill for foreign language learners when interpreting metaphors as it involves experimenting with a number of possible interpretations. This constitutes a type of active 'language play', an activity that has been associated with successful foreign language acquisition (Cook, 2000). We return to the issue of language play in Chapter 10.

3.3.4   Analogical reasoning

As we saw in section 3.2, successful metaphor comprehension frequently involves making maximum use of the context. In order to understand a metaphor the first time one comes across it, one first needs to identify and then use the target domain to identify which of the features associated with the source domain term are to be accessed. This relationship is likely to involve a degree of 'analogical reasoning'. Analogical reasoning is a process whereby partial similarities or relationships are observed between concepts, so that the characteristics of one can be used to shed light on the other (Holyoak and Thagard, 1995). It has been argued that the capacity to perceive correspondences between apparently dissimilar domains is central to all kinds of metaphoric processing, and that the basis of similarity may lie in shared attributes or that it may involve relational similarity (Paivio and Walsh, 1993).

Strong empirical support for the role of analogical reasoning in metaphor comprehension and appreciation is provided by Trick and Katz (1986), who found that participants who scored highly on a test of analogical reasoning found it especially easy to interpret, and appreciate, metaphors in which the source and target domain were conceptually distant.

As with associative fluency, we argue that analogical reasoning could usefully be employed by foreign language learners to help compensate for gaps in their salient source domain knowledge. Whereas native speakers can rely heavily on intuition, cultural knowledge and the activation of relevant networks of features, for language learners the process may be more arduous and mundane. In order to hit upon the correct interpretation, it may be useful for them to draw as many analogies between the source and target domains as they can.

Some support for this position is offered by Mori's (2002) study of Japanese who were learning kanji compounds. His findings offer some evidence for the effectiveness of a combined strategy, where foreign language learners use contextual cues together with knowledge of the network of features surrounding the source domain term. A kanji compound consists of two characters that are combined to make a single word. Mori found that students who combined the use of contextual cues with a figurative analysis of the properties of the characters themselves were significantly more likely to determine its meaning than students who used either the context or the word's morphology alone. Interestingly, Mori discovered that the combined strategy was only effective if students actually believed that it would work. This strongly suggests that foreign language learners need to be shown examples of how metaphoric thinking can be used to work out the meaning of new vocabulary, and need to be convinced of its efficacy, before they are actually asked to do it for themselves.

3.3.5 Image formation

A number of researchers have been suggesting for many years that mental imagery plays an important role in the comprehension and production of figurative language. Much of the following discussion is based on research connected with Paivio's Dual Coding Theory (DCT) (Paivio, 1983). The key claim in DCT is that verbal data is stored separately from non-verbal, especially visual, data. The two types of data differ, in that verbal data tends to be sequential while non-verbal data can be accessed in a parallel fashion – meaning that it is easier to connect or superimpose two (mental) images than two words or sentences. The two types of data are, however, linked, in that concrete words or expressions, it is argued, readily trigger (or call up) images, whereas it is far harder to create images for abstract words. As concrete terms regularly receive imagistic support, they are said to be double, or dually, coded. Dual coding is claimed to enhance memorability by a factor of two; concrete expressions are thus remembered twice as well as abstract words.

Attempts have been made to explore how DCT relates to metaphoric comprehension. Paivio and Walsh (1993), for example, claim that the two elements of metaphor (i.e., target and source/topic and vehicle) are fused by means of an interactive image (see also Reichmann and Coste, 1980). They argue that imagery helps the speaker or listener make the comparisons necessary for metaphor production or comprehension, and that imagery can generate novel, integrated representations for metaphor production, as well as increase the efficiency of the search for relevant information for metaphor comprehension. It is precisely the fact that images from the non-verbal store can be superimposed and combined so rapidly and easily (as a result of being accessed in parallel fashion) that renders this fusion of source and target so effective. Pedagogically, the converse situation is of particular interest: that consciously activating, or fusing, mental images might lead to (a) improved understanding of metaphoric expressions – many of which do involve relatively concrete source terms – and more importantly, (b) improved recall and learning. There is substantial empirical support for the role of imagery in L1 metaphor comprehension. For example, Gibbs and Bogdonovich (1999) found evidence, based on self-report data, to suggest that concrete mental images play a prominent role in the comprehension of poetic metaphors. Again, Harris *et al.* (1980) examined subjects' use of imagery in encoding metaphoric expressions in comparison with non-metaphoric ones. They found that subjects used images significantly and more frequently to encode metaphoric sentences than non-metaphoric ones. Some of these images were surreal and interactive, as Dual Coding Theory predicts (Paivio and Walsh, 1993). The surreal nature of these interactive images, and the fact that they enable the interpreter to fuse the source and target domains means that in many ways they echo Fauconnier and Turner 's 'blends', which were mentioned in section 3.2. There is neurological support for the role of imagery in metaphor comprehension. Bottini *et al.* (1994) found that a significant contribution is made by the right hemisphere prefrontal lobe. According to Bottini *et al.*, this area of the brain is responsible for manipulating imagery.

It is difficult to say what the exact relationship might be between imagery and the other psychological processes as outlined previously. If, as Paivio and Walsh (1993) propose, imagery helps the drawing together of conceptual referents then it may well be linked to analogical reasoning. As we have just seen, the idea of image formation also ties in quite neatly with blending theory, which requires the conceptual integration of the source and target domains in a third 'blended space'. It could be that, when they comprehend or produce metaphors, some individuals form a mental image that combines features of the source and target domains with a number of additional features (as with Harris *et al.*, 1980, and Gineste *et al.*, 2000).

Li's (2002) study is one of the few to explore the role of mental imagery in the learning of foreign language idioms. As we saw in

Chapter 2, he conducted a range of experiments focussing on the best ways to teach imageable metaphoric expressions, idioms and proverbs (all relating in a fairly clear-cut way to common conceptual metaphors). In all cases the experimental groups which had been (a) shown diagrams, (b) asked to draw diagrams of the body and a container, (c) asked to describe personal images holistically via 'what image is in your mind' or (d) asked to explore and describe the transferred 'image' structure performed significantly better than control groups on one-week delayed post-tests (DPT) of meaning. Retention of the form of the expressions was, however, less common and less marked.

Li's results need to be interpreted with a degree of caution, as all the five groups with higher DPT (meaning) scores were asked to engage actively with the materials, querying them, drawing them and questioning them, and it may simply have been the *existence* of such engagement (rather than the nature of the engagement) that provoked learning. However, it can confidently be concluded from Li's studies that a combination of imaging and engaging actively with the images and the words led to an increase in short-term retention of the meaning of linguistic metaphors, fixed idioms and proverbs. The active engagement is a good example of exactly what we are calling 'figurative thinking', carried out in a teacher-led scaffolded situation.

To sum up, we have seen in this section how the psychological processes of noticing, schema activation, associative fluency, analogical reasoning, and imagery may be usefully employed by foreign language learners when dealing with metaphor. An example of how such learners might be helped to employ these processes is given at the end of this chapter.

3.3.6 Spontaneous processing and metaphor production

The ability to break down metaphor comprehension into the psychological processes as described before should help foreign language learners to focus on the range of possible associations between the source and target domains, and lead to more successful metaphor interpretation. However, if they had to employ all of these psychological processes each time they wanted to understand or produce a metaphor, this would interfere considerably with their fluency in the target language. There may therefore be times when it is more beneficial for them to adopt a more spontaneous approach. By spontaneous, we mean one that emphasises the non-analytic perception of relationships between the source and target domains of a metaphor.

Spontaneous processing is likely to be particularly appropriate for the comprehension of synaesthesic metaphors. As we saw in Chapter 2, these involve mappings across sensory domains, and are more difficult to analyse and explain than other metaphors. Very often synaestheisic mappings cannot be explained by a listener, they are simply felt. For example, expressions such as 'sweet music' or 'speak softly' are very difficult to analyse. Synaesthesic metaphors such as these are more likely than other types of metaphor to rely on spontaneous processing.

The same may be true for novel metaphor *production*. L1 Research has shown that if people are given instructions that encourage spontaneous *gestalt* processing, they are better at producing appropriate novel metaphors than if they are given step-by-step instructions based on analogical reasoning (Pitts *et al.*, 1982). These findings suggest that novel metaphor production is enhanced by an ability to engage in spontaneous *gestalt* processing. For language learners, the ability to produce novel metaphors appears to be statistically unrelated to more receptive abilities such as ability to find meaning and metaphoric fluency (Littlemore, 2001a). One reason for this might be that novel metaphor production is more dependent on spontaneous processing, whereas metaphor comprehension is (or can be) a more analytic process, involving associative fluency and analogical reasoning.

For both native and non-native speakers, a large part of *conventional* metaphor production is likely to consist of exemplars or 'chunks' (Skehan, 1998). According to Skehan, language is first received in chunks, which are then broken down and analysed syntactically. They are then reformulated into these chunks for productive purposes. For metaphor, the syntactic analysis might be accompanied by a degree of semantic analysis in which the semantic features of the source and target domains are analysed using the processes as outlined previously. The metaphors might then be reformed into automatic chunks for productive purposes.

3.4   Psychological processes that foreign language learners might use to understand metonymy

In conceptual terms, metaphor involves the perception of relationships between a source and target domain, whereas metonymy involves the perception of a relationship between two features of a single domain. For example, in the expression 'Blair bombed Iraq', Tony Blair is being used to refer metonymically to some members of the armed forces who were under his command. In this expression, the one part of a single domain provides 'access' to another part of it. It is also possible for a whole domain to stand for a part ('Your country needs you'), for part of a domain to stand metonymically for the whole domain, or for a domain to stand for something closely associated ('I need a hand' – where hand implies the associated action of helping and a whole person to give it). Kövecses and Radden's (1998) model of conceptual metonymy suggests more complex possibilities, but the 'traditional' relations of part-whole and close association are adequate for present purposes.

It is uncertain whether metonymy poses as many problems for non-native speakers as metaphor does. The problems may lie more with production than with comprehension, but to the best of our knowledge, no research has yet addressed this issue. We have found that native speakers often find it extremely difficult to notice metonymy, even when they are perfectly capable of understanding it. One reason for this may be that metonymy often serves more of a straightforward referential function than metaphor, and that it may therefore not be signalled as often, or in the same way.

Despite the fact that native speakers are less likely to notice metonymy than metaphor, the psychological process of noticing may help language learners in some situations. For example, the use of 'Blair', or 'Bush', to add agency to unpopular decisions that were in fact voted for by the entire government makes them appear solely responsible, and the technique of 'cite the responsible baddie' is a basic tool of propaganda, from Islamic fundamentalism to *The Sun*. The responsible learner needs to learn to think about the use of Person/Institution for actual actors. In cases such as these, the skill of noticing becomes more important, and language teachers could usefully point this out to students.

Metonymy comprehension is also likely to involve the activation of domain knowledge (as we saw in Chapter 1, metonymy is usually thought to involve a relationship between two aspects of the same domain). This is likely to be followed by a degree of associative fluency, for we need to search the domain to find out what is actually being referred to. But the associative searches involved in metonymy comprehension are likely to differ from those involved in metaphor comprehension. Whereas in metaphor comprehension, it is useful to search the network of *connotations* that the source domain term may have, in metonymy comprehension it is more useful to search for related concepts within the same domain. For example, in order to understand the metonymic use of *eye* in 'Ken was assessing her with the eye of a practised womaniser', we would need to understand that the eye stands metonymically for 'seeing' (although the metonymy starts to shade into metaphor when we consider issues of 'taste' and 'desire'). This example illustrates the importance of contextual clues in metonymy comprehension. The contextual clues in this example, such as the presence of the word 'womaniser', and one's knowledge of the genre in which the sentence appeared (perhaps a romantic novel) are crucial. A reader would probably be able to use these clues to infer that Ken was appreciating her beauty, and that he was weighing up his chances with her.

Because similarity is not one of the main components of metonymy, analogical reasoning may be less central to metonymy comprehension. On the other hand, it is likely to be marginally involved, to the extent that in order to interpret metonymy a reader or listener needs to relate their interpretations to the context in which the metonymy appears.

The use of imagery may also help language learners to interpret and use metonymy in the target language. Metonymic relationships that are particularly easy to visualise may include ones in which THE MEANS STANDS FOR THE ACTION (for example, 'he sneezed his glasses off'); ones in which THE PART OF BODY INVOLVED IN THE ACTION STANDS FOR THE ACTION (e.g., 'she elbowed him out of the way', 'he headed the ball', or 'she eyed the chocolates'); and ones in which THE DESTINATION STANDS FOR THE ACTION (e.g., 'she floored her opponent', or 'he cornered the ref.'). Verbs such as these are sometimes referred to as 'manner of movement verbs', and research has shown that they are understood and learned better if they are acted out (Lindstromberg and Boers, 2005).

3.5   Using psychological processes to help foreign language learners understand metaphor and metonymy: two examples

This section looks at how the activation of source domain knowledge, associative fluency, analogical reasoning and image formation can be developed in the context of foreign language learning. We will give one anecdotal example of an individual foreign language learner being helped to use these processes to understand metaphor, and another anecdotal example of a group of learners using them to understand metonymy.

We begin with metaphor, and look at an instance (reported in Littlemore, 2002) in which a Spanish speaking upper-intermediate student of business English came across the sentence:

By the late 1990s even big names such as IBM and Hewlett-Packard had *jumped on the bandwagon*. Intel's logo appeared on the computers of more than 1,600 manufacturers and its chips held a 75 per cent market share. (The Essence of Building An Effective Brand, The *Financial Times*, 18 December 2000).

In order to help her to *notice* the metaphor, Littlemore asked her to circle any incongruous or difficult-to-understand expressions. She circled the term 'jumped on the bandwagon'. Littlemore began by asking her to separate out the words 'band' and 'wagon' and asked her to picture a wagon carrying a band playing music. She then explained that the expression probably originated in an old-fashioned scenario, where the arrival of a bandwagon in a town generally attracted a large following. She then asked her to picture the scene (a large group of people following the bandwagon) and to think of words and concepts associated with this image. When she came up with ideas, Littlemore kept pushing her for more and more associations. By doing this, Littlemore was asking her to engage in *image formation* in order to *activate her knowledge of the source domain* and to develop her *associative fluency*. The concepts that she came up with were *popularity, crowd, movement, noise, publicity, enthusiasm, togetherness, old-fashioned clothes, a fair ground*. She then asked the student to think about how these concepts might apply to the context in which the expression appeared. This was the *analogical reasoning* part of the exercise. In effect, Littlemore was asking the student to use a 'mapping process' from the source domain to the target domain. This led her to pick out concepts such as *popularity, crowd, movement, noise, publicity, enthusiasm, togetherness* from the above list.

Finally, Littlemore encouraged the student to employ a blending process, whereby she attempted to blend the concepts of bandwagons and big business, by means of an interactive image (*Intel* sitting on the bandwagon, *IBM* and *Hewlett Packard* in the crowd behind). Although the student claimed to find this part of the exercise difficult, she was able to identify a wider variety of concepts, which included preconceptions that she may already have had about IBM and Hewlett Packard. For example, she thought that they might be *large, push the other companies out of the way and kick some of the weaker ones off the bandwagon*. As we saw above, according to blending theory, metaphor comprehension involves a blending of domains, rather than a simple mapping from one domain to another. This blending process may result in novel 'mental spaces' that may include elements that are not intrinsically part of the source domain. So when this student said that IBM and Hewlett Packard might be large, push the other companies out of the way and kick some of the weaker ones off the bandwagon, she was relying on part of her own elaborate conception of the target domain, therefore moving away somewhat from the source domain.

We can see from this example that the student was able to achieve a rich understanding of the term 'jump on the bandwagon' through the use of figurative thinking processes. Moreover, when tested five weeks later, she had no difficulty whatsoever in recalling the meaning of this item. This is a promising result, although it must be remembered that is was a one-off example. Further research is needed to identify how many of these types of examples students are able to remember. It must be borne in mind that by using this technique students run the risk of reaching incorrect or inappropriate interpretations. It would therefore be useful to check their interpretation against an authority. Nevertheless, the advantage of trying to work out the meaning for themselves first is that they are much more likely to remember it when they have done so (Boers *et al.*, forthcoming).

Now let us look at an example of how figurative thinking processes can be used to understand metonymy. Let us imagine, for example, the difficulties that are presented to a language learner by an expression such as 'water cooler moments' as in the following extract from a TV guide:

> Harry Hill (above centre) returns for a second series of his amusingly daft, surreal and unpredictable Late Review for telly junkies. The large-collared comedian will be on hand to cast a typically absurdist glance at the soaps, the stars making headlines and the latest *water cooler moments*, as well as dispensing the odd quirky aside involving badgers. (*The Times*, 30 October 2003, italics added)

Here the term 'water cooler' is used metonymically to refer to a type of activity that often occurs in the vicinity of a water cooler in a typical office, that is to gossip about recent and interesting happenings. This is a linguistic metonymy. As such, it is a surface feature of discourse that forms part of a more general conceptual metonymy. The conceptual metonymy in this example might be described as THE OBJECT STANDS FOR AN ACTIVITY THAT IS CARRIED OUT WHILST USING THAT OBJECT. The best way to access this conceptual metonymy might be through a group brainstorming activity, where students are encouraged to vocalise the first idea that comes into their head, and where no ideas are rejected in the first instance. Their ideas could then be tested against the context of the utterance. There are other interesting dimensions to this example. For example, the word 'dispensing' becomes ambiguous by juxtaposition with 'water cooler': it becomes literal and metonymically related to coolers. Thus metonymy seems to create resonances, just like metaphor – a point that we will pick up on in Chapter 7. Also, 'water cooler moment' draws much of its humorous and negative effect from paralleling other 'moment' expressions, like 'senior moment', or 'moment of madness'. Although each of these features probably merits further study, our current focus is on the attempts made by a group of mixed-nationality students (all of whom were advanced learners of English) to work out the meaning of 'water cooler moments' as it appeared in the above context. Here is an extract from their discussion (Box 3.1):

Box 3.1 Extract of students working out the meaning of the expression 'water cooler moments' in an advanced level English language class given at the University of Birmingham (2003)

Student 1	Water cooler moments
Teacher	Yeah, water cooler moments, do you know what a water cooler is?
Student 2	It's a machine
Teacher	Yeah, it's a machine in reception, or maybe in the office, and you put a beaker under it, and water comes out of it.
Student 3	Icy? With ice on it? Icy moments? Not friendly.
Teacher	Icy? I can see where you're coming from with icy moments, but there's another meaning here. Water cooler moments?
Student 2	I can suggest only that somebody's doing something, that somebody's pouring cold water on them, refreshing
Student 4	By putting cold water on them
Student 2	Or putting people in a stupid situation (Mimes throwing water over another student's head)
Student 2	In the previous sentence, it says 'the stars making headlines' so you know like doing something
Teacher	It's got that idea a little bit ...
Student 1	We have an expression which is like 'disturb water' which is do something that make some attention or interest. May not be good but may not be bad, but 'stir water', you know it reminds me of that.
Student 2	I think the one more thing is that people meet in office, they usually talk about other people in the office doing such interesting things, then they go to the water cooler to do that.
Teacher	Yes, that's it. Are they talking about important or not important things?
Student 1	Not important things
Teacher	Yeah that's right, gossip.

The figurative thinking processes in this extract are immediately apparent. The first interpretation, offered by student 3 is metaphoric (*water cooler moments are icy moments, which are possibly unfriendly*). The second interpretation, offered by student 2, is more metonymic (the water is *refreshing*). The third interpretation, also offered by student 2, is also metonymic (*people are made to look stupid by having cold water poured over them*). The fourth interpretation, offered by student 3, is based on a comparison with a related idiom in her own language (*to disturb water is to do something that attracts attention*). This fourth interpretation appears to serve as an impetus for student 2 to offer a fifth interpretation of the expression. He observes that people go to the water cooler to talk about other people in the office doing 'interesting things'. He thus identifies the metonymic relationship between the water cooler and the act of gossiping.

The students appear to be employing the psychological processes of noticing, activation of source domain knowledge, associative fluency, relating to context, and image formation in this example, although to varying degrees. They all noticed an incongruity between the term 'water cooler moments' and the context of the TV review. The activation of source domain knowledge and role of associative fluency were also apparent in these interpretations. The students associated the idea of a water cooler with the ideas of unfriendliness, freshness, being made to look stupid, attracting attention and participating in office gossip. In the third, fourth and fifth interpretations, there is also evidence of analogical reasoning, as the students were trying to relate their interpretations to the context of a TV chat show. In the third interpretation, where the student mimed water being thrown over another student, he appeared to be appealing to his classmates' ability to form an appropriate mental image, but we can only infer this.

In this example, it is the teacher who serves to cut off the brainstorming process when the appropriate attribute is found. Up until this point, she remains in 'stand-by mode' (Samuda, 2001), allowing the students to develop their hypotheses in a co-operative manner, until they hit upon a satisfactory interpretation.

3.6   Conclusion

In this chapter, we have seen that figurative thinking involves the psychological processes of noticing, activation of source domain knowledge, associative fluency, analogical reasoning and image formation. It is important for both students and their teachers to be aware of these processes if they are to develop their figurative thinking ability in the L2. They also need to develop a degree of *autonomy* over these processes if they are to function without a teacher present. Chapter 4 considers the issue of autonomy, and looks at how a range of potentially limiting factors to autonomy might be dealt with.

4
Developing Learner Autonomy in Figurative Thinking

4.1 Introductory comments

So far we have seen that figurative thinking is likely to play a fairly important role in foreign language learning, and that it can be beneficial for language teachers to help their students develop their figurative thinking capacity, in order to facilitate their comprehension and retention of L2 figurative language. However, inasmuch as learners need ultimately to be able to operate without the support of a teacher, one important part of this process must involve helping learners to identify and understand figurative thinking processes, and exercise a degree of control over them. In other words, learners need to develop a degree of *autonomy* over them. Just how much autonomy is possible or productive, though, is a complex question. The aims of this chapter are therefore to examine what is meant by 'autonomy', to assess the extent to which foreign language learners can develop autonomy over their figurative thinking processes, and to consider how at least some of the barriers to autonomy might be surmounted. We argue that an awareness of the existence of such barriers can in many cases be a first step towards dealing with them.

4.2 Developing students' autonomy over their ability to work with figurative language

Learner autonomy involves 'a capacity for detachment, critical reflection, and independent action' (Little, 1991: p. 2), and entails a 'readiness to take charge of one's own learning in the service of one's needs and purposes' (Dam, 1995: p. 1). In general, it has been found that language learners who are able to engage in self-directed, strategic and reflective learning tend to develop better communicative abilities than those who are not (e.g., Legenhausen, 1999; Dam, 2000). In other words, language learners are more likely to be successful if they know about their own thinking processes, and are able to use this awareness to regulate their learning. This is likely to be equally true of figurative language comprehension and production. In order to develop autonomy over their ability to *understand* figurative language, students would need to be able to: recognise it when they see it[1]; understand, at a basic level, the cognitive processes involved in interpreting it; and predict, to some extent, the misinterpretations that they may make as a result of gaps in their knowledge of both the source and target domains. In order to develop autonomy over their ability to *produce* figurative language, they would need to recognise situations in which it might be appropriate to use it, be aware of possible problems in terms of phraseology and register; and then signal their use of novel figurative expressions in an appropriate manner. Raising students' awareness of the psychological processes of noticing, activation of source domain knowledge, associative fluency, analogical reasoning and image formation ought to go some way towards helping them develop their autonomy in these areas, although there will be limitations. Furthermore, it may encourage them to play with the language in ways that will help them to learn (Cook, 2000), and help them to continue learning beyond the classroom.

One way to raise students' awareness of the role played by their figurative thinking processes in their language learning might simply be to show them concrete examples, such as those presented at the end of Chapter 3, of students making metaphoric and metonymic connections between ideas, and to use this as an opportunity to discuss the various psychological processes involved. This approach has the advantage of relying on 'near-peer role models', that is other students, who are of a similar level and background to them, performing the activities (Murphey, 1996). Murphey found that the ability of his language students to complete language learning activities improved significantly if they were shown videos of other students performing apparently difficult tasks. He argued that this was because the approach gave them the necessary levels of confidence and self-belief to learn.

A more interventionist approach might be for the teacher to note down the various attempts made by students (e.g., during collaborative oral work) at working out the contextual meaning of figurative language, and then to draw their attention to the figurative nature of their reasoning.

As we saw in Chapter 2, preliminary findings suggest that language learners can be trained to exploit the potential of their figurative thinking capacity in order to work out the meaning of new expressions in the target language. An important component of this training involves providing them with opportunities to develop the strategy in an individualised way (Littlemore, 2004b; 2004c). This implies that they should be encouraged to think of the networks of senses that are in *their own* source and target domains – which will in all probability be a mixture of L1, individual and partially understood L2 components – and to apply these to the contexts in which the figurative language appears.

In terms of production, learners could be encouraged to operate a quick probability check procedure. A Chinese student of English might ask herself: if I refer metaphorically to the 'Wuzhi mountains',[2] are the English likely to know what or where they are? (Personal Communication with Xin Yu, MA Language Learning and Education student). They can also be taught to be generally wary of any animal references in an L2, and to gloss with expressions, such as 'as we say'. Alternatively, in low-consequence situations, learners can be encouraged to use higher risk strategies, such as trying out figurative extensions of word meaning potential by signalling them appropriately (or with even higher risk by not signalling them), and seeing what kinds of response they get from their interlocutors. People vary in their sensitivity to listeners' reactions, so for the strategy to work, teachers may well need to train speakers to attend to listeners' reactions. This training of course does double duty, given the importance of co-construction in oral discourse of metaphor (Cano Mora, 2005; Cameron and Stelma, 2005).

Even though it may be desirable for language learners to develop a degree of autonomy over their figurative thinking processes, such autonomy is unlikely to be possible for all learners, in all situations. There are a number of factors that are likely to limit the ability of language learners to think figuratively without the help of a teacher. Furthermore, it is important for teachers to assess what level or type of guidance or instruction their learners will need to successfully interpret and master figurative instances in the L2. To make well-informed choices, a language teacher needs to be able to estimate the degree of semantic or pragmatic transparency that particular figurative instance is likely to present to a learner. That degree of transparency is the outcome of a complex interplay between the characteristics of the type of figurative language at hand and the assumed characteristics of the learner, including his or her cultural background and cognitive style. In the remaining sections of this chapter, a number of factors are discussed which may limit the ability of a students to work out the meaning of figurative language for themselves, or to produce appropriate metaphors and metonymies. Where relevant, possible ways of dealing with these factors are suggested.

4.3 Possible limiting factors to autonomy

The first eight limiting factors to autonomy are discussed in sections 4.3.1–4.3.8. These factors relate mainly to the nature of words and expressions in the target language itself, and the students' knowledge of these words and expressions. These include the students' lack of knowledge of the 'basic' senses of the words; limitations in the students' culturally embedded encyclopaedic knowledge; the centrality of the expressions to a conceptual metaphor or metonymy; word class; the length of time involved in the process of interpretation; the lack of predictability of the derived senses; and the metaphorical nature of technical language. The remaining three factors relate more to general personality and cognitive characteristics of the students themselves that might affect their ability to think figuratively.

4.3.1 Lack of knowledge of the basic senses of the words

A first obstacle is that, in order to have complete autonomy over the metaphor and metonymy *interpretation* process, the student must have some knowledge of the 'basic' sense(s) of the word, and this may not always be the case. For example, if a student comes across the expression 'the company fell at the first hurdle' and has never encountered the word 'hurdle' before, he or she may have difficulty in identifying the expression as a metaphor. On the other hand, initial studies suggest that learners, especially at advanced level, *are* often aware of the more basic senses of many of the words that they encounter, and that the difficulties tend to lie in extending these senses to come up with a contextually appropriate interpretation (Littlemore, 2001b; 2002). Furthermore, it has been noted that metaphorical processes account for the majority of meaning extensions of lexical items (Dirven, 1985), so the strategy of working out an abstract sense of a word by metaphorically extending its more basic sense is likely to have a reasonably broad application. The pedagogical implication would seem to be that if there is a valid curricular reason to teach basic senses of words first, then it is probably worth doing so.

4.3.2 Limitations in the students' culturally embedded encyclopaedic knowledge

Another problem is that figurative language often relies heavily on encyclopaedic knowledge that is so deeply embedded in the culture that it is difficult, if not impossible, for foreign language learners to access it without the help of an authority. We will explore the relationship between culture and figurative language in depth in Chapter 5, but for now it will suffice to say that for a variety of cultural reasons, learners may bring partial or inaccurate domain knowledge to their understanding of metaphor. Gaps in their domain knowledge may apply equally to both the source and target domain (Cameron, 2003). Sometimes figurative language can be traced back to conceptual metaphors that are universal (e.g., GOOD IS UP), but at other times, they can be traced back to richer, more elaborate source domains that are culturally loaded. When this is the case, their meaning is likely to be less accessible. Metaphor and metonymy often involve shared cultural perceptions that are not necessarily factual, and that can be unpredictable, not widely known, or even obsolete.

For example, the expression 'up the spout', which means to be completely ruined, useless or damaged beyond repair, originally referred to a pawnbroker's method of checking articles by passing them up a spout to the back of the shop (Kirkpatrick and Schwarz, 1993). This sort of information is unlikely to be available to most language *teachers*, let alone *learners*. On the other hand, research suggests that such complete semantic opaqueness is relatively rare (Gibbs and O'Brien, 1990). There is empirical support for a 'continuum of analysability' which stretches between instances of figurative speech that reflect general universal structures and instances that reflect specific cultural and historical references (Bortfeld, 2003). An awareness of these cultural and historical references has been shown to be a key determinant of successful idiom comprehension and retention (Boers *et al.*, 2004b) and of the ability to interpret the evaluative function of metaphors (Littlemore, 2001b, 2003a). However research by Boers *et al.* (forthcoming) suggests that it does not always matter if the language learner accesses the incorrect source domain; the fact that they have attempted to identify some sort of source domain results in deeper cognitive processing, which, in turn, leads to deeper understanding and longer retention. In Boers *et al.*'s study, the participants were told the correct sense of the idiom after they had tried to work it out for themselves. This underscores the fact that increased learner autonomy does *not* mean that the teacher will become redundant in the classroom. Students still need input from their teacher, or some other source of authority, such as a dictionary or textbook, if they are to identify the correct sense of an idiom, as they do for many other aspects of the target language. The essence of Boers's argument is that it is beneficial for students to try and work out the origin and the sense of the idiom *for themselves*, before being told what it is by the teacher. It is this 'deep-processing' which results in the all-important long-term retention. For Boers, the initial role for the teacher in language focus activities such as these seems to be that of a passive spectator, at least until the learners have had a good go at identifying the meaning for themselves.

With regard to metonymy, Littlemore (2005) reports on a student's inability to work out the meaning of the expression 'he's a bit of an anorak' used of an acquaintance, to imply that he is somewhat unfashionable and has a strong obsession with a particular hobby. In order to understand this expression, it is necessary to access quite a wide range of (largely culturally determined) features that one might associate with an anorak, and the type of person who wears an anorak. These include (among others) the fact that it is an unstylish item of clothing that might be worn by a person (often male) who has an obsessive enthusiasm for a particular (often solitary) hobby (originally train spotting). It is then necessary to identify a metonymic relationship between the item of clothing and the type of person who usually wears it, and to understand that the expression has negative connotations.

Foreign language learners would probably need a great deal of help from their teacher to understand this expression. The teacher could help the students to access the relevant underlying conceptual metonymy THE POSSESSED STANDS FOR THE POSSESSOR, and draw the students' attention to clues in the context, such as the words 'self-confessed', which suggest that the word 'anorak' has negative connotations *in this context*. He or she might then ask the students to think of the possible negative qualities that a person who habitually wears an anorak might have, particularly in terms of fashion. This would be a very difficult task for students who have had little contact with English-speaking people, for whom an anorak might be a much more neutral item of clothing. For such students, it would be necessary to think of connotations that an anorak *might* have, but which it does not necessarily have for them at present. Perhaps the best way to approach this would be through a teacher-led brainstorming session, where students were encouraged to vocalise the first idea that came into their head, and where no ideas were rejected in the first instance. Their ideas could then be tested against the context of the utterance.

A further barrier to complete autonomy in the area of metaphor and metonymy interpretation is that the connotations and semantic prosodies of words change over time, and may become unrelated, or even run counter to their original, literal meanings. For example,

Channell (1999) points out that the negative connotations of 'par for the course' cannot be predicted from its original, literal meaning in the context of golf. Finally, it has been suggested that some languages, such as Malay, simply do not contain as much metaphor as English, and that they rely much more on metonymy (e.g., Charteris-Black, 2002; Goddard, 2004). If this is the case, then speakers of these languages may need more help in developing metaphoric processing strategies if they are to become fluent in English. These problems and differences highlight the extent to which it is important for learners to make maximum use of the context when employing figurative thinking processes to work out word meaning.

4.3.3 Centrality of the expression to a conceptual metaphor or metonymy

Related to the topic discussed in section 4.3.2 is the issue of an expression's centrality to the relevant conceptual metaphor or metonymy. The link between a linguistic metaphor and its corresponding conceptual metaphor is sometimes obvious. For example, if you understand the spatial sense of 'top', it is not difficult to find the relationship between 'He's on top of the world' and the corresponding conceptual metaphor HAPPY IS UP. On the other hand, some linguistic metaphors are based on elaborations of the source domain, and this makes them more difficult to interpret. For example, the expression 'step on it' meaning 'hurry up' refers to the conceptual metaphor PROGRESS IS FORWARD MOTION. But here the conceptual metaphor has been elaborated into something along the lines of PROGRESS IS FORWARD MOTION *BY CAR OR MOTORBIKE*, and the expression 'step on it' means to put one's foot down on the accelerator. Similarly, the expression 'I'm running out of steam' might be said to reflect the conceptual metaphor PROGRESS IS FORWARD MOTION *BY STEAM TRAIN*, and the expression 'he's soaring through it' might be said to reflect the conceptual metaphor PROGRESS IS FORWARD MOTION *BY A BIRD*. The further an expression gets from the basic source domain, the more susceptible it is to cross-cultural variation.

4.3.4 Word class

As we saw in Chapter 3, it has been shown that verb metaphors are more difficult to detect and harder to interpret than noun metaphors (Cameron, 2003). Cameron found that her students (ten-year-old *native* speakers of English) were likely to discuss the source domains of noun metaphors at some length, engaging in substantial vehicle/target domain development and contextualisation, but when they encountered verb metaphors, they usually resorted to repetition and relexicalisation, and did not seem to acknowledge the fact they were in fact metaphors. According to Cameron, her students were almost unaware of verb metaphors, or at least that they did not perceive them to be metaphors as such. Learners may therefore need to be helped to notice verb metaphors, and recognise them as such. The practical problem is that verb metaphors frequently shade into seemingly non-metaphoric verbs with general reference (like 'take (a break)', 'hold (an opinion)', 'run (a company)', 'give (recognition)' and 'have (a word)'), are, in our experience, generally the hardest class to agree about in a metaphor identification exercise, and are not generally recognised as figurative in reference books that learners encounter.

The potential problems posed by verb metaphors in English are also emphasised by Slobin (2000), who proposes an interesting categorisation of languages into two types in terms of the way in which they habitually describe movement. In 'satellite-framed' languages (such as English), the manner of movement is expressed within the verb, and the direction of movement is expressed through a preposition, as in 'to dash in', 'to slip out', 'to creep up' and 'to eat away'. Many of these expressions are metaphorical or metonymic, and are often synaesthesic. In 'verb-framed' languages (such as Spanish), only the actual direction of movement is expressed in the verb, and the manner of movement is expressed as a non-finite verb as in 'entro en la casa corriendo' (he entered the house running); and 'Sali corriendo a la calle' (I exited running into the street). These expressions tend to be more literal.

Slobin even goes so far as to suggest that speaking a satellite-framed language predisposes a speaker to cognitively encode motion events in a different way from speakers of verb-framed languages. As a test, he asked 14 Spanish speakers and 21 American English speakers to give an oral report of a passage from Isobel Allende's House of the Spirits – the English translation had few manner-encoded verbs. The Americans added manner-encoded verbs like 'stumble', 'stagger' and 'trudge' to their reports and 95 per cent claimed to have mental images of various types of movement. The Spaniards and South Americans' reports did not focus on the manner of the movement and only 14 per cent reported having images of movement, although they visualised the path, the physical details of the surroundings, the man's inner state and his trajectory of movement.

There were a few bilingual subjects in the experiment who reported distinctly different imagery in their two languages, with more manner imagery when reporting on the text in English – but still much less than the monolingual speakers of English.

These findings suggest that, for some language pairs, it may not be sufficient to simply draw students' attention to the presence of verb metaphors. It may be necessary to alert them to the fact that satellite-framed languages, such as English, have a fundamentally different way of describing (and possibly conceptualising) manner of movement than do verb-framed languages. In order to produce authentic-sounding language, learners may therefore need to learn to imitate the way in which speakers of the target language conceptualise movement. Receptively, they also need to learn the strategy that any movement verb is likely to have a manner component built in.

4.3.5   The length of time involved in the process of metaphor and metonymy interpretation

Another possible impediment to autonomy is the amount of time involved in the process of metaphor and metonymy interpretation. Accessing a word's core or 'basic' sense in order to interpret its meaning in a given context can be a lengthy procedure and the student may still come up with an inaccurate interpretation at the end of this procedure. Language learners may not always have time to engage in the process, especially if it does not always guarantee success, and may prefer simply to look the word up in a dictionary, infer its meaning from context or ask the teacher. On the other hand, as we saw before, in the 'targeting' example, the pay-off for taking the time to think figuratively about word meaning appears to be quite significant in terms of vocabulary retention and the learner's ability to fully appreciate the semantic content of words and expressions. Furthermore, a student is significantly more likely to remember the meaning of a word if s/he has worked it out by engaging in figurative thinking, than if s/he worked it out by simply inferring from the context (Boers, 2000b). Figurative thinking is therefore likely to be of more use as a *learning* strategy than as a *comprehension* strategy.

4.3.6   Technical language

Technical terms are another potential problem area, since what is the 'basic' term to an expert is unusual to a non-expert, who immediately interprets it as figurative. Cameron (2003) found that her ten-year old (L1) students did exactly this. When dealing with a text about the human heart, containing the expression 'muscular walls', they immediately began to apply notions of rigidity, which for them was probably one of the salient properties of a wall, whereas all they needed to do was to draw on the notion of enclosure. Given their age, they were most probably employing a strategy of transferring descriptive rather than structural, abstract attributes. Adults may be more aware that scientific analogies, when not tongue in cheek, like 'charm' in Physics, tend to focus more on structural and functional properties, but if they are not, teachers can teach this as an interpretive strategy to adopt. Non-technical explanations and even technical texts play on this difference in meta-phoricity and can repeatedly activate and deactivate a technical metaphor through a text. Establishing the intended tone can thus be very hard for the foreign language learner.

4.3.7   Lack of predictability of the derived senses

So far in this chapter, we have talked mainly about comprehension, but there are two potentially very significant barriers to autonomy in the area of figurative language production. The first is that, although the derived senses of many words are usually figuratively motivated, it does not follow that they are always fully predictable (Kövecses, 2002). Figurative thinking processes offer a great deal of potential for meaning extension in a variety of different directions, but only a few of these possible derivations *actually do* occur in the language. Such occurrence depends largely on culture, circumstance and fate, and as such is highly unpredictable. This means that language learners may figuratively extend the meaning of a piece of vocabulary to produce an expression that is completely alien to native speakers, and this may be problematic. However, exploratory research by Boers (2004) shows that native speakers are remarkably tolerant of figurative extensions of word meaning, and that the more unrelated an expression is to the conventional figurative expressions, the more creative it is deemed to be, and the more likely it is to be 'accepted' as appropriate English. Furthermore, if language learners are able to signal their use of such novel expressions appropriately, using terms such as *sort of, kind of* and *as it were* (Goatly, 1997), then they are more likely to be accepted. It is therefore important that students be taught appropriate signalling devices. We shall consider these further in Chapter 7.

4.3.8   Conventionalisation and phraseology

The second barrier to autonomous production relates to phraseology. Although language permits a certain amount of creativity, expressions do at some point become conventionalised in terms of their phraseology, and language learners need to know which expressions are conventional and which are not. When words are used figuratively, they tend to occur in relatively fixed phraseological patterns, which differ from the phraseological patterns that are used with their literal senses (Deignan, 1999a; 1999b; 2005). For example, the word *price* often collocates with *heavy* when it is used figuratively, but this collocation is rare when it is used in its literal sense. Moreover, these differences are particularly marked when we look at the grammar. For instance, when the expression *at a price* is used literally, it is generally post-modified by a clause, such as *at a price that does not even include costs*. When *at a price* is used figuratively, it is rarely post-modified in this way (Deignan, 2005; p. 209). Thus phraseology can provide important clues, which allow the native speaker to decide whether a figurative or a literal interpretation of a particular word or expression is intended. It is therefore important for language learners to be made aware of this. When they produce figurative language they will need some sort of guidance, either from a teacher or another authority, concerning the conventional phraseological (and grammatical) patterns that surround figurative uses of target language vocabulary. This represents a significant limitation to their autonomy as it restricts their ability to produce whatever expressions they like in the target language. On the other hand, with the development of sophisticated *noticing* skills and exposure to large amounts of the target language, they should not only be able to identify permissible figurative uses, but also detect the patterns that conventionally surround those uses. The role of the teacher is to help learners develop these skills.

4.3.9   Individual differences in figurative thinking ability

Having seen a number of possible limitations that relate to a student's existive knowledge of the target language and culture, we now turn, in this remaining section, to the cognitive and personality-based characteristics of the students themselves that may affect their ability to think figuratively. It is important for teachers to be aware of the fact that their learners will vary in terms of their ability to think figuratively. Indeed, there is a strong body of research showing that individuals vary significantly in their ability to deal with metaphor, a trait which is broadly defined as 'metaphoric competence'. Unfortunately, to date, no research has investigated individual differences in one's ability to deal with metonymy. The absence of any research into 'metonymic competence' (or indeed any other type of figurative competence) is a significant gap in the literature that will hopefully be filled in the near future. In the meantime, this section will necessarily be somewhat biased towards metaphor and the notion of 'metaphoric competence'.

'Metaphoric competence' is an umbrella term that has been used to refer to an individuals' ability to understand and produce metaphors. The term means different things to different people. The narrow view (e.g., Kogan, 1983; Danesi, 1986; 1992a; 1995) sees metaphoric competence simply as the ability to comprehend and produce metaphor. The broader view (e.g., Low, 1988) sees metaphoric competence not only as the ability to comprehend and produce metaphors, but also as including: knowledge of the boundaries of conventional metaphor, awareness of acceptable topic and vehicle combinations, the ability to comprehend and control hedges, an awareness of 'socially sensitive' metaphors, an awareness of multiple layering in metaphors, and interactive awareness of metaphor. The main difference between these views is that the former focuses on the cognitive processing aspects of metaphor, whereas the latter is more concerned with its socially interactive functions. Although we feel that the latter view is of more relevance to language teachers and learners, those who have conducted empirical research have tended to work within the narrower view of the construct. It is to this work that we now turn.

Somewhat stable individual differences have been found in the area of L1 metaphoric competence. The most wide-ranging study was carried out by Kogan (1983), who, after completing a comprehensive study of a number of tests of metaphoric processing that had been carried out on children (including tests of metaphor interpretation, production and appreciation), drew the conclusion that the ability to understand and produce metaphor functions as a relatively stable 'individual difference' variable. Kogan's findings gain support from research showing that individuals vary in terms of: their ability to comprehend novel metaphors (Pollio and Burns, 1977); their ability to produce novel metaphors on demand (Pollio *et al.*, 1977); their ability to provide original responses when asked to explain novel metaphors (Pollio and Smith, 1980); their ability to find meaning in metaphor (Pollio and Smith, 1979); and the assessments that they make of metaphor comprehensibility, ease of interpretation, degree of metaphoricity, metaphor goodness, metaphor imagery, felt familiarity, and semantic relatedness (Katz *et al.*, 1988). All of these researchers have found their respondents to be largely consistent in their responses.

Significant variation in metaphoric competence has also been found amongst foreign language learners. For example, language learners have been found to vary significantly in their ability to offer sophisticated or numerous interpretations for a given metaphor (Johnson and Rosano, 1993); their ability to find meaning in metaphor (Littlemore, 1998;

2001a), the speed with which they find meaning in metaphor (Littlemore, 1998; 2001a); their ability to produce novel metaphors (Danesi, 1992a; 1992b); and their ability to use the core sense of a word to work out its more metaphoric sense in context (Littlemore, 2004b; forthcoming). There also appears to be variation in the *types* of figurative thinking processes that language learners employ when working out the meaning of new vocabulary. For example, they appear to vary in the extent to which they like to use imagery to support the process, in the extent to which they like to rely on contextual clues, and in their preference for either a simultaneous or a step-by-step process (Littlemore, forthcoming). The ability to use metaphor, the preference for using it and the way in which it is used therefore appears to constitute substantial individual difference variables. These findings suggest that, despite a teacher's best efforts to help their students develop their ability to deal with metaphor, there will always be some who respond well to the approach and others who 'just don't get it'.

Although these appear to be different skills, some interdependence has been revealed between the different aspects of metaphoric competence (Pickens and Pollio, 1979; Littlemore, 1998). Furthermore, researchers have found that metaphoric competence in the L2 relates not to language proficiency but to a range of cognitive factors (Johnson and Rosano, 1993; Litlemore, 2001a). These findings suggest that metaphoric competence relies as much on generic cognitive abilities as it does on linguistic ones, which leads us onto the possible sources of variation in metaphoric competence.

One factor that may account for variation in these different aspects of metaphoric competence is a learner's cognitive style. A cognitive style is a person's habitual way of perceiving, processing and acquiring information (Riding and Cheema, 1991). Researchers are divided over the issue of stability: earlier researchers (e.g., Kogan, 1983) claimed to have found evidence that cognitive styles remain stable over time, but more recent researchers (e.g., Bloomer and Hodkinson, 2000) have found that they do not. It would therefore be foolish to suggest that learners remain prisoners of their cognitive style, and we must tread very carefully when making recommendations in this area. On the other hand, it may be helpful if learners, and their teachers, are at least aware of their cognitive style and of the barriers that it might put in the way of the development of their metaphoric competence, and by extension their figurative thinking ability. If they are equipped with such awareness, they are in a better position to remove any potential barriers that their cognitive styles present. Two cognitive style dimensions have been found to have an impact on a student's figurative thinking ability: the holistic/analytic dimension; and the verbaliser/imager dimension.

The holistic/analytic cognitive style

The holistic/analytic cognitive style contrasts holistic processing, in which parts are considered together as a whole, with analytic processing, in which the whole is broken down into parts. Researchers investigating the holistic/analytic distinction point out that holistic processing involves drawing together pieces of information and treating them as a whole, perceiving similarity and togetherness, whereas analytic processing emphasises the perception of difference and separateness. Language learners with a holistic, as opposed to analytic, cognitive style have been found to be better at the rapid identification of meaning in novel linguistic metaphors (Littlemore, 2001a). The ability to interpret metaphors quickly in conversation can be a crucial element of interaction. Often, in conversation, there is not enough time for learners to process every L2 utterance analytically before responding. When one's interlocutor uses an unfamiliar metaphor, one must process the metaphor spontaneously and holistically, rapidly identifying one or more possible meanings in order to respond quickly and thus maintain the flow of the conversation.

At the level of conceptual metaphor, research suggests that a person's holistic or analytic cognitive style may determine whether they are more likely to employ a blending or a mapping process when interpreting conceptual metaphors. When they asked a group of students to interpret the conceptual metaphors, ECONOMIC COMPETITION IS RACING, AN ECONOMY IS A MACHINE and ECONOMICS IS HEALTH CARE, Boers and Littlemore (2000) found that students with a holistic cognitive style were significantly more likely than students with an analytic cognitive style to deviate from the source domain in their explanations (by attributing elements to the source domain that were actually part of their rich conception of the target domain). Such 'deviations' from the source domains included the following examples: 'Economic competition is talked about in terms of racing because it is a merciless jungle where only the fittest survive'; and 'Economics is talked about in terms of health care because economies can never recover without consulting a doctor / an economist' (disregarding the source domain feature that many people resort to self-medication, especially in cases of minor ailments). This suggests that students with a holistic cognitive style may favour blending processes, whereas students with a more analytic cognitive style tend to favour mapping processes. These findings indicate that holistic students are perhaps more capable of coming up with more unusual or elaborate interpretations than their more analytic peers.

The verbaliser/imager cognitive style

The verbaliser/imager dimension is one of the most widely studied cognitive style dimensions. It has been found that people vary significantly in their ability to process information verbally or visually (Riding and Cheema, 1991) and in their tendency to favour one of these modes of processing (Katz, 1983; Paivio and Harshman, 1983; Thompson, 1990). As we saw in Chapter 3, imagery is often involved in metaphor comprehension and production, which suggests that a person's ability or tendency to think in terms of mental images may contribute to their ability to create and understand metaphor. This contention is supported by the finding that foreign language learners with a strong imaging capacity are significantly better at producing novel metaphors than individuals with a strong verbalising capacity, both in their native language and in the target language (Littlemore, 1998). Language learners who favour image-based ways of thinking are also significantly better at using metaphoric extension strategies to work out the meanings of unknown words than those who favour a more verbal way of thinking (Littlemore, 2004b). These findings suggest that language learners will vary both in their capacity to engage in figurative thinking and in their willingness to do so, and that part of this variation will be due to their ability (or tendency) to form mental images.

One possible explanation for these findings comes from exploratory research into the relationship between the verbal/imager cognitive style and conceptual metaphor interpretation. The responses given by imagers to the conceptual metaphors ECONOMIC COMPETITION IS RACING, AN ECONOMY IS A MACHINE and ECONOMICS IS HEALTH CARE, in the Boers and Littlemore (2000) study mentioned above, suggest that they were forming stereotypical mental images from which they could then generalise. Imagers may therefore associate a whole experiential domain with one typical scene, which they then employ as a metonymic representation of the metaphor. Verbalisers, on the other hand, may be more likely to adopt a more propositional approach. In terms of the psychological processes discussed in Chapter 3, this suggests that imagers may have more facility with image formation and associative fluency.

Other cognitive style dimensions

We have just seen that a high level of metaphoric competence appears to be a characteristic of students with holistic and imager cognitive styles. In addition to this, there are a number of other cognitive styles that may impact upon a student's level of metaphoric competence. We now consider two further cognitive style dimensions that may well be linked to metaphoric competence (tolerance of ambiguity, and level of intuition), although to date no research has been carried out to confirm or disprove such links.

We might expect there to be a relationship between figurative thinking ability and tolerance of ambiguity. Tolerance of ambiguity is a measure of the extent to which a person feels comfortable in unfamiliar or ambiguous situations (Norton, 1975). As figurative thinking involves dealing with new and ambiguous stimuli, one might expect it to be related to tolerance of ambiguity. It may be predicted that a learner's tolerance of ambiguity will affect their reaction to the learning process and the strategies they use to deal with it. Indeed, in foreign language learning contexts, tolerance of ambiguity has been found to be a significant predictor of strategies such as looking for overall meaning in reading, guessing a word from its context and using mental images to aid memory. It has also been found to be a significant negative predictor of strategies such as looking for similarities between new words and L1 words and of various strategies that involve focusing on individual language elements (Ely, 1989). It has also been found that people who can tolerate ambiguity are more likely to take risks in language learning (Beebe, 1983; Ely, 1986). One might therefore expect students who are more tolerant of ambiguity to carry out more extensive searches of the source and target domains in order to find meaning in metaphor. Students with stronger risk-taking tendencies may be more inclined to test the potential of a word's possible figurative meaning extensions. Further research is required to assess these relationships.

Another style dimension that may be related to figurative thinking ability is the sensing/intuition dimension on the 'Myers Briggs Type Indicator'.[3] Intuitive people apparently seek out patterns and relationships among the facts they have gathered. They are thought to trust hunches and their intuition and look for the 'big picture', whereas sensing people prefer organised, linear and structured input, and, apparently, tend not to stretch their imaginations. One might therefore expect intuitive students to display higher levels of metaphoric competence than sensing students, but again, no studies have yet investigated this relationship.

Although research suggests that metaphoric competence is related to cognitive styles, and some would argue that cognitive styles are fairly immutable, preliminary studies suggest that, with imaginative teaching techniques, learners can be helped to overcome the handicaps presented by their particular cognitive style when it comes to metaphor interpretation and memorisation. For instance, Stengers *et al.* (forthcoming) used the *Idiom Teacher* programme, outlined in Chapter 2, to explicitly train students to form mental images in order to guess and remember the meaning of idioms. They found that the training worked equally well for learners with imager *and* verbaliser cognitive styles. More research is needed to assess whether this type of training can deal with other cognitive style dimensions, such as holistic and analytic, but as an initial generalisation, we suggest that all language learners be taught to generate mental images. The activity again lends itself to collaborative work (those who find it easy can help those who do not) and reflective periods, where learners engage actively with meanings and images: both generally accepted as aiding language acquisition.

4.4   Conclusion

In this chapter, we have seen that it is desirable for language learners to develop a degree of autonomy in their ability to understand and use figurative language in the L2. However, there are many possible barriers to the development of this autonomy, both in terms of the language with which students are confronted, and in terms of the psychological characteristics of the students themselves. These barriers explain why figurative language can, at times, be such a difficult aspect of the target language to master. An awareness of the existence of such barriers should indicate to language learners where their difficulties might lie, and as such, is a first step towards dealing with these difficulties, and developing autonomy over their ability to deal with figurative language in the L2. Teachers also need to recognise that learners will vary in terms of their ability to understand and produce figurative language, which at the current state of research means with metaphor, and that this variation will not necessarily be related to L2 proficiency. Training in mental imaging appears to be a helpful solution to part of this problem.

Part I of this book has been dedicated to defining figurative thinking, outlining its relationship to foreign language learning and discussing how it might be developed in language learners. It has focused mainly on the role of figurative thinking in comprehending figurative extensions of word meaning, and in producing appropriate figurative language. Part II will expand this theme, by discussing ways in which figurative thinking might contribute to a wide range of aspects of communicative language ability with Bachman's (1990) model. More specifically, we focus on the contributions that figurative thinking might make to: sociolinguistic; illocutionary; textual; grammatical; and strategic competence in an L2 context. Bachman's model is used because it provides opportunities to discuss how figurative thinking can help language learners to perform a wide variety of functions in the target language. The model also allows room for a discussion of roles played by figurative thinking in the learning of grammar, and in the formulation of communication strategies.

Part II

Figurative Thinking and Communicative Language Ability

5
Figurative Thinking and Sociolinguistic Competence

5.1 Introductory comments

In Chapters 1 to 4, we saw that engaging in figurative thinking can in many cases help language learners work out a reasonable approximation of the meaning of unknown vocabulary, as well as extend the variety of things that they can talk about with their existing vocabulary. We also saw that although learners are likely to vary in their ability to engage in figurative thinking, several of the skills involved appear to be trainable, and that under appropriate instructional conditions, figurative thinking can lead to learning. The focus in Chapters 3 and 4 was very much on psychological processing; what we have not discussed in any detail is the role that figurative language, and by extension, figurative thinking, might play in performing (and acquiring mastery over) communicative functions. In the next five chapters, we will do precisely this, taking as a framework the model of communicative language ability proposed by Bachman (1990).

Several models of communicative competence have been devised in the last thirty years, but the most pedagogically influential form a rough family. The family derives ultimately from Hymes (e.g., 1971), which was extended for language teaching and testing purposes by Canale and Swain (1980) and Canale (1983). The model was modified slightly in Bachman (1990) and Bachman and Palmer (1996). Douglas (2000) then adapted the list of strategic skills and reduced the role of figurative language by replacing Bachman's 'figures of speech' with 'idiomatic expressions' (2000: p. 35). Of all these models, Bachman's is the most straightforward and unproblematic (particularly with regard to its formulation of strategic skills). We have therefore chosen to use Bachman's (1990) model to structure the remaining chapters of the book.

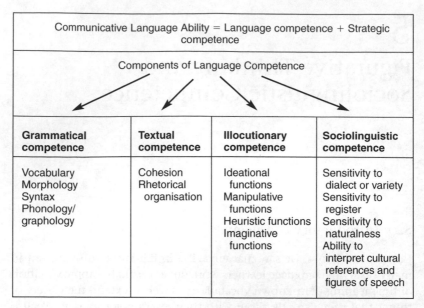

Communicative Language Ability = Language competence + Strategic competence			
Components of Language Competence			
Grammatical competence	**Textual competence**	**Illocutionary competence**	**Sociolinguistic competence**
Vocabulary Morphology Syntax Phonology/ graphology	Cohesion Rhetorical organisation	Ideational functions Manipulative functions Heuristic functions Imaginative functions	Sensitivity to dialect or variety Sensitivity to register Sensitivity to naturalness Ability to interpret cultural references and figures of speech

Figure 5.1 Bachman's (1990) model of language competence (adapted). Reproduced by permission of Oxford University Press. From *Oxford Applied Linguistics: Fundamental Considerations in Language Testing* by Lyle F Bachman, © Lyle F Bachman 1990.

Bachman (1990, ch.4) takes a broad definition of the term 'competence', which includes, amongst other things, the ability to deal with knowledge-based components of language that have been isolated as theoretical areas, such as 'syntax' or 'cohesion'. Speakers draw on their language knowledge, using a range of strategic skills to link the message appropriately with the social purpose and situation. Bachman argues that communicative language ability consists of language competence and strategic competence (Figure 5.1).

Language competence includes four sub-competences: grammatical, textual, illocutionary and sociolinguistic. Grammatical competence refers to the ability to use the grammar of the target language, with grammar being used in a broad sense to include systematic aspects of word meaning (what Radden (2005) calls 'lexical grammar'). Textual competence is again broad and concerns the ability to appreciate the overall conceptual and rhetorical structure of discourse. Illocutionary competence describes the ability to interpret the ideational, interactional and manipulative functions of discourse. Finally, sociolinguistic competence concerns our 'sensitivity to, or control of, the conventions of language use that are determined by the features of the specific language use context'. (Bachman, 1990: p. 94). Strategic competence includes the ability to use language interactively, and to convey a message, despite gaps in one's knowledge of the target language.

The only overt reference to figurative language or thinking in Figure 5.1 is the 'ability to interpret cultural references and figures of speech' under 'sociolinguistic competence'. In Chapters 5 to 9, we argue that figurative language plays an important role in all five areas of competence, not just sociolinguistic. In each chapter, we will take one of Bachman's categories and discuss the importance of figurative language, examine some of the pedagogical implications and suggest how language learners can be helped to develop their skills and knowledge through figurative thinking processes. In doing this, we will evaluate existing research on the contributions that figurative thinking makes and identify areas where research is lacking. We should emphasise that our aim is not to promote or to critique Bachman's model; indeed we accept that there is considerable overlap between some of the categories. The point is to take a model developed specifically to illustrate the breadth of knowledge and skills needed when learning a foreign language, and use it as a vehicle to explore the extensive role that figurative thinking can play in communicative language ability.

5.2   Figurative thinking and sociolinguistic competence

Bachman is to some extent right to place 'figures of speech' alongside the ability to interpret cultural references. Figurative expressions often contain cultural references, and knowledge of them is necessary if they are to be understood appropriately. To 'understand appropriately', learners need to appreciate the extended meanings given by a specific culture to particular entities, characteristics, actions, events, places or institutions. The acquisition of sociolinguistic competence thus requires a high degree of cultural awareness, or as Lantolf (1999) puts it, an ability to *appropriate* the target culture. In this chapter, we focus on the question of cross-cultural differences, and the need for learners to see behind particular phrases and to establish how conceptual metaphors and metonymies are exploited in the target culture.

Bachman's definition of sociolinguistic competence not only embraces culture at a national level, it also includes more local cultures by talking about sensitivity to dialect, variety, register and naturalness. Therefore, we also examine the role that figurative language and figurative thinking can play in gaining access to different speech and discourse communities. We thus move from culture in language to what Kramsch (1995) calls language *as* (an aspect of) culture.

We use 'culture' in its broad sense, to refer to the behaviour and lifestyle that characterise a social group, and 'a culture' as a shorthand label for that group. The relationship between language and culture is clearly complex and a detailed examination is well beyond the scope of this book. Language and culture can be coterminous, when a language has a single socially coherent group of speakers, or a social group emphasises a language as a key marker of identity. The two can, however, be very different where numerous social groups with very different characteristics employ the same language (like Arabic across the Moslem community). For the purposes of this book, we allow that any speaker of a language will belong concurrently to several social or 'cultural' groups, where (a) some groups are broader than others, (b) the extent of shared behaviour or belief systems can vary markedly and (c) the degree of membership in any one can often vary from peripheral to central. We also make the default assumption that a language has a socially or institutionally coherent group of speakers associated with it. This is clearly a technically inaccurate idealisation, as not only, for example, do many Belgians and Swiss speak French as a first language, but they have also left their mark on it, both lexically and phonetically. However, the assumption is sufficiently valid to allow a degree of explanation that is adequate for much foreign language learning.

5.3 How is culture absorbed into a language and how do cultures vary in this respect?

The encoding of culture in language involves the continuous internalisation of information from our environment. Native speakers extract from their environments elements and associations that appear to be relatively constant, which they use to build a series of representational networks or 'schemata' (Cook, 1997a). As we saw in Chapter 3, schemata are the representations of the world that speakers already have in their minds, and which they use to understand and interpret incoming information (Cook, 1997a).[1] In short, we use schemata to help us concentrate on a manageable amount of relevant input, rather than getting lost in a practically infinite number of stimuli. One part of a comparative analysis of different cultures is therefore a comparison of their different schemata.

The schemata that cultures have for many *concrete* phenomena are relatively literal and are unlikely to involve figurative thinking. However, according to conceptual metaphor theory, the schemata that cultures have for *abstract* phenomena are thought to consist largely of conceptual metaphors or metonymies, as we tend to encode abstract concepts figuratively, in terms of our concrete embodied experiences (Gibbs, 2005). These often appear to group together into narrative-like clusters, generally called 'cultural' or 'cognitive models'.[2] Many conceptual metaphors, such as STATES ARE LOCATIONS and PROGRESS IS TRAVEL are considered to be universal, as they reflect universal bodily experiences (Kövecses, 2002). On the other hand, as we stated briefly in Chapter 1, there are often significant cultural differences in the ways in which these metaphors are elaborated and exploited, particularly in the case of more complex conceptual metaphors. For example, although 'THE BODY IS A CONTAINER FOR THE EMOTIONS' (e.g., 'Anger was building up inside him') appears to be universal, languages locate particular emotions in different parts of the body. As stated earlier in Chapter 1, in Hungarian culture, for example, anger is often in the head, while in Japanese it can rise from the stomach via the chest to the head (Kövecses, 1995). Western cultures seem to assume that most so-called higher emotions involve the heart (e.g., 'I've got a heavy heart', 'heartfelt contempt', 'He broke her heart'), but in Malay these associations are commonly made with the liver (Charteris-Black, 2002).

Differences have also been found in discourse. Boers and Demecheleer (1995), for instance, looked for evidence of conceptual metaphors in economic discourse in English, French and Dutch. They scanned comparable economic publications from Britain, France and Holland for examples of three metaphoric source domains that are often used to talk about economics. These were journeys (e.g., 'The *moves towards* privatisation and liberalisation', ibid., p. 679), health (e.g., 'The *diagnosis* was established with little difficulty', ibid., p. 686) and fighting (e.g., 'The Bank of England is *flexing its muscles*', ibid., p. 687). Their research revealed distinct patterns of metaphor use. The British publication used more journeys, whereas the French one talked of fighting and to a lesser degree, health. The Dutch publication referred equally to journeys and fighting, but much less frequently to health than the British or French publications. In short, Britain, France and Holland are geographically close and the languages are related, yet the nature and use of metaphors and metonymies in comparable journals differed markedly. From a pedagogical perspective, it would also be useful to know whether this difference relates generally to talking about health, or whether it relates purely to written texts in journals.

It has been argued that familiarity with the ways in which conceptual metaphors are elaborated by the target language community is likely to provide access to its conceptual system (Danesi, 1992a). If language learners are able to use these metaphors appropriately, then their use of the target language is likely to sound much more natural. Where the conceptual metaphors of the target language coincide with, and are elaborated in the same way as, those of the learner's L1, a process of transfer can usefully take place. However, when the two languages favour different conceptual metaphors, or elaborate them in different ways, learners may find it more difficult to make appropriate use of those that are conventional in the target language but not in the L1.

Cultural differences in terms of metaphor and metonymy need to be considered from a linguistic angle as well as a conceptual one. The reason is that even when languages employ the same conceptual metaphors, there can be differences in the types of linguistic metaphor that are produced, in the degree of conventionalisation of these metaphors and in the scope of the conceptual metaphors themselves (Barcelona, 2001). In a comparative study of metaphor between English and Polish, Deignan *et al.* (1997) identified a number of cross-linguistic differences between conceptual metaphors and their linguistic variations. They classified these differences into four types:

1. same conceptual metaphor + equivalent linguistic expression;
2. same conceptual metaphor + different linguistic expression;
3. different conceptual metaphors used in the two languages;
4. words and expressions with the same literal meanings but different metaphoric meanings.

Variation at the linguistic level appears to be particularly marked where metonymy is concerned. For example, the word 'eye' in English and French often stands for seeing or watching. Thus, in both languages, children can play under the watchful eye of their mother ('sous l' oeil' in French). But if the watchfulness decreases, things happen 'under' or 'before' your eyes' (plural) in French ('sous/devant les yeux'), but only 'before your eyes' in English. Being observant involves repositioning the eyes in both languages, but the position is different. In English you have eyes in the back of your head, but in French you take them out of your pocket ('ne pas avoir les yeux dans sa poche').

One explanation for cross-cultural variation at the linguistic level is that different features of a word are salient in different cultures, making them more susceptible to selection for figurative transfer or use (Gyori, 2000). For example, in Japanese, the words 'asa*gohan'*, 'hiru*gohan'*, 'ban*gohan'* and 'yu*gohan'* refer respectively to breakfast, lunch, dinner and supper. 'Gohan' means 'rice' and is a reflection of the fact that for Japanese people, one of the salient properties of rice is that it is their staple food. So, in Japanese, the word 'rice' is used metonymically to refer to meals in general.

An awareness of the ways in which the target language elaborates its commonest conceptual metaphors and metonymies is likely to be very useful to foreign language learners as the knowledge may help them to predict types of expressions that are common in the target language, and assist them in deciding which expressions from their native language can be transferred (i.e., literally translated) to the target language. They may also give some insight into ways in which speakers of the target language think (bearing in mind the need to disentangle use from belief), and reveal a degree of systematicity in aspects of the language that might otherwise appear arbitrary.

Some research has been carried out into the transfer of figurative thought systems from the L1 to the L2. For example, when Danesi (1995) conducted a small exploratory study in which he looked at the type of language produced in a free composition exercise in the target language, he found that his elementary, intermediate and advanced English-speaking students of Italian all tended to use conceptual metaphors that were alike in both languages, a finding which he took to mean that the students had developed 'no new ways of thinking conceptually' as a result of their language learning experiences (1995: p. 12). Charteris-Black (2002) reported similar findings for Malay learners of English.

Although these studies are small, and their results have to be interpreted with caution, their findings do lend some support to Danesi's (1995) suggestion that we could usefully introduce a modified form of contrastive analysis (CA) into language teaching and learning. Contrastive analysis involves the comparison of language systems in order to predict the types of difficulties that learners might encounter. CA is an approach that went out of fashion during the 1980s, mainly because it attempted to be too all-embracing. Nevertheless, Danesi argues that there may be some mileage in using a weak form of CA in which figurative thought systems, rather than discrete grammar points, are contrasted. Contrastive analysis has also been criticised for portraying the process of language acquisition solely in terms of a flow from the native to the target language, assigning no active role to the individual learner in the process (Danesi, 1995). In order for the approach to work, a degree of learner-centredness would therefore be necessary. For example, learners would ideally be encouraged to reflect on their conscious transfer of L1 and idiosyncratic thought systems to the target language, and made aware of transfers of which they are less conscious. Language teachers would ideally draw students' attention to the ways in which the conceptual metaphors are used by the target language community. Learners could then be encouraged to reflect on differences between these, and the ways in which they are used in their own language. They could be helped to reflect on the ways in which their own world knowledge is built around conceptual metaphors and metonymies, and employ figurative thinking to make new types of connection that rely on different aspects of the source domain from those that they are used to working with. There are clearly limits to the amount of such 'awareness' and 'reflection' that a busy teacher can introduce, but we are simply arguing here for the general idea, not the replacement of all activities in the L2.

5.3.1   Sources of cross-cultural variation

Before turning to the language teaching implications of all this, we would like to briefly consider some possible reasons for the types of variation outlined before. If abstract concepts emerge metaphorically from basic human experience, then differences in human experience are likely to lead to variation in conceptual metaphors. Although research in the area is limited, three categories of experience appear to have led to differences in the way cultures build their conceptual metaphors. These are: differences in history and behaviour; differences in social organisation; and differences in the physical characteristics of the landscape.

History and behaviour

Differences in the conceptual metaphors employed by different cultures often reflect behavioural and historical differences between those cultures. The best example of this is a piece of research carried out by Boers and Demecheleer (2001), who found that English uses more idioms based on the domains of *hats* and *shipping* than French, whereas French uses more idioms based on food. These differences are probably due to historical and behavioural differences between the British and the French: Britain has long seen itself as a seafaring nation, and historically, hat wearing was perhaps more common until recently in Britain than in France. On the other hand, the French traditionally attach more importance to food than the English.

When Boers and Demecheleer looked at the ability of French learners of English to interpret imageable idioms in English, they found that they had significantly more difficulty understanding idioms that were based on hats and shipping (e.g., 'to keep something under one's hat' or 'to get someone on board') than they did when trying to understand idioms based on food (e.g., 'to have egg on one's face' or 'to cry over spilt milk'). These findings suggest that historical and behavioural differences between cultural groups can affect the conceptual metaphors used, and that cross-cultural differences between these conceptual metaphors can be a stumbling block for language learners.

However, Deignan (2003) warns that we must be careful not to make too much of these kinds of links. There is often a significant time lag between the metaphorical expressions that are used and the circumstances that gave rise to them, so that the knowledge that gave rise to the expressions is no longer directly experienced by the people who use them; 'metaphorical expressions are a cultural reliquary, and an incomplete one' (ibid., p. 255). The pedagogical implications of this recognition are unclear (in press). One answer would be to teach a 'postcard' view of English culture, focusing on the technical details of sailing ships, small farms, castles, fox hunting and steam engines. This would, however, go very much against the modern trend of linking foreign language teaching to communication in the contemporary world.

Teachers also need to be acutely aware that using a conceptual metaphor is not the same as believing it. Saying 'I didn't catch what you said' does not commit you to believing the conduit metaphor, just as saying 'you seem pretty sanguine' or 'I'm feeling a bit phlegmatic this morning' does not commit you to a belief in the old medical theory of bodily humours. Learners, like native speakers, may well need at times to work out how to get round the limitations of conceptual metaphors, but this is to move into illocutionary competence (see Chapter 6).

Social organisation

The way in which a society organises itself and constructs its values may have an effect on the conceptual metaphors and metonymies that it employs. This means that language learners from a society that is organised differently, or has different sets of values from their own, may find it difficult to understand expressions that are based on these conceptual metaphors and metonymies.

Cultures have been found to vary in terms of social organisation in a number of ways. For example, Trompenaars (1993) argued that cultures vary markedly in terms of how appropriate it is for people to reveal their true feelings in their relationships with others. This difference appears to be manifested in the conceptual metaphors employed by different cultures. For example, in Japanese culture, where one is often expected to keep one's feelings to oneself, many conceptual metaphors relate to 'hara' (literally 'belly'), which is a combination of truth, real intentions and the real self. This contrasts with 'tatemae', or one's social face. Anger is metaphorically located in the belly, so when Japanese people keep their anger under control, they are hiding their most private, truthful, innermost self. This conceptual metaphor results in expressions such as 'hara ga tatsu' ('stomach stands up'), which roughly means to lose one's temper and 'hara ga suwatte iru' ('stomach is sitting'), which roughly means having guts, being resolute or being strong willed. These Japanese expressions do not translate easily into English, precisely because the word 'hara' carries the additional idea of the emotions being hidden.

The physical environment

It has been argued that a physical environment can have a powerful effect on the thought processes of the people who live there, and that environmental features contribute to the conceptual metaphors employed by members of different cultures (Kövecses, 2002). For example, when Dirven (1994) analysed the source domains used in the Dutch spoken in Holland versus those used in Afrikaans, he found far more references to wild animals in Afrikaans than in Dutch. This may reflect the fact that historically the South African settlers were much more likely to encounter greater numbers of wild animals than people who lived in Holland.

Research has also shown that the climate can play a role in a culture's use of conceptual metaphors. For example, Boers (1999) systematically counted all expressions reflecting the conceptual metaphor THE ECONOMY IS A HEALTHY/UNHEALTHY PATIENT in the editorials of *The Economist* over a ten-year period. He found that the average number of such expressions increased significantly during the winter period. Boers' findings describe a phenomenon that is likely to be very widespread, namely that subconscious representations of our interactions with our environment can affect the language that we use.

5.3.2 Implications for foreign language learning

We are unaware of any research studies on promoting the ability to interpret cultural references and figures of speech through the use of figurative thinking in L2 contexts. However, one way in which it could be done is through the use of poetry. It has been argued that poetry, as well as literature and song lyrics can act as a powerful change agent by developing language learners' intercultural awareness while at the same time nurturing empathy, a tolerance for diversity and even emotional intelligence (Ghosn, 2002). Furthermore, crossing the language/ literature divide in the language classroom is likely to help learners to appreciate the more poetic elements of everyday language (Carter and McCarthy, 1995). Poetry allows the teacher to expand metaphorical themes in different contexts. Modern poetry can help language learners gain insights into the target language culture, and much poetry, whether modern or not, aids discussion of the relationship between universal and culture-specific themes. By discussing how the metaphorical themes are developed in a particular poem, language learners can be helped to get a feel for the different ways in which conceptual metaphors are elaborated in the target language. They might then be encouraged to consider the extent to which these elaborations would work in their own languages, and whether different elaborations might be more appropriate.

A poem that makes extensive use of metonymy, providing access to a range of aspects of British or American culture is Auden's (1936) 'Funeral Blues'. In it, the narrator protests that everything in the world should stop because his lover has died. It may also be satirical in origin, being sarcastic about the public funeral of a politician.[3] The poem draws heavily on the cultural connotations of words, a fact which could be heavily exploited in the language classroom.

> Put crepe bows round the white necks of the public doves [7]
> Let the traffic policemen wear black cotton gloves [8]

To understand line 8, students could be asked to note their associations with 'black' and to describe their image of a traffic policeman. They could then understand how in British culture, black not white is the primary symbol of mourning. A similar exercise ('Who would wear a crepe bow?', 'What do you associate with doves? With white doves?') would get at the greater complexity of line 7, with its echoes of the black and white of (Victorian?) funeral parades, pigeons as stereotypically associated with public places and the dove as the Christian incarnation of the Holy Spirit or the soul, as well as a common symbol for love until death.

Learners could also be asked to identify metaphors and metonymies that are likely to be universal, but which are expressed in different ways in their language. For instance, 'Stop all the clocks, cut off the telephone' (line 1) expresses both the feeling on numbness at the loss and the habit of publicly remembering the dead with a few minutes silence. Time (in the form of the sun or a clock) stopping to mark a deeply significant event has been a conventional literary conceit for thousands of years in western European culture (from the Bible, through the *Song of Roland* in the Middle Ages), but it is likely to be expressed differently in languages with different cultural connections.

Finally, learners could be asked to work out which metaphors and metonymies in the poem are conventional in English, and which represent novel extensions or creations by the author. Even intermediate level learners could consider the metonymic implications of substituting 'doves' for 'pigeons', or using 'telephone' as an image of happiness, noise and sociability. Such activities would provide learners with an opportunity to develop their associative fluency and analogical reasoning skills.

A useful source of material that could be exploited in order to explore the boundaries between conventional and creative metaphor is cartoons. Forceville (2005) shows how ANGER IS HEAT OF A FLUID IN A CONTAINER is creatively exploited in *Asterix* comics. Pictorial signals of anger include bulging eyes (presumably representing a build-up of interior pressure), a tightly closed mouth (presumably to prevent the anger from escaping), and smoke or steam coming out of the ears (presumably representing the ultimate evaporation of the fluid). These cartoons could be shown to students, who might then be asked to describe the scenes verbally. This would give rise to a variety of conventional and novel metaphors for anger. It might also be useful to encourage them to look up words such as *explode, steam, burst*, and so on, in a large corpus, such as the Bank of English or the British National Corpus.

A final source of authentic material for the analysis of cultural references is advertising. This is because, in advertisements, several messages often have to be conveyed as concisely as possible, meaning that the metaphors they use are often multi-layered. We saw in Chapter 3 how the wording of a beer advertisement 'Boddingtons: The Cream of Manchester' posed problems to a group of Japanese learners of English. Students could be encouraged to discuss with their teacher the many connotations 'cream' might have, such as: its texture, the fact that it usually refers to the best, it comes at the top, is pure and wholesome, and so on. They might be asked to identify the different possible interpretations, and consider the different audiences at which they might be aimed. They might then go on to think of other ways in which the word might be used, thus developing their metaphoric extension abilities. In short, advertisements such as this can provide a rich source of teaching material designed to sensitise learners to cultural differences in association patterns.

5.4 The relationship between figurative thinking and dialect and variety

We have focused thus far on the role of figurative thinking in interpreting cultural references and figures of speech that are employed by the idealised notion of the target language community as a whole. But sociolinguistic competence includes 'sensitivity to dialect or variety', 'sensitivity to register', and 'sensitivity to naturalness', which implies an ability to cope with the language of smaller groups. However, it is when we consider smaller groups that the serious pedagogical problems begin to arise. Any language teacher who is interested in covering dialect and variety in their classes will need to consider at least three potentially problematic issues: First, there is the fact that small-scale variation adds enormously to the complexity of the target language and also localised figurative expressions are frequently of very restricted application. Second, learners differ markedly in the degree to which they want or need to affiliate with the social and cultural groups involved. Third, since the language of topics such as fighting, sexual attractiveness and a lack of intelligence seem particularly prone to local variation, many figurative expressions that one could justify pedagogically on the grounds of relevance or usefulness may well offend the sensibilities of teachers, learners, parents or government education departments. On the other hand, with advanced adult learners, teaching the types of figurative language that are used by different speech communities may be a more worthwhile endeavour.

There is certainly clear evidence of 'small-scale' social and cultural variation with respect to both metaphor and metonymy. Variation can be explored in terms of the user (e.g., lawyers, Glaswegians), the language (dialect, register), or the behaviour / product (speech events, genre). We begin by focussing on the user, using Swales's (1990) rough division between more 'purposeful' groups where membership is achieved with some effort (Discourse communities) and less 'purposeful' groups where membership is more due to chance, for example, where people live on the same street (Speech communities).

Speech communities may be purely geographic, though in the United Kingdom at least, the existence of a more or less clear national standard results in a frequent association between regional dialect and social class. Ethnic groups that settle in a country can also generate dialects and then mixtures between the ethic variety and local varieties. While ethnic/local mixes are increasingly being recognised in Britain (Rampton, 1995), there is as yet little research on the metaphor or metonymy involved.

At a general level, however, it is fairly easy to see how localized varieties reflect specific details of the local environment. 'Meaders' meaning socially undesirable people refers metonymically to the rough South Mead area of Bristol (BBC, 2005). Or the metaphoric, metonymic and euphemistic 'Kirby kiss' in working class Liverpool speech, meaning a head butt (Kirby is a deprived area of Liverpool). Again in Liverpudlian slang, someone unintelligent can be described as being 'as thick as a docker's butty'; Liverpool was famous for its docks until relatively recently and a 'butty' is fairly common across much of northern England to mean a sandwich – where buttered is a PART FOR WHOLE metonymy.

Teenagers represent a speech community based on age. The situation here is complex as, although the use of figurative expressions can vary regionally, the extent of lexical variation is frequently unknown (Upton, 2005). Thus a British teenager might describe an undesirable person, especially from a sexual point of view' as a 'minger', or an attractive person as 'fit', but quite how general or localised these expressions are is unclear. Older people also constitute a speech community, but while there has been some research on idiom and proverb comprehension ability of the over fifties (Qualls, 2003), we could find little on patterns of figurative language use. Anecdotally, they may (unlike younger people) have *a night out on the tiles*, ask what's on at *the pictures*, or decide to *give it a whirl*.

Gender groups are roughly classifiable as speech communities, though they have elements of social bonding (e.g., feminist 'sisterhood'). Kövecses (2004) notes the use of differing metaphors of endearment/attraction by men and women in English: ATTRACTIVE MEN ARE LARGE FURRY ANIMALS (cuddly, bears) while ATTRACTIVE WOMEN ARE SMALL SOFT ANIMALS (chick, kitten, bunny). So far, we have looked only at speech communities, which fall under the heading of 'dialect' and 'variety'. Our discussion of discourse communities, in the following section, will take us into the realm of 'register'.

5.   The relationship between figurative thinking and register

Discourse communities, like academics, architects, or lawyers, have ways of doing and talking about their work (their 'practices'), ways of presenting it to outsiders and often rites of entry to the group. The types of communicative activity undertaken are called 'genres' and the functional varieties of language involve 'registers'.[4] All three concepts; social groups, genres and registers: are highly flexible and can be broadly or narrowly based.

A good example of a very broadly based register used by academics is academic English. Formal variants tend to employ words that are derived from French, whereas less formal variants tend to have a greater proportion of words that are of Germanic origin, many of which are idiomatic phrasal verbs. Thus, formally points are 'raised', issues are 'investigated', problems 'arise' and people 'intervene', whereas in less formal variants, points are more often 'brought up', issues are 'looked into', problems 'turn up' and people 'step in' or 'barge in'. Figurative thinking plays a particularly important role in identifying the relationship between the formal and informal instantiations of the same concept. We discuss this issue in more detail in Chapter 8.

Discourse communities tend to generate large numbers of technical terms, which are frequently metaphoric and/or metonymic. Some are fairly general, thus all academics need to know how to distinguish between 'a stand', 'a view', 'an observation', 'a conclusion' and 'a reflection', but others are more narrowly based; it is largely ethnographers who talk about 'projecting' an opinion and quantitative researchers or statisticians who talk about 'Y hat' (for $\hat{y}$).

Two important points may be made about technical terms. First, when experts use them 'within the group', they are generally treated as non-figurative and the non-literality is rarely signalled (Knudsen, 2003). The figurative dimension tends to remain activatable, however, and academics will signal metaphoricity and develop further metaphoric expressions around them when writing for non-expert readers (Low, 1997). Second, scientific metaphors are recognised by the expert group as highly metaphoric when newly coined and a theory is being developed – indeed academics fight over whose metaphor will be the one finally accepted (Knudsen, 1996) – but writers also explain them in articles, making comprehension 'at the cutting edge' somewhat easier for learners.

The exact degree to which disciplines differ in the creation of new metaphors or the extending of old metaphors and metonymies is not clear. But the broad area of economics, politics and business seems particularly rich. Creativity involves the creation of single technical terms, like 'dead cat bounce', as well as the extension of common conceptual metaphors ('the green shoots of recovery' extends

AN ECONOMY IS A PLANT). Such extensions can be taken up and repeatedly played with as ideas are developed internationally (witness the national and emotive variations on EUROPE IS A HOUSE (Schäffner, 1996; Chilton,1996) and EUROPE IS A FAMILY (Musolff, 2000). The sources of such creativity are numerous; Arleo (2000), for example, found metaphors from biology, catastrophe theory, chaos theory and quantum physics to be frequent in texts about entrepreneurship.

It is arguable whether user groups constitute speech or discourse communities, but they often generate considerable amounts of figurative language, which function as technical terms and serve to mark the speaker as a member of the group. Terms used by drug users are a good example: drugs are often named metonymically (and sometimes metaphorically) after the physical and psychological sensation they create: 'ectasy' (whence 'Es'), 'eye opener' (crack cocaine), 'black bomber' (amphetamine) (http://surrealism.50megs.com/slang; (see Neaman and Silver (1991: pp. 215–227) for terms from the 1960s to 1980s). Descriptions of the process of drug taking are also highly metonymic ('a fix', 'to shoot up', 'cut a line'). Youth and user-group expressions seem to move fast from their original community and drug terms spread quickly around the world.

Social and cultural communities vary markedly in the degree to which there are rules and rites for entry and exit, or even who can talk when (Briggs, 1986), and to which sanctions can be imposed. At the 'tight' end of the spectrum are teenage gangs and fundamentalist religious groups, while at the 'loose' end are interest groups, like 'computer users', 'keen photographers' or 'hip hop listeners'. There is frequently a close relationship between language use and group membership: using certain words at all, or with high frequency displays core membership, or a desire to join, whereas avoidance displays peripheral membership or rejection (LePage and Tabouret Keller, 1985). Learners need to know the sort of claims they are making if they use particular figurative expressions and to develop some idea of whether they are failing to claim if they make grammatical or collocational errors.

Learners will vary about which speech and discourse communities they wish to be associated with and about the degree to which they wish to affiliate with them. Learners may well also construct a series of slightly different identities when using the L2 (Lam, 2000), and teachers need to recognise that individuals may quite validly wish to retain, possibly despite the teacher's enthusiasm, a sense of 'me' which holds back from full integration. While individuals will probably find ways of retaining an L1 dimension to their L2 by themselves, teachers can help them establish an appropriate L2 identity by training them to accommodate linguistically and conceptually to (or distance themselves from) particular groups.

From a teaching point of view, there is no ethical problem with exposing learners to technical terms, teaching them to talk like over-obsessed wine buffs, or helping them master hidden assumptions in order to 'play the academic game'. But there are serious implications about devoting valuable class time to highly localised language unless the learners are likely to come across the group concerned, say when studying abroad. The high proportion of figurative expressions devoted to swearing, insults and derogatory expressions of various sorts constitutes a major ethical problem even in these situations. It is a brave teacher who says, 'here's how to sound young' or 'here is what you may encounter' and 'here is how to get your own back'.

5.5.1   Using figurative thinking to promote sensitivity to register in the English for Academic Purposes classroom

Littlemore (submitted) looked at how graduate students of English for Academic Purposes (EAP) at a UK university might be sensitised to the variety of language employed by their relevant discourse community. She first attended a lecture in International Development alongside the group of 20 students, and recorded it. Key parts involving figurative language were transcribed and a handout was prepared based on the transcript (Box 5.1). Later in the same day, she helped the students to work through the handout, in the presence of the lecturer. This approach addressed the issue of *noticing*, which was discussed in Chapter 3. It enabled the students to perceive the ubiquity of metaphor in the lecture, and allowed both the students and the lecturer to discuss the meanings being asserted or implied. The students discussed with the lecturer a number of conceptual metaphors that they had identified in the text. By doing so, they were able to gain more insight into his conceptions of government. The students reported that in subsequent classes, this lecturer made his use of figurative language much more overt, and that they were better able to understand the content of the lectures. They claimed to be more able to detect the lecturer's not-so-hidden agendas, and thus better able to debate issues with him. In terms of comprehension at least, they reported being able to turn declarative knowledge into procedural knowledge. This led to a deeper understanding of lectures given by this lecturer. The students had thereby *begun* to enter the discourse community, at least as far as this lecturer was concerned.

Box 5.1   'Academic language': Extract from student handout

Language and critical thinking
Extracts from the lecture are in italics.
[...]

And I sometimes tease my British colleagues. We're becoming more and more like Chinese you know! The Chinese have, since ancient times, run their governments by metaphors. Or certainly the public interface.

Which conceptual metaphor lies behind the lecturer's use of the word 'interface'?
What does this word suggest about the relationship between government and the general public?
[...]

And that was the basis of liberalisation. New liberalisation. Go to the World Bank and there are words and words and words and words. But Deng Xiaoping managed to put it into words that are more related to the farmyard and to the household.
Why do you think Deng Xiaoping used this kind of language?
What equivalent kind of language does the Bangladeshi Government use when talking to the general public about its policies?

So, that's that. This group is now going to be Ministry of Industry. Assuming that you're top ministerial level. You're doing strategic management exercise in the Ministry and first stage is mission statement and objectives.
What is the difference between 'mission statement' and 'objectives'.
[...]

Your job is to examine, to tackle, not to examine, to tackle the arsenic in water problem.
Which conceptual metaphor lies behind the lecturer's use of the words 'to tackle'?
How is 'tackle' therefore different from 'examine'?

Ministry and water affairs. You are to work out your mission and your objectives. And the left hand group is going to be the Bangladeshi handloom board, who are already and then you are asking yourselves, right 'where do we go from here?' Strategic management exercises are done from time to time.
Which conceptual metaphor lies behind the expression 'where do we go from here'?
[...]

When you come to objectives, this 'SMART'. The 'SMART' way of categorising objectives is to think about something which is, for the organisation, stretching, you know challenging in that sense, measurable, achievable, realistic and achievable. Realistic and achievable are close cousins here. And time-bound. Why do we have time bound in there? It's to stop you bureaucrats from putting it onto a committee which will meet for the next 10 years.
What are the literal meanings of 'stretch' and 'bound' (as in time-bound)?
What does 'close cousins' mean?
[...]

Organisations may turn round and say, we've run out of time. But in reality organisations should be able to re-shape and re-focus.

Box 5.1 Continued

What do the words 're-shape' and 're-focus' say about the lecturer's attitude towards organisations (think about the three big Civil Service metaphors that we saw on Monday)
[...]
By definition, sustainability is almost by definition, not time-bound. So I have a quarrel with this methodology. Erm, which all goes to show that we shouldn't be slaves.
What does he mean by this?
Can you find examples above of the following conceptual metaphors?
Sport:
Fighting/the army:
Computing:
Religion/official doctrine:
Path:
Flexible material (e.g., clay):
Human beings:
What implications might each of these metaphors have?

The apparent success of this approach is likely to be due to its contextualised, student-centred nature. The students could see actual examples of figurative language in use, and to assess their ideational and evaluative content. The team-teaching approach was also valuable, lending support to Dudley-Evans and Johns' (1981) claims for the effectiveness of team-teaching in EAP. Although they are time consuming, it would be worth conducting team-teaching sessions, like the one described earlier, at the beginning of the academic year for students from different disciplines. Further research would be required to establish what the long-term gains of such an approach might be, for a larger number of lecturers, across a wide variety of disciplines.

5.5.2 Using figurative thinking to promote sensitivity to register in the general English language classroom

Littlemore (2004d) attempted to sensitise learners to differences in register between tabloid and broadsheet journalism in the United Kingdom. The following activity was piloted with a group of ten mixed-nationality advanced adult learners of English in the United Kingdom, who were introduced to the figurative animal adjectives: 'bullish', 'foxy', 'catty', 'cocky' and 'ratty'. The learners were shown pictures of the animals and asked to think of the attributes that they normally associate with them. This could be described as a 'bottom-up' strategy, consisting of focusing on the word itself and pursuing any concepts that the word might generate. The next step was to discuss the linguistic and social differences between British broadsheet and tabloid newspapers. The students were then asked to employ a 'top-down' strategy where they inferred meanings from concordance lines for each term. To illustrate tabloid usage, the following concordance lines were taken from *The Sun* sub-corpus of the Bank of English:

> Stubborn Taurus still looking BULLISH? The characteristics of this
>   star sign ...
> We admit we're very BULLISH. We will stay the way we are ...
> Fergus McCann was equally BULLISH. He refused to withdraw his
>   comment ...
> The man Mexico calls El Matador, is in BULLISH mood. He'll be a
>   real threat to ...
> With his short, cropped hair and BULLISH neck, Davies looked like ...

To illustrate broadsheet usage, the following concordance lines were taken from *The Guardian* sub-corpus of the Bank of English:

> While market sentiment is not exactly BULLISH, traders are fairly
>   optimistic ...
> ... well it would stand up in a more BULLISH market.
> ... from recruits. BNFL is most BULLISH about staying nuclear. It is ...
> The pound has swung from crazily BULLISH to almost crazily
>   bearish since ...
> Nomura is taking a BULLISH stance. It forecast profits this ...
> ... percentages up again. The market is BULLISH and prices are looking up.
> NHS chiefs are in a BULLISH mood after securing acceptance of ...
> ... an impassioned, and at times BULLISH appeal from John
>   Major to 'let me ...

The learners were asked to work in small groups to determine the different meanings of the five words in the two publications. The object was not to find hard and fast rules governing different patterns of usage, but to identify tendencies and patterns. During a post-task discussion, the students were encouraged to think of possible sociolinguistic reasons for the differences between the ways these words were used in the two newspapers, and differences in the ways in which the equivalents were used in their own languages. An important aim of this activity was to sensitise learners to the fact that the meanings of idiomatic expressions can vary according to the social context.

In *The Sun*, 'bullish' referred to a person's character, mood or physical appearance, and drew on a bull's physical size or the difficulty of stopping it when angry. In *The Guardian*, it was used less personally, to describe a rising stock market, drawing on the notion of a bull having great energy. Eight of the ten students were able to identify the main difference between the two publications, but some of them were put off by difficult vocabulary in the concordance lines, which distracted them from the main task. In future studies, the concordance lines would need to be more carefully edited to avoid this problem.

One advantage of this approach is that it encourages learners to use both images and contexts to work out possible meanings of the words, implying that it should in theory accommodate both visual and verbal learners. This corresponds to the dual coding theories outlined in Chapter 3. The study did not investigate the relation with cognitive style, but this would be a useful follow-up study. Further research is also required to assess long-term effectiveness, and to look at whether the approach could be adapted to teaching other aspects of idiomatic language, such as different connotations of colour.

5.6 The relationship between figurative thinking and 'naturalness'

Bachman's third aspect of sociolinguistic competence is 'sensitivity to naturalness'. This presumably reflects the fact that even small errors of syntactic form, metaphor mixing or figurative extension can make it clear that one is not a native speaker. In part this means learners need to recognise the boundaries and limitations of metaphoric expressions – something far more complex than just knowing what they mean, or the conceptual relationships underlying them (Low, 1988; Deignan, 2005). It also means they need in practice to recognise where translations of basic meanings from their L1 would be inappropriate. Linguistic variations in the use of delexicalised nouns and verbs (which involve metaphor in conceptual metaphor theory) is a good example. Learning problems may arise where L2 versions diverge rather than converge. Thus Chinese learners of English regularly overgeneralise 'way' in place of 'method', 'means' or even 'type'. At other times, language preferences seem almost random: 'to go for a walk' in English, 'dar un paseo' (give a walk) in Spanish, but 'faire un promenade' (make a walk) in French. Delexical word errors seem to be persistent and our experience of even very advanced EAP classes is that one repeatedly has to teach 'take' or 'do' a course or an exam, not 'make' it. Coping with this sort of variation as a learner requires the learner to accept the L2 variants as perfectly reasonable alternatives to whatever expression is used in the mother tongue. This is also likely to require a certain tolerance of ambiguity, as we discussed in Chapter 4.

5.6.1   Using figurative thinking to promote sensitivity to naturalness in the language classroom

We are not aware of any studies that have looked at how sensitivity to naturalness might be promoted through the use of figurative thinking. Indeed, much conventional phraseological patterning lies beyond the limits of what can be achieved through figurative analysis. Highly delexicalised expressions, like 'make an error' may well be better taught by exposure, rote memorising and repetition. The use of multitext and multitask exercises for more obviously figurative expressions was suggested in Low (1988), so that learners had to change formality level, genre and/or register as part of the activity, but their effectiveness has not been empirically tested. Another instructional technique that is potentially productive is the use of associative group analysis. Associative group analysis involves listing all the spontaneous associations that one has for a given stimulus word (see e.g., Szalay, 1984). This is a technique that could be adapted to the language classroom in order to get students to examine their own semantic networks and to make hypotheses about how they may differ from those of a native speaker of the target language. This is likely to be useful as paradigmatic and syntagmatic associations are involved in metaphor, metonymy and collocation. One might begin by asking the students to brainstorm the associations that they have for a given word. They could then be shown a list of typical native-speaker associations for that word (or encouraged to find such a list via an email exchange project). They could then look for the word in an Internet search engine in the target language, and analyse the first 20 hits to see whether the collocations of the word overlap in any way with the set of native speaker associations. They could then be encouraged to think of possible reasons why some overlap and others do not. This type of activity could be used to extend the range and scope of meanings that they normally attach to individual words, and help them to be more creative (though perhaps not more 'natural-sounding') in the target language. The effectiveness of such an approach, however, remains to be tested.

5.7   Conclusion

In this chapter, we have shown that metaphor and metonymy are involved to some extent in all four of Bachman's subareas of sociolinguistic competence, and not just in the obvious one of 'interpreting cultural references'. In many cases, competence relates to understanding how something is conceptualised generally 'in English', or draws on some aspect of culture at national, or international, level. However, we noted the paradox that while knowledge of the practices of smaller cultural and social groups is necessary in order to sound 'natural' or to claim membership of the groups, the restricted applicability and the derogatory nature of many of the figurative expressions (or conceptualisations) concerned can pose serious problems to the teacher. There has been little published research into how best to teach figurative aspects of sociolinguistic competence, but we have suggested several ways in which figurative thinking might be used and summarised two exploratory studies where it appeared to be effective.

6
Figurative Thinking and Illocutionary Competence

6.1   Introductory comments

Illocutionary competence refers to one's ability to understand the message behind the words that one reads or hears, or to make clear one's own message through careful use of words. Illocutionary competence is what (usually) prevents us from 'getting the wrong end of the stick' when people talk to us. It consists of ideational functions, manipulative functions, heuristic functions and imaginative functions. According to Bachman, ideational functions refer to our use of language to exchange information and our feelings about that information. Manipulative functions serve a primary purpose of affecting the behaviour of others. Heuristic functions involve our use of language to extend our knowledge of the world around us. Finally, imaginative functions involve our ability to play with language in order to entertain others.

In the following sections, we will discuss the roles that figurative thinking might play in performing each of these four functions, bearing in mind the fact that there is a great deal of overlap between them. We will also outline a number of techniques that might be used in foreign language classrooms to help language learners develop these different aspects of illocutionary competence through figurative thinking processes. We will evaluate the effectiveness of these techniques, and identify areas where further research is needed.

6.2   The role of figurative thinking in performing ideational functions

Ideational functions, according to Bachman, refer to the use of language to exchange information and our feelings about that information.

Figurative language is involved in ideational functions, as we often use it to convey our evaluation of a situation. An inability to understand the language used can thus lead a listener or reader to misinterpret the evaluation offered by the speaker or writer. Some figurative language simply reports in a fairly neutral way: 'The Conservative Party held the view that ...', 'A few people 'spoke up for him', or 'He touched on a number of topics'. However, large amounts of figurative language, whether innovative or conventional, like 'spill the beans', 'a hard life' or 'a tough cookie', contain both an information-reporting component and an affective or evaluative component. Indeed, the listener has a much greater need with figurative language than with 'literal' language to be able to tell whether an affective or evaluative component is intended. In terms of production too, the ability to use figurative language to convey one's standpoint is likely to contribute significantly to a student's communicative language ability.

The most important thing about ideational functions is that they are used to convey our feelings about that information. The word 'feelings' can have a wide range of applications. It can be used to refer to particularly high levels of emotion, feelings of dissatisfaction, as when we are complaining, evaluative comments or political ideology. In this section we will review research which has identified strong roles for figurative language in each of these areas.

Emotions are subjective experiences and, as such, are difficult to capture. Also, they are complex, and figurative language can be used to succinctly express this complexity. Indeed, research has shown that speech addressing topics that are emotional is likely to result in the production of significantly more figurative language (in particular metaphors) than, for example, narratives, statistics and examples (Corts, 1999; Fussell and Moss, 1998; Gibbs and Nascimento, 1996; Williams-Whitney *et al.*, 1992). There are particularly high instances of figurative language use when people are talking about negative emotions (Fainsilber and Ortony, 1987).

It has been argued that people use overt figurative language to distinguish a particular emotional state from other similar types of states (Fussell and Moss, 1998). These differences may be qualitative and/or quantitative. For example, Fussell and Moss (ibid.) carried out a study in which they asked the participants to look at a series of film clips featuring sadness. Although the literal expressions that speakers used were fairly similar across clips, their idioms and metaphors were tailored to specific clips and to specific points in the characters' emotional experiences. They found that people used significantly more metaphors when categorising *specific personal* instances of sadness than they did when simply describing sadness in general. These findings are in line with the idea that speakers produce creative utterances to individuate personal emotional experiences from the general concepts encoded in the lexicon (Gerrig and Gibbs, 1988).

Further evidence of the role of overt figurative language in expressing our feelings and attitudes is provided by Drew and Holt's (1998) finding that people are most likely to employ idioms when they are complaining to, or about, another person.

This reflects a broader view that figurative language is most likely to be found in the context of negative evaluations (Moon, 1998). Findings such as these show that there is a degree of systematicity governing people's choices of when to use idioms and when not to. A speaker's decision to choose a particular idiom from their linguistic repertoire will, at some level, either consciously or subconsciously, reflect their subjective positioning. This has also been found in university lectures where the lecturer will use figurative language to convey his or her evaluation of the subject being discussed (Littlemore, 2001b). Littlemore found that international students sometimes missed the evaluative component of the lecture because they had misinterpreted the lecturer's use of figurative language. For example, when one lecturer suggested that Government policy was going to 'begin a new chapter', this was understood by a number of students to mean that there was simply going to be a new version of what went before, rather than a completely new approach. These students had picked up on the wrong part of the source domain, leading them to focus on continuity, rather than change and the lecturer's enthusiasm for this change.

As well as conveying emotions and evaluation, figurative language, particularly metonymy, is also involved in the interpretation of implicatures and indirect speech acts. It is generally accepted that the identification of a speaker's communicative intention in an indirect speech act requires some inferential work on the part of the hearer. For example, if there is a cake on the table in the dining room and a visitor to the house utters 'mmm, that looks good', the chances are that they are trying to convey the message 'can I have a piece?'. Speech act theorists rarely discuss the nature of the inferential work involved in interpreting utterances such as these, but recent work in the area of cognitive linguistics suggests that metonymic shorthand may be involved (Gibbs, 1994; Panther and Thornburg, 1998; Perez-Hernendez and Ruiz de Mendoza, 2002).

In order to account for the role of metonymic thinking in understanding indirect speech acts, Panther and Thornburg (1998) propose a useful distinction between 'propositional metonymy' and 'illocutionary metonymy'. Propositional metonymy includes both traditional *referential* metonymy, in which words are used to refer to related concepts (e.g., *the White House thinks*), and *predicational* metonymy, in which potentiality stands for actuality (e.g., where *they were able to get a small farm in the West* stands for *they got a small farm in the West*). Illocutionary metonymy is what allows people to understand the illocutionary force of indirect speech acts. In the cake example, the utterance 'mmm that looks good' stands metonymically for the scenario in which the host offers them a piece of cake, they eat it, and enjoy it. This would be a 'comment for request' metonymy. The widely cited utterance 'it's cold in here', which, in certain contexts, means 'please close the window', may involve a similar type of 'comment for request' metonymy. In a conversation about a possible trip to the cinema, the utterance 'Star Wars is on' may be intended to mean 'let's go and see Star Wars', which would constitute a 'comment for suggestion' metonymy.

Illocutionary metonymies are likely to be involved in the comprehension of many, if not all implicatures, that is, things that are implied in conversation, but not expressed directly. For example, if someone were to ring up their partner and say 'I'm standing right outside the fish and chip shop and it smells fantastic – I was wondering if you'd put the dinner on yet', this might reasonably be inferred to mean 'would you like me to buy us some fish and chips for dinner?' If someone asks 'have we got any biscuits left?' and receives the reply 'I don't know, but Joe was on his own in the kitchen for a very long time yesterday evening', he or she may well infer that Joe has eaten all the biscuits, so there probably aren't any left.

From what we have seen just, it is likely that people engage in metonymic thinking in order to understand the contextual clues (Gibbs, 1994). In the fish and chips example given earlier, the listener needs to form a metonymic connection between the fact that their partner is standing outside the fish and chip shop and the fact that he or she wants to know if they have put the dinner on. In the biscuits example, a metonymic connection needs to be drawn between Joe's presence in the kitchen and the fact that the biscuits may be finished.

Implications for foreign language learning

We can sum up Section 6.2 by saying that figurative thinking is likely to contribute to ideational functions in two main ways. First, we have observed that figurative language is often used to convey emotions and evaluation, particularly negative evaluation, and second, we have seen that metonymic mechanisms lie behind the interpretation of indirect speech acts. But how can we help language learners to develop their figurative thinking potential in order to acquire both of these skills?

One way of sensitising learners to the role of culture in understanding implicatures (particularly ones that convey evaluation) is through the study of poetry. A poem that makes good use of metonymic shorthand, and which contains language that is easy enough for lower level students, is 'Hair Today, No Her Tomorrow', by Brian Patten (see Box 6.1). This poem appears to revolve around a simple discussion of a hair, but in fact it is dealing with complex issues of love, hate, jealousy and faithfulness. Very little is said, but a great deal is implied. This poem could be used to explore the ways in which metonymy acts as a kind of shorthand for both universal and cultural-specific assumptions and schemata. Before reading the poem, students could be asked to conduct an associative group analysis for words such as 'hair', 'black', 'white' and 'bed'. They could be asked to read the title and predict what the poem is going to be about. They could then be asked to identify the metonymic links between the objects referred to in the poem, and the actions and ideas that they encapsulate. They could then be encouraged to reflect upon parallel metonymies in their own language, and on possible cultural equivalents to the ideas expressed in the poem. Another more overarching metaphor that could be exploited is the fact that this poem sets up a kind of tennis match between the two speakers, a pattern that more advanced students could perhaps be asked to imitate.

6.3   The role of figurative thinking in performing manipulative functions

The primary purpose of manipulative functions is to affect the world around us. They help to get things done, to control the behaviour of others, and build up relationships. As one might expect, the manipulative use of figurative language is particularly prevalent in the world of politics. The way in which a politician's choice of metaphors can affect the world order is demonstrated by Rohrer (1995), who examines the effects of George Bush's use of the 'political rape' metaphor to describe Iraq's invasion of Kuwait. He argues that the practical outcome of accepting Bush's metaphor and his metaphorically projected inferences was the 1991 war in the Persian Gulf. Also in the UK political domain, substantial damage may have been done to the Conservative leader Michael Howard's image by Anne Widdowcombe's comment that 'there is something of the night about him'.

Box 6.1   Hair Today: no Her Tomorrow.

Hair today, no her tomorrow

I've been upstairs-she said
Oh yes?-I said
I found a hair-she said
A hair?-I said
In the bed-she said
From a head?-I said
It's not mine-she said
Was it black?-I said
It was-she said
I'll explain-I said
You swine-she said
Not quite-I said
I'm going-she said
Please don't-I said
I hate you!-she said
You do?-I said
Of course-she said
But why?-I said
That black hair-she said
A pity-I said

Time for truth-she said
For confessions?-I said
Me too-she said
You what?-I said
Someone else-she said
Oh dear-I said
So there!-she said
Ah well-I said
Guess who?-she said
Don't say-I said
I will-she said
You would-I said
Your friend-she said
Oh damn-I said
And his friend-she said
Him too?-I said
And the rest-she said
Good God-I said

What's that?-she said
What's what?-I said
That noise?-she said
Upstairs-I said
Yes-she said
The new cat-I said

Box 6.1   Continued

A cat?-she said
It's black-I said
Black?-she said
Long-haired-I said
Oh no-she said
Oh yes-I said
Oh shit!-she said
Goodbye-I said

I lied-she said
You lied?-I said
Of course-she said
About my friend?-I said
Y-ess-she said
And the others?-I said
Ugh-she said
How odd-I said
I'm forgiven?-she said
Of course-I said
I'll stay?-she said
Please don't-I said
But why?-she said
I lied-I said
About what?-she said
The new cat-I said
It's white-I said

© Brian Patten (c/o Rogers, Coleridge and White, 20 Powis Mews, London, W11 1JN)

The salience of metaphor in political rhetoric is also highlighted by Charteris-Black (2005), who demonstrates how metaphor is used in the language of leadership to mediate between 'conscious rational ideology' and 'unconscious myth'. He shows how metaphor was used by Churchill to create a myth of Britain as a heroic warrior; by Martin Luther King to create a myth of himself as a messiah; and by Margaret Thatcher to activate a myth of Boadicea. Charteris-Black also reveals how Tony Blair developed a conviction rhetoric in which he is a dynamic agent in a mythological struggle between good and evil. On a more sinister note, Chilton (1994) shows the powerful role of metaphor in racist discourse, in which the container schema is used to emphasise notions of externality, otherness and difference, and rejection, through the repeated use of words and expressions such as '*in* our country', 'invasion' and 'barbarians'.

In the calmer world of business writing, we again find evidence of the crucial role of figurative language in performing manipulative functions. In the following extract, popular business guru Tom Peters (1994: p. 5) uses a metaphor of a dynamo to cast a certain type of worker in a good light (the 'dynamos') and to exaggerate the worthlessness of the average worker (the 'cruisers').

> Only 10 to 20% [of workers] are ... dynamos ... always working to learn something new ... continually building their practices in new and challenging areas. The rest of the partners are 'cruisers', who don't stand out as special talents. The bottom line: The long-term success of any professional service company depends on nurturing a high share of intellectual-miracle-building dynamos

Peters' use of the word 'nurture' clearly implies that a high proportion of dynamos must be maintained and have valuable resources devoted to them. The simple fact of 'not stand[ing] out' is equated, via the relative clause, with 'cruising', which implies going along aimlessly, slowly or even worse, pleasurably. As they are also 'partners', which is placed just one word away, the strong implication is that they are failing morally, as well as intentionally. The fate of such people is omitted, but the reader may treat the omission as significant and, by implication, the opposite of being 'nurtured': they are not to be cherished, they should have few resources devoted to them and they may even be sacked.

These metaphors, supported rhetorically by collocation and various types of implication, become highly persuasive, taking on moral overtones too. The idea that workers who do not 'stand out' are morally defective and should be ignored or made social outcasts is convincing precisely because the reader is asked (i.e., manipulated) to generate the conclusion him/herself. It may be that workers have indeed been sacked as a direct result of their managers reading Tom Peters' book. If this is the case, then the metaphor has performed both an instrumental function and a control function. We might also note that the manipulation centrally involves the writer asking the reader to construct an emotional stance or evaluation. Although the writer in this case can deny responsibility for the overtones thus generated, to all intents and purposes the situation is tantamount to the previous category – metaphor serving an evaluative function. The link between manipulation and covert evaluation is thus a close one; indeed it lies at the very heart of propaganda. In short, the ability to identify metaphors and metonymies that serve these functions contributes directly to one's communicative language ability.

In the light of these findings, the ability *not* to be swayed by another person's use of figurative language is an equally important part of communicative language ability. In order to avoid being positioned by the writer or speaker, a reader, or listener, needs to identify the conceptual metaphors and metonymies underlying the arguments. He or she will then be able to assess their limitations by identifying aspects of the source domains that do not transfer easily to the target domains, or even come up with alternative conceptual metaphors and metonymies.

Manipulative functions can be performed in conversation by picking up on and extending the metaphors used by one's interlocutor. An excellent example of this is given by Mio (1996), who quotes a televised exchange between a Lithuanian and a Russian representative at the time of Lithuania's imminent independence from Russia. The Russian representative compared the separation of the two countries to a divorce, claiming that, as they had been married for such a long time, any separation would take time and a period of separation was necessary before any full-scale divorce could be considered. To this, the Lithuanian representative replied that the two countries were 'not going through a divorce because we were never married, Lithuania was simply raped'. (Mio, 1996: p. 136). The second speaker thus picks up on the metaphor being used by the first and extends it, twisting it slightly to lend force to his argument. Mio asked listeners to rate the persuasive force of this metaphoric extension response, compared with that of a response based on an unrelated metaphor (Lithuania as a prisoner), and a literal response. The extended metaphor was found to be significantly more persuasive than the unrelated metaphor and the literal response.

Numerous examples of the persuasive role of metaphor can be found in the work on forensic linguistics, otherwise referred to as 'the language of the law'. For example, Cotterill (2003) shows how the Defence's use of a jigsaw puzzle metaphor was apparently responsible for the acquittal of O. J. Simpson. The Defence managed to convince the jury that the whole jigsaw needed to be present if they were going to find him guilty. This is a largely unrealistic expectation in any court case.

In other academic fields, researchers are beginning to appreciate the importance of choosing the 'right' metaphor to describe a given process and to change what is going on in that area. For example, Boers (1997) showed that business students made drastically different recommendations, depending on what metaphors are used to describe a business's problem. If the business was presented as a fortress then they argued for increased protective measures, whereas if the business was presented as an ailing athlete, then they argued for more injections of capital.

There are probably a number of reasons why figurative language is particularly good at performing manipulative functions. One is the fact that in some cases it can produce strong imagery, which makes the message much more memorable. It has been demonstrated that paragraphs with metaphoric conclusions, as opposed to literal conclusions, consistently lead to higher (immediate and long-term) memorability of both the conclusion and its context (Reynolds and Schwartz, 1983). Another reason is that figurative language allows speakers to hide behind shared values, allowing a speaker to voice his or her own opinion without being strictly accountable for it (Moon, 1998). This shared common ground allows speakers to get the interlocutor or the listener on one's side (McCarthy, 1998), and nowhere was this more evident than in the Watergate tapes, where not so innocent references were made to 'smoking guns' and 'cancer in the Whitehouse'.

Implications for foreign language learning

It may seem somewhat ambitious to expect language students to be able to use figurative language manipulatively in the L2, though adults at least will have been exposed to the fact of metaphor extension in their first language. Nevertheless, we can cite verbatim one example of students having the confidence to create and play with extended metaphor in a foreign language classroom. The aim of the class was to train a group of Japanese language teachers in spoken academic English, prior to their attendance on a Masters course in teaching English as a Foreign Language. After having spent some time preparing the subject, the students were participating in a debate *for* and *against* the explicit teaching of grammar in the language classroom. About five minutes into this debate, the following exchange (Table 6.1) took place between three of the five students:

Table 6.1 Extract from grammar debate

Student arguing against explicit grammar teaching	Student arguing for explicit grammar teaching
It is best for the students to be *showered* in a lot of English	
We are not *throwing them in the water,* they are just *in the shower*	But we don't want to *throw them in the water*
But grammar teaching is like *sitting on the tatami mat, and not getting in the water* And *there is few [sic] water in Japan,* this is why the classroom atmosphere is more important	We need to *get them used to the water before swimming*

These students appear to be playing with the metaphor LEARNING A LANGUAGE IS IMMERSION (IN WATER). Immersion was elaborated to swimming in a pool and extended to include the social activities surrounding it (including not swimming!). Students on both sides of the debate extended the basic metaphor in order to strengthen their arguments, making their utterances serve a strong manipulative function.

In our experience, the spontaneous use of extended metaphors such as these by non-native speakers is a somewhat rare occurrence, but there is some evidence that, with explicit training in the use of extended metaphors, intermediate students are able to employ them effectively, and to order, in academic debate. For instance, in order to assess whether or not language learners can be taught to tap into their figurative thinking processes to perform manipulative functions, Littlemore (2005) conducted a study in which students were actively encouraged to use extended metaphors in class debates. The students, who were all upper-intermediate and advanced non-native students of economics, were told that they would be participating in a debate, arguing for and against government intervention in the economy. They were then introduced to the conceptual metaphor THE ECONOMY IS A CAR, and asked to brainstorm possible arguments for and against intervention, based on this metaphor. When asked to do this, they first expressed concern that the activity might be too difficult. One of the students even commented that she did not know anything about cars and so would not be able to contribute. However, when they actually began the task, each student was able to come up with at least one argument for or against intervention. Arguments for intervention included the fact that one sometimes needs to change the wheels of a car, the fact that you need somebody at the wheel, namely a good driver, as soon as there is a problem in the economy you need to be able to hit the brakes, the economy needs regular checks, and if you haven't got the right skills then the economy will crash. Arguments against intervention included the fact that car thieves can do just as good a job as a driver, implying that having the wrong person in control is worse than having no one in control, the driver is just pumping the accelerator and the car is doing the rest, and that automatic cars are better than non-automatics. They then suggested that established economies are like automatic cars, and that economies in transition are shifting from automatic to manual.

After the brainstorming session, the students were split into two groups. One group was told that they would be arguing for Government intervention in the economy, and the other group was told that they would be arguing against the idea of Government intervention. They were then introduced to the conceptual metaphor THE ECONOMY IS A PLANT and given five minutes to prepare their arguments, based around this conceptual metaphor. An extract from the debate is presented in Table 6.2 below. As we can see from this extract, both sides were able to exploit the source domain in order to come up with a variety of arguments.

About ten minutes into the debate, the students were asked to reach a consensus using the same metaphor. An extract from this part of the debate is presented in Table 6.3.

Table 6.2 Extract from a student debate about Government intervention employing the metaphor THE ECONOMY IS A PLANT

For government intervention	Against government intervention
I think that the proper government intervention is quite important or essential for the some development of the economy just like the economy is a plant, it's just like a plant which needs a lot of sunshine very good condition to be planted. So when you plant something, flowers or plants, sometimes we use a greenhouse to seek a special temperature or special humidity to keep the plants growing even in some special areas still in Winter times …	But sunshine is not a kind of invention, it's just natural you can nurture it everywhere, it's just self-growth.
Right but at the same time, if you want to take cutting of your saplings, there won't be light for all of them. They will just be stuck and die old so	Well I think that the intervention of the Government just destroy the normal way of the plant's growth. Not helpful. The plant can grow healthy even without any other forces empowered on it.
	You only need sun, water and air for plants to grow properly.
Plant will grow properly if watered regularly in appropriate amounts.	Yes but look at the Amazon, I mean plants have been growing there for millions of years and the human intervention caused their destruction and deterioration, which is sort of similar to government intervention in the economy.

Table 6.3 Extract from the debate in which students were asked to reach a consensus

For government intervention	Against government intervention
Well I was always for the monetarist approach with the limited intervention of the government. There should be intervention but it should be limited to a certain extent, to let the invisible hand grow or stop.	Yeah it's like we can say that the government can sort of trim the tree of economy but not interfere in the photosynthesis.
Anyway the household plant need the gardener but maybe not the wild plant so much. It depends of different types of the government.	
Wild plant need less government I think. I think Government stil needed to maintain the economy. So the plants will be protected, but not absolutely by government. It can change, refers to the times, refers to the circumstance surrounding the plants something like that.	OK yes, sometimes you have garden roses and sometimes you have wild roses so some differences.

It is clear from Table 6.3 that the students were able to reach a consensus by agreeing that some plants, such as saplings (= infant industries) needed more protection than others and that at some times of year more protection is required (= cyclical recession and seasonal unemployment).

These findings suggest that the approach was useful in helping the students to develop the argument. By engaging in figurative thinking, they appear to be extending their critical thinking capacities. In informal post-task discussions, the students indicated that the approach had encouraged them to think about the topic in new and different ways. However, there was one weakness in the approach, which we can see in Table 6.4.

In this extract, the students appear to have merged the source and target domains, and they are now talking about the Government's role in caring for the *environment*, rather than the economy. This suggests that, although they were exploiting the source domain well, they were not monitoring their analogical/metaphorical reasoning to a sufficient extent. They were therefore not making enough mappings onto the target domain. It is difficult to know whether this is a general weakness of the 'explore a conceptual metaphor' approach, or whether it is

Table 6.4 Extract from the debate about the economy in which students merged the source and target domains

Against government intervention	For government intervention
There are plants for every climate. Everywhere there are plants.	And again, the government can't control all the plants.
Government is not God.	That's why deserts are so far spreading just because people don't care about anything in the nature, and if you don't if you stop, if in certain climates you don't care about the plants as the government doesn't care about the economy, the whole countries are deserted.
Well actually, deforestation is caused by modernisation. The forest fire of the Amazon river, we look at this movie, it is because some people destroy or make fire of this forest for the purpose of profit.	
Yeah that is the point.	It is individual action, but the intervention of the Government to protect the forest, so the Government intervene to create the ways to protect the natural plants.
But before that, a man intervened in the nature, which was ...	Yes but we saw in the same movie, in Brazil you have a project by the government called Brazilia something.
This project is to create roads in the Amazon forest. So by doing that they are deforesting large areas of the forest so it's expected to deforest 40% of the forest of the Amazon. That's government action. 40% of the forest is very hard to replace.	Erm maybe it's a certain period but that's ...

specific to this particular group of students (they may simply have been interested in these ecological issues, and wanted to discuss them); however it does appear to be a problem that needs to be looked out for. Another important point to bear in mind is the fact that these examples emphasise performance not learning. We do not know what kind of debate the students would have had if they had *not* been asked to exploit a conceptual metaphor. On the other hand, the examples do suggest that conceptual metaphors can be productive in a language use situation, and that in the above examples they appear to be acting as a kind of scaffolding, allowing learners to explore their potential whilst remaining well within their zone of proximal development. Moreover, by using conceptual metaphors in this way, the students appear to have been using at least five of Bachman and Palmer's (1996) communication strategies. They were: planning what they were going to say; moving the subject onto areas that they felt more comfortable with; making use of rhetorical skills in order to sound persuasive; using language skilfully in order to sound intelligent; and adjusting their speaking style to match that of their interlocutor. The use of communication strategies such as these is likely to increase the students' opportunities for learning. The subject of communication strategies, and their relation to learning, will be picked up and discussed in much more depth in Chapter 9, under the heading of 'Strategic Competence'.

6.4   The role of figurative thinking in performing heuristic functions

It has been shown that figurative thinking (particularly metaphor) can serve a powerful heuristic function in general educational contexts (see, for example, Spiro *et al.*, 1989; Low, forthcoming). Heuristic approaches to education involve the students discovering solutions for themselves, by a process of trial and error. For example, it has been shown that students of statistics who were taught through metaphor were significantly more able to transfer their knowledge to an unrelated domain than students who had not been taught through metaphor (Evans and Evans, 1989).

Cameron (2003) offers some interesting insights into the role of metaphor as a heuristic device. She is particularly interested in the ways in which metaphor contributes to the construction of opportunities for learning and participation. She looked at various lessons in British schools, including a geology class, two mathematics classes, a dancing class and a grammar class, and found that in all these classes the teachers used what she called 'stepping stones' to help pupils cross the gulf between their current levels of understanding and the levels of understanding desired by the teacher. The use of metaphor in these stepping stones often played a role in constructing values and attitudes between teachers and pupils. The main point seems to be that, in educational contexts, metaphor often has some kind of alignment function, whether this be to promote shared values, to simplify, or to mitigate potentially face-threatening situations. Her findings reveal the important role that metaphor plays in creating understanding, and managing relationships.

Implications for foreign language learning

Figurative thinking may help foreign language learners to perform heuristic functions, particularly in the area of English for Academic Purposes (EAP). This is because different discourse communities often rely on particular sets of conceptual metaphors, and in order to gain access to them EAP students will need to make use of Cameron's 'stepping stones' in order to reach a full understanding of these conceptual metaphors. Moreover, EAP students might usefully be asked to use and evaluate different conceptual metaphors in order to learn from each other. An attempt to use EAP students' figurative thinking processes for heuristic purposes is given in Littlemore (2005). In this study, a group of International Development students were each asked to teach the other students in the group about their place of work using one or more conceptual metaphors. The students were asked to think of a conceptual metaphor which best described their organisation, to draw that object, and to give a short talk about their organisation, explaining why they had used that particular metaphor. Whilst they were making their presentations, other students in the group were encouraged to ask as many questions as they could.

A particularly interesting metaphor was chosen by one of the students to depict the Russian Economic Development Agency, which he had worked for prior to attending the course. The student drew a picture of a ray of sunlight shining down from the heavens (to represent the way in which the agency sees itself) and of a burnt out candle (to represent the way in which the agency is seen from the outside). The extract from his presentation in Box 6.2 shows how an intervention from another student in the group forced him to consider the future of his organisation in more practical terms.

Another student depicted his organisation, the Tanzanian Prime Minister's Office, as an elephant. This was interesting as it revealed a significant cross-cultural difference in word connotation. He chose an elephant because it is a strong, powerful and respected animal in Tanzania. During the presentation it emerged that, in Tanzania, elephants do not have the same connotations of clumsiness and slowness that they do in developed countries. This is presumably because in Tanzania, people find themselves in closer contact with elephants in the wild, and they are therefore more familiar with their actual characteristics. People in the

---

Box 6.2   The Russian Economic Development Agency

There are actually two metaphors for describing my organisation. The upper ... the metaphor that I'm using is the ray of light in the kingdom of darkness, so what I'm thinking is the economic development agency is a ray of light in the dark kingdom or for the governmental organisations area in general. And the other metaphor, which was used by other critics to the same character, was the poor remains of the candle because the scale of my organisation is really small ... so that could be one of the overall general opinions of the general public about the activities of the agency.

Other student: Your metaphor seems interesting. However, it seems to me that the second one there is not sustainable. It seems after some times like it's going to fade away this last one. Maybe it should be electric light or something ...

I mean you're absolutely right, I mean er it's very unsustainable in the this sense because if I want to go to the ... City Council, and not defend the money that I'm supposed to get as a pay cheque for my employees, then I won't get anything. There won't be any light at all, I mean it's very shaky. So in a certain way there is also some kind of instability which is showing in here.

West, who only see elephants in zoos are perhaps more likely to perceive them as clumsy and slow. On the other hand, this may just be a residual folk memory, in the same way that in English the terms 'old goat' or 'cow' reflect a past that current speakers use but do not experience any longer.

A third interesting metaphor was proposed by a Lithuanian student, who chose a spider to represent her organisation, the Lithuanian Cabinet Office. She used the image of a spider to connote 'happiness in the home'. This reveals the interesting fact that, in the Lithuanian mindset, a spider can be seen as a homely, sympathetic creature, and that it does not have the same negative connotations as it does in English. A student intervention: 'Who are the flies that get caught in the web?' forced the student to consider who the enemies of the Lithuanian Government might be. She replied 'the criminals, I suppose'. Again, this shows how being asked to think metaphorically about their organisations encouraged the students to engage in critical thinking and comparative reflection.

Although these examples show performance rather than learning, they do suggest that the explicit use of conceptual metaphors in EAP contexts may make it easier for students to use metaphor as a heuristic device. Moreover, the afore-mentioned activity fits well into the task-based language learning framework, as it provides the students with plenty of opportunities to negotiate meaning, since they need to explain and recast the metaphors carefully, which is likely to develop their vocabulary and inter-language (Skehan and Foster, 2001). It is also, potentially at least, a good example of co-operative learning, as the students explore and develop the metaphors together. This type of learning has been found to increase peer motivation, learner autonomy and intrinsic interest (Ehrman and Dörnyei, 1998).

6.5 The role of figurative thinking in performing imaginative functions

Imaginative functions are all those functions that involve playing with the language for humorous and aesthetic purposes, and they often contribute to relationship building. They link quite closely to what Cook (1997b; 2000) calls 'language play'. Cook makes the important point that the reason why children play around so much with their first language is that language play has a crucial cognitive function in first language acquisition. He goes on to argue that if this is true for L1 acquisition, then it is likely to have far reaching implications for L2 learning and acquisition. Indeed, Cook makes a powerful case for the idea that foreign language learners should be given opportunities to play around with the linguistic forms of the target language in the classroom, and to see examples of it being played with by native speakers.

Language play can be an expression of creative freedom. Cook (2000) describes two types of language play: play with language form; and semantic play – the latter being 'play with units of meaning, combining them in ways which create worlds which do not exist: fictions' (ibid.: p. 228). Cook goes on to argue that language play may contribute to language learning, as it destabilises the language system, thus opening it up to development. Play takes thus place within Vygotsky's (1962) 'zone of proximal development'; an area in which the learner is able to try out new behaviour with appropriate scaffolding and support. Indeed, research suggests that language learners engaging in creative activities produce far more target language (in terms of quantity) than learners engaging in less creative activities (Broner, 2001). It has also been suggested that the emotional excitement accompanying language play increases the depth of memory for those aspects of the language that are played with (Stevick, 1976; Schumann, 1999). All of this suggests that it is likely to be beneficial to encourage language learners to play with the target language, on both a syntactic and a semantic level.

One aspect of language that provides native speakers with numerous opportunities for play on both of these levels is *idioms*. Native speakers regularly play with idioms by making ironic references to their literal senses, changing the syntax, and adapting them to other contexts (e.g., 'it's raining *homework*', instead of 'it's raining *cats and dogs*'). Recently heard examples of such playfulness by native speakers of English include 'I've been sitting on the fence so long my bottom is beginning to hurt'; 'I grasped the nettle so hard that all the spiky bits got stuck in my hand'; and 'she always says that she wants to be kept in the loop, but she's in so many loops that she's going to end up hanging herself'.

Many jokes rely on the existence of two possible interpretations, one of which might be figurative, the other literal (Ritchie, 2004). Indeed, a common technique for conveying humour is to re-literalise figurative uses of language. A real-life example is given in Box 6.3, of an email circulated by a head of department at Birmingham University where the figurative use of the word 'iron' was re-literalised, to comic effect:

Implications for foreign language learning

The main opportunities for language play that are offered by figurative language appear to be: altering the syntax of fixed expressions; adapting fixed expressions to different contexts; and the re-literalisation of figurative expressions for comic effect. If foreign language learners were able to play with conventional and novel forms of figurative language, this would help improve their communicative language ability, and moreover, if we follow Cook's argument, it would also help them to *learn* the language.

Very few researchers have investigated this aspect of foreign language learning in any detail. In one article that we have found, Prodromou (2003) recommends encouraging language learners to experiment syntactically with conventional idioms. For example, he recommends encouraging them to interpret and produce expressions such as 'it's raining kittens and puppies' (if it is only raining a little), or 'one more TV

Box 6.3 Email at Birmingham University involving the re-literalisation of the word 'iron', for comic effect (with author's permission)

'There are solutions to managing your workload and one, according to XXXX, social psychologist and life coach at XXXX University, is to imagine it as a pile of ironing. The temptation with ironing is to dive straight in, he says, but you should resist this. You need to divide it into three piles – cool, medium and hot ironing, to be done in that order. XXXX suggests you divide your workload the same way ...'

Wendy suggests we invite him to the Department to give us a demonstration. And bring our ironing?

And then we could suggest what he might do with his iron ...

cook will spoil the broth' (to argue that there are too many TV cooks) (ibid.: p. 27). Also, he observes that native speakers rarely employ the whole idiom, for example, 'ah well, it never rains does it?' 'well the early bird ...', and that foreign language learners need to be taught to understand and produce these sorts of abbreviated idioms. Unfortunately, Prodromou does not give any details concerning how foreign language learners might be helped to manipulate idioms in this way.

In order to test out some of Prodromou's ideas, we showed his examples of manipulated idioms to a group of advanced learners of English, and asked them to come up with their own adaptations. The idioms, and the contexts to which we asked them to adapt them, are presented in Table 6.5.

A few of the students in the study managed to produce appropriate answers, such as: 'bring home the dirty bacon' for item 2; 'give him a hand and he will take your arm' and 'give him a drop of water and he will bring home the whole sea' for item 3; 'a few pillars short of a house' and 'a few bricks short of a wall' for item 4. However, we found that the majority of the students found this activity very difficult indeed. Very few were able to think of plausible adaptations, and the majority of the students did not write anything. The answers given were often inappropriate, suggesting that the students had experienced difficulties understanding the objectives of the activity. For instance, answers included: 'to bring the boss a gift' (item 2); it's not as easy as falling off a log (item 5); and throw the drug away, it stinks to high heaven (item 6). These findings indicate just how difficult it can be at times to get students to

Table 6.5 The six idioms and the contexts to which students were asked to adapt them

Idiom	Adapt to the Context of
1. To keep up with the Joneses.	Tony Blair's positioning in relation to the United States.
2. To bring home the bacon.	To refer to a person who earned a lot of money for their family.
3. Give him an inch and he'll take a yard.	Someone who does this to excess.
4. He's a few sandwiches short of a picnic.	A builder whose stupidity stops him from doing his job very well.
5. It's as easy as falling off a log.	To refer to something that seems easy but isn't.
6. To stink to high heaven.	To refer to something that smells extremely bad.

work with figurative language in the language classroom. Another important consideration here is the fact that language learners are likely to vary significantly in their receptiveness to this type of activity. Whereas some students may see it as an interesting opportunity to experiment with the target language, others may find it more difficult to see the point of what they are doing, or relate it to their own language learning goals. One would also need to consider simplifying the activity significantly in order to make it manageable by lower level students.

6.6. Conclusion

In this chapter we have seen that figurative language can be used to perform ideational, manipulative, heuristic and imaginative functions, and that figurative thinking is therefore likely to contribute to a student's ability to perform these functions. We have outlined a number of techniques that might be employed to help students with these aspects of their language learning, but one thing that has become apparent is the shortage of conclusive empirical research in this area. Such research would be well worth conducting as it may reveal new ways in which foreign language learners can manipulate figurative language in order to perform a wide range of essential functions, thus contributing to their overall communicative language ability.

7
Figurative Thinking and Textual Competence

7.1 Introductory comments

So far we have discussed the role that figurative thinking can play in helping language learners develop sociolinguistic and illocutionary competence. In this chapter we turn to the third section in Bachman's model, namely textual competence. As we saw in Chapter 5, textual competence refers to one's ability to appreciate the overall conceptual and rhetorical structure of oral or written discourse. We will continue to use 'discourse' as a general term and 'text' for the specifically language-related components of it: whether spoken utterances or written sentences. Essentially, we will consider how the figurative pieces of the jigsaw discussed earlier are brought together by speakers and writers, to handle entire texts, or at least large stretches of text. The way figurative expressions or notions contribute to a text as a whole is closely related to distribution, so part of our argument concerns how figurative expressions, or the realisation of underlying figurative notions, are spread across the resulting text.

We begin by noting three problems that impact markedly on language teaching and learning. The first concerns the fact that if we recognise that a figurative phrase contributes to a message, we tend to assume that it was used deliberately, or at the very least that the writer would accept the interpretation if we presented them with it. But demonstrating deliberateness is extremely hard to do in many cases, even where a pattern recurs in numerous texts, so we might well end up teaching learners to be deliberate where native speakers are not. This may not be a problem if the learner's output proves effective; it may be more of a problem receptively, if the reader reads 'too much' into the text.

The second problem is that most 'use' represents a choice. Since the speaker/writer could arguably choose *not* to use a figurative expression to achieve a rhetorical purpose, there is much less urgency about teaching figurative language productively. Or again, while some uses of figurative language stand out and need to be interpreted if the main lines of the message are to be understood, others are extremely subtle and are unlikely to be noticed by any but the most critical and nit-picking of native-speaker readers. The question then becomes, just how critical, and aware of being critical, do we want learners to be about foreign language discourse? At times there will be institutional or political reasons for limiting instructed critical awareness, but at a general level, the question is hard to answer.

Lastly, we would emphasise, with Holme (2004) and Philip (2005), that learning to *produce* figurative language is very different from working out a reasonable interpretation of what an expression means when someone else uses it. Some expressions you will use just because they are part of the target language vocabulary, but even here, you need to establish that an expression is appropriate to contextual factors, like formality and genre. You also need to make it fit grammatically and be aware of which words are modifiable and whether there are limits on the modification. Many figurative expressions tend to have restricted uses or a limited range of collocations (see Chapter 8), so a fine sense of lexical possibilities is needed. In order to develop this sense, learners need, at the very least, repeated exposure to a range of figurative expressions in meaningful contexts where both the use, the grammar and the words themselves are varied. Given the large number of expressions and the enormous number of possible variations, this is unlikely to be a viable option in most teaching situations. To date, it is perhaps unsurprising that almost no rigorous empirical research has been published about learning to cope receptively or, particularly, productively with metaphor in foreign language texts. We are, as a result, largely unable to review research as we do in the other chapters, so we will instead pause at intervals and try to draw a number of educational implications.

To keep the argument to manageable proportions, we will argue that figurative thinking can contribute to the development of textual competence in three ways. We will hypothesise that it can first, aid in the detection of *figurative clusters*, second, lead to an appreciation of the role of figurative language in *topic transition* and third, help learners detect and use *overarching conceptual metaphors* to structure discourse.

7.2 Figurative clusters

Researchers have repeatedly claimed that figurative language is not distributed evenly through oral or written discourse, but that it often appears in clusters. The nature of the clusters remains somewhat controversial, though. Corts (1999) and Corts and Meyers (2002) reported that clustering across the four American university lectures and three religious sermons that they examined comprised primarily metaphor, simile and analogy. This is perhaps unsurprising, given that metaphor (both linguistic and conceptual) has been found to be the most frequently occurring figure in texts in general (Low, 1997). On the other hand, a recent report by Cano Mora (2005) on oral and written texts from the British National Corpus reports frequent clusters of hyperbole. The safest solution at the current stage of research is to simply suggest that clusters can be predominantly metaphoric, or hyperbolic (or both).

The 'or both' represents an important proviso, which has serious, if rarely addressed, implications for developing L2 communicative competence. This is that even metaphoric clusters often contain, as will be shown, things other than metaphor and that metaphor frequently needs to be seen as operating collaboratively in discourse with a range of other devices, *not* as an isolated stand-alone feature (Carter and MacCarthy, 2004; Cameron and Low, 2004; Low, 2005; Low, in forthcoming; in forthcoming).

While there is consensus that figurative clusters exist, there is rather less consensus on precisely how to find them. Both Corts and Meyers (2002) and Cameron and Stelma (2005) did, however, conclude that for most research purposes, adequate reliability could be achieved by using simple visual recognition rather than complex statistical methods. Basically, this is good news for teachers and learners, as it suggests that they can be trained to recognise clusters fairly easily, without having to first acquire a set of highly technical and statistical skills.

For researchers, life is unfortunately not quite so simple, and the nature of one's identification procedure seriously affects the results. Say you encounter the sentence,

(1) His *hackles rose* as the Secretary for State *gave* a prepared answer.

If you identify metaphorically used words, using the Pragglejaz technique[1] (Steen, 2005), and you accept 'gave' as metaphoric, in line with cognitive linguistic analyses by Lakoff or Kövecses, you have three items.

If you reject 'gave' (with Goatly, 1997), you have just two. If you base your identification on metaphor Vehicles, like Corts and Meyers (2002) or Cameron (2003), you would treat 'hackles rose' as a single unit, giving you the possibility of recognising only one figurative item in the sentence. Statistically, the more you include as metaphoric and the smaller your unit of identification, the greater the chances of finding a cluster.

What do metaphoric clusters contain? Corts and Pollio (1999: p. 94) and Corts and Meyers (2002) emphasised that the clusters they found were highly coherent, with metaphoric expressions organised around either one or two metaphors, or particular concepts. The following cluster (or 'burst') is cited by Corts and Pollio (1999: p. 91) from a university lecture on aging:

81   That fact that there are many jokes about aging means that it is a topic which *stirs up conflict* within us.

83   There are two reasons why aging *stirs up* those *conflicts* within us.

84   The first is that aging, thinking about aging, makes us *face* the *hollowness* in that *image* of ourselves getting bigger, stronger, and smarter every day ...

86   ... we don't just *grow*, we also *decline* ...

87   it makes us *face* that *painful* reality; it's a kind of *attack* on our narcissism ...

89   Our parents didn't get married to have us ... that *Copernican revolution* in object relations, that you have to begin to *swallow* that *bitter* knowledge that you're not ... *the universe doesn't revolve around us.*

90   If you wake up in the morning, and nothing *hurts* ... you're *dead.*

95   It brings into clear opposition two value systems within us.
     (Italics are ours. They represent metaphorical expressions)

The most noticeable feature, apart from the consistent attempts to align with the audience ('we', 'us'), is the central metaphoric core of AGEING IS AN EMOTIONAL ATTACK, which is made explicit (and given a clear marker, 'a kind of') in 87. Other expressions, like 'stirs up' and 'conflict' are connected with warfare. (Emotionally) 'hurt', 'painful', 'dead' and even the verb 'face', though quite conventional and from unrelated metaphors, are drawn together and given coherence within the attack scenario. 'Revolution' might be connected, but part of the effect here may derive from the metaphoricity of the other words. The 'Copernican' part is ambiguous; on the one hand, the listener can take it literally, but the revolving also applies metaphorically to individuals' emotional and social perceptions of themselves. Cameron and Stelma (2005), discussing this extract, point to the repetition of 'stirs', 'face' and 'conflict', plus the use of polar opposite terms which could be seen as metaphoric ('grow', 'decline'), plus the late introduction of 'attack', so that it summarises what has previously been introduced in more conventional terms ('conflict'). Despite the fact that there are rather more thematically unrelated metaphoric expressions than the 'one or two' that Corts and Pollio (1999: p. 91) claim, and the fact that the coherence is developed in quite a complex way, the cluster nevertheless can be seen as involving a range of phenomena, which work together to give it a loose functional unity.

A second example comes from Cameron and Stelma's (2005) Northern Ireland reconciliation dialogues between Pat Magee, an ex-IRA bomber and Jo Berry, a mother whose father was killed. The cluster involves numerous underlying metaphors italicised, but the bolded terms all involve variations on the theme of *ceasing to be separate:*

12 Jo: (...) on that day it was like suddenly I was *thrown into*
     the conflict
     it was suddenly my conflict
     and it felt like *my heart was broken*
15   *through* the conflict
     and (.) the suffering was my suffering
     I couldn't **separate** it
     I couldn't be **detached** any more
     and that that er
20   that *pain* that *loss* was **shared by** (.) **everyone**
     and you know and after that
     (.) the *pain* **on every side**
     you know
     I felt it

Cameron and Stelma (2005)[2]

To emphasise the point (or the emotion), the key phrase 'I couldn't separate it' is almost repeated, but not quite ('I couldn't be detached'). The result adds slightly to the message and the pair of utterances function together as a sort of emotional centre of the discourse. Not only do words like 'thrown', 'broken', 'separate' and 'detached' represent completed actions, but Jo Berry also uses extreme terms like 'suddenly', 'any more', 'everyone' and 'on every side' to emphasise the intensity and sense of integration. Just as in the lecture extract (given earlier), the speaker juxtaposes terms of opposite polarity ('detached' ~ 'shared') and the key metaphor pair only occurs after the content has been prepared by 'I was thrown into the conflict' and 'my heart was broken'. In sum, the cluster works as a functional whole, via a range of related and unrelated metaphors that share a semantic theme or domain (that of integration).

Studies of interaction show that metaphor is often repeated, or echoed, across turns by different participants for a short period and then dropped. At times this relates to a key topic that participants are developing metaphorically, but at others the metaphors are conventional and the co-construction is purely for social bonding, or involves a recency effect. An example of co-construction using conventional metaphor comes from Todd and Harrison (2005); two members of a book group are discussing a novel and the following five expressions occur in fairly close proximity. The underlining is Todd and Harrison's and the numbers represent turns.

373   JT   ... (better once) they started to *join up the characters*.
376   JB   'How's he gonna *link them together?*'
385   JR   ... you just cannot *keep track of them*.
399   JB   ... (the story line) nothing *was connected*.
402   JR   ... *drawing people* together.

It may be noted in passing that even here the back and forth recurrence involves positive and negative / opposite terms.

Many clusters contain peripheral, or 'non-core' expressions, like 'revolution' in the lecture extract. These 'outliers' can often be related to what Cameron and Low (2004) call 'resonance' or 'attraction'. Resonance is where words that might not be taken metaphorically are given possible metaphoric interpretations, or greater metaphorical intensity, by occurring near a clearly metaphoric term (Sayce, 1953), as in the following sentence from an article in *The New Scientist* on the Snowball theory of evolution:

This specialisation turned the *creep* of evolution into a **sprint** as complex creatures *competed* to *find* ever more *imaginative* ways of *exploiting* the world's resources. (Walker (2003: p. 30))

The five words italicised might be read as minimally metaphoric and coherent, but the introduction of the highly agentive 'sprint' leads to the five becoming far more animate and agentive and functioning as a much more cohesive, and thus coherent, set of ideas.

Resonant outliers pose an interesting problem for teaching productive skills. The rhetorical impact of such clusters is generally subtle and at times subjective, in that not everyone may even accept the metaphoricity, so the need to teach them as part of reading may not be compelling, though McGlone and Bortfeld's (2003) finding, that L1 readers often reacted to metaphors which they appeared not to have consciously noticed, might argue for including resonance in reading instruction, at least at advanced level (Low, in press a). It is also frequently far from clear whether the authors included the resonant terms deliberately or intentionally – it could just be the result psychologically of a recency or 'spreading activation' effect – so it is entirely unclear whether it is desirable or worthwhile teaching them as an aspect of writing.

Attraction is said to occur when one metaphoric expression triggers other metaphoric expressions from the same broad conceptual domain. A good example of attraction appears in the following cross-paragraph cluster from an explanation of new multi-layer semiconductor technology from an anonymous article in *The Economist*:

> Think of a *freezing cold sandwich* with *the thinnest of fillings*. It is **not an appetising thought**; but understand it and you know, more or less, how a superconducting quantum interference device (SQUID) works.
>
> The two outer layers, *'the bread'*, are made of ...
> (© *The Economist Newspaper Limited* (11 June 1988: p. 129)).

The target domain here is clearly food, and the core analogy is the highly conventional one of a multi-layer device as a sandwich. This is intensified by referring to details of actual sandwiches. The joke (bolded) in the middle, 'not an appetising thought', however, is peripheral to the core argument and comes from a different metaphor (GOODNESS IS HUNGER); it remains within the core domain of food and has been 'attracted' by the main sandwich metaphor. The result is similar to the 'separation' cluster (given before): related and unrelated metaphors grouped together within a general theme.

It is perhaps worth reiterating yet again at this point that although some clusters may be based around a single underlying metaphor, many are not. A very negative book review in *Philosophy of Science*, for example, contains the following section:

> [the book] *pretends* single-handedly to resolve a debate that is still *raging* in the philosophy of social science. Worse is the *arid* assumption that with a little Foucault and Habermas, one can show that whole disciplines in the social sciences *melt away* as *pure* methodological *bravado*. (McIntyre (2004: p. 421))

The metaphors here all contribute to the intensification function of the two-sentence block, along with the sarcastic metonymy (and perhaps understatement) 'a little Foucault and Habermas' and the relatively intense, extreme or completion terms ('single-handedly', 'resolve', 'whole'), yet they come from different underlying metaphors and very different source domains.

It is noticeable that the sandwich and philosophy clusters both involve the same intensification techniques as the lecture and reconciliation extracts (given earlier): first, making the metaphoric words themselves extreme ('freezing' and 'thinnest' in the sandwich extract; 'raging', 'arid' and 'pure' in the book review), second, adding extreme or completion words and third, grouping them (creating a small-scale cluster) at the end of a sentence to help generate a climax. In the sandwich extract, the aims are to align with the readers, offer them an explanation and save the readers' face(s) by subtly implying (by mentioning a familiar concept and sharing a joke) that they will be able to understand, despite being economists. The book review has no such benign intention! This brief demonstration of the convergent rhetorical use of multiple devices within a cluster brings us to perhaps the main reason why clusters impact on foreign language learners and learning: their function.

Clusters have been found to serve several textual functions and these appear to be roughly similar in both spoken and written discourse. Perhaps the most obvious and unsurprising role is that they flag what we will call later 'edge effects', serving to mark the start and end of a text, paragraph changes in written texts and topic changes in both spoken and written discourse (Low, 1997; Corts and Meyers 2002; Cameron and Low, 2004; Cameron and Stelma, 2005). Second, they have been found to highlight key points in a text, such as important explanations (Cameron, 2003, Low, 2005 and the lecture extract), points that are particularly problematic to convey, either because the producer feels emotional – positively or negatively – (Low, 1997 and the reconciliation extract), or because s/he disagrees with someone else's argument or study (Low, 1997). Cameron (2003) also found her primary teachers using metaphor clusters to set the agenda for the lesson – which could be seen as a type of (lesson-initial) edge effect. Clusters may serve to flag a producer's continuing purpose in speaking, or conceptualisation of a topic, but they may equally flag the opposite: a *change* of purpose, or a *new* conceptualisation (Corts and Meyers, 2002). In a similar vein, the philosophy review (given before) shows the cluster as intensifying and attacking, but the same corpus of reviews found clusters being used as often to tone down attacks and/or threats to the original author's face (Low, in forthcoming b). The general implication is that metaphor in clusters frequently has some sort of evaluative role, so it is hardly surprising that it often occurs in the evaluation sections of what Hoey (1983) called 'problem-solution-evaluation' discourse (Koester, 2000: pp. 177–180). This is a cyclical pattern of discourse, in which a problem is identified, a solution is proposed, the solution is evaluated and a new problem frequently emerges.

In short then, metaphoric clusters do tend to have significant functions in oral and written discourse, but the precise function in any given sentence or utterance can be variable and there may well be more than one. The reader or listener therefore needs to work to establish both the nature and the number of the functions.

7.2.1 Implications for foreign language learning

Several of the findings about clusters appear to have implications for language teaching and learning. First, figurative clusters in monologues like lectures and sermons often serve key explanatory or conceptualising functions. When they do, they are largely metaphoric, and the metaphoric expressions relate either to a small number of underlying conceptual metaphors or semantic domains. The reality is a bit more complex than this, but the finding still suggests that, if learners can locate the clusters, they can usefully apply the sort of figurative reasoning procedures described in Chapters 2 and 3 to aid understanding. The question is, how can learners locate these clusters?

One way to help learners to locate figurative clusters is to teach them to recognise how they are signalled. Clusters in spoken discourse are sometimes signalled by the use of physical gestures which indicate a speaker's attempt to make that segment of the lecture stand out as figurative (Corts and Pollio, 1999).[3] Reported that gestures were associated either with a specific narrative or with a particularly challenging metaphor. Interestingly, the gestures in their data always related to the source domain rather than the target domain, but how far this connection can be generalised to other genres and speakers is not known. From an educational point of view, exploring the use of gesture and aligning it with metaphoric expressions is hardly problematic, as it lends itself beautifully to the language class: collaboration, use of physical gesture, reflective periods, individual creation, puzzle setting and resolving, and generally having fun.

The other ways in which figurative clusters can be detected are by noticing repetition and/or relexification and by attending to verbal markers. We saw the use of relexification in the reconciliation extract ('separated', 'detached') and of verbal markers in the lecture extract (given earlier), with 'a kind of attack'. It is worth devoting a few lines to verbal markers. Markers mark individual metaphoric expressions, not clusters, and as we saw with the lecture extract, they may well not occur until the middle of the cluster, after the speaker has engaged in a degree of prefacing work.

There has been some systematic research into the use of markers in discourse, though we still know little about (1) their flow through an entire text or interaction, beyond being matched to the developing knowledge of the receiver, (2) which ones can be used to signal metonyms as well as metaphors or (3) how their use varies cross-culturally or cross-linguistically. However, Cameron and Deignan's (2003) study of two corpora – Cameron's classroom data and the Bank of English – suggested that markers serve three main functions (which can co-occur). First, they can direct attention to whether something should be taken figuratively or not (2, 3, 4, 7; see following extract). Second, they can increase or decrease the strength of the metaphor (3–6, and possibly 7). Third, they attend to the producer's or receiver's face and sensitivities (4–7). The examples are from Cameron and Deignan (2003, pp. 153–158); the metaphoric expressions are italicised, the markers are set in bold face. 'BofE' stands for Bank of English.

(2) ... the majority of   people ... take it *on the chin* **so to speak** (BofE)

(3) He **literally** went *through the roof* (with anger) (BofE)

(4) Fryer he was the he was er **in a way** our *midwife* because he was Secretary of the Agricultural Research Council.

(5) Teacher (dancing): Can you go back **just** *a whisper*

(6) Monday and Tuesday I'm usually **a bit of** *a vegetable* ... and Thursday I'm out in the evening so it's nice having this **sort of** *island* in the middle of the week. (BofE)

(7) ... but when men are **sort of** *chained* **as it were** to a female they lead a different life.

The downtoners in particular are used to do 'face-saving' work: to lower imposition (5), to stop the speaker looking pretentious for using a word from a different register, or looking stupid if the listener cannot in fact successfully match source and target, where the expression is unexpected (4). Example (7) may be double marked to show that the speaker is slightly embarrassed or threatened by the very thought of chaining. Downtoners also flag that the listener need not try and read too much into a metaphor ('in a way our midwife'; 'a bit of a vegetable').

The use of markers has at least two interesting implications for language learning: First, many do not have fixed meanings; 'actually' and 'really' can indicate figurative or non-figurative senses; 'as it were' may just mean a pun, but may also flag an aside or a peripheral point. Learners need to be helped to use context and to apply the balance of probability to guess whether a figurative sense, or a key point (versus an aside), is intended. Second, we hypothesise that many of the basic skills of using markers are likely to be available to learners from their L1, especially if the learners are adult. It therefore only takes one marker and a couple of words known to have a figurative and non-figurative sense for a learner to make an ironic aside for the purposes of social bonding. ('I'm OK /fit /sad /easy, as it were'). There would seem to be no inherent reason why this should be a purely advanced skill.

Teaching learners about markers is likely to be relatively straightforward receptively, but can become difficult productively, as the expressions carry subtly different overtones and expectations. From a production point of view, the speaker also needs to think about whether a metaphor that has been coined will be recognised by the addressee and given a roughly similar cultural value. If not, it will need a marker like 'as it were'.

Another pedagogically important point about metaphoric clusters is the fact that in interactions they are often co-constructed (as we saw before). Research is currently exploring the precise ways in which this happens, but even at this early stage, it is clear that such clusters serve social bonding (including word play) functions as well as being explanations and evaluations. Not only do learners need to learn to pick up a speaker's metaphors and respond for a few turns, but they need to be able to do so using both repetition and relexification and modification. The figurative thinking involved is less complex, simply requiring the flexibility to think fairly rapidly of an appropriate phrase and to decide when to repeat an utterance and create a pairing effect. These activities lend themselves fairly easily to class groupwork, both controlled and involving unpredicted content.

A final point is the finding that metaphoric clusters frequently have complex structures, involving metaphor and other figures like hyperbole, plus resonant and attracted items. While it is not entirely clear whether it is cost effective to teach resonance phenomena in outliers, it does seem both useful and quite feasible to teach structures where a figurative item establishes an overall position, then the speaker (or writer) qualifies it, or explains it (literally, or using figurative terms). In class terms, this might mean starting with simple conversations, then repeating them to move figurative terms into desired positions and give them appropriate intensity, and finally working on the discourse immediately surrounding the idiom to add the right kind of 'build up' and 'acknowledgement' sequences. The use of authentic, native speaker dialogues for modelling purposes would increase the effectiveness of this approach.

7.3 Marking the edges of the text

As we noted in Section 7.2, one of the main uses of figurative expressions, and especially metaphor, is to mark out the edges of text 'units'. They are sometimes used to mark the start and end of a text, or to mark paragraphs and topic changes within paragraphs. There is some evidence to suggest, though, that whatever the unit, positioning is less crucial in writing; because the impact of white space and paragraph marking is visually very marked, the need to position the figurative item at the precise point of transition is not crucial, and there is a degree of leeway. There is also no need to ask the reader's permission before a change can be made. On the other hand, in interactive spoken discourse, the issue of topic change is more complex, as it has to be negotiated, and it is to this area that we now turn.

7.3.1 The role of figurative language in topic transition in interactive spoken discourse

It has been observed that, in dialogue, people often use idioms, and particularly proverbs and sayings, to summarise what they have been saying, and to indicate to their interlocutor that they would like to terminate the topic about which they have been talking (Drew and Holt, 1995; 1998). Indeed, English-speaking listeners in both the United Kingdom and United States have been found to treat such examples as largely unambiguous and to react immediately in terms of whether they want to change the topic or not. This change mechanism seems to be a very basic and ingrained part of language users' practices – so ingrained in fact that speakers may not be consciously aware that they are using it. As such, we can be reasonably confident that it is an area that would probably benefit from teaching and practicing.

Why proverbs and idioms are used to change topic is an interesting question. Drew and Holt (1995) argue that idioms like 'Well, that's life' or proverbs like 'No use crying over spilt milk' are so general that they serve to detach the talk from previously discussed matters of factual detail, connecting back to turns before the immediately preceding one. They are frequently figurative and often connected with concrete imagery and/or intensified or extreme modifiers (Drew and Holt, 1998). Many are also fairly clichéd, which further implies that there is little more of interest to be said about the topic. One effect of using an idiom or proverb like this is that the speaker begins to detach the talk from the current argument, making it hard for the listener to continue with it, except by explicitly rejecting the idiomatic term. The proverbs and idioms thus summarise, evaluate and draw the topic to an end. A second effect is that the utterances are easily interpreted as salient and as something requiring a response. A smooth transition involves the listener agreeing with the speaker, followed at times by an acceptance of the agreement by the speaker and a rapid change of topic. Only where the listener refuses to accept a change is there complexity – with, for example, the speaker repeatedly throwing idioms on proverbs into the conversation.

This use of idioms to indicate a desire for topic transition has also been observed by Cameron (2002) in her studies of doctor–patient dialogue. As we can see in Box 7.1, in her data the use of idioms to signal closure was usually carried out by the more powerful member of the dyad (the doctor).

The role of figurative language in topic change and evaluation can sometimes take on an even more strategic role. One way in which figurative expressions are used strategically is in the context of 'tactical summaries', which are frequently used in business negotiations (Charles and Charles, 1999). These are short summaries of the preceding discussion, used by negotiators to move the discussion in a particular direction. They often refer to the hidden agendas of the two negotiating parties, generally allow the speaker to put his or her own gloss on events and may, as a result, not always accurately reflect the discussion that has gone before. In short, they allow the shared past to be shaped and interpreted in a way that is favourable to the speaker. Figurative

---

Box 7.1 Doctor–patient topic change (Cameron, 2002)[4]

Doctor: yeah, lots of people suffer with intermittent problems like that we call it sciatica when you get pins and needles and lower back pain

Patient: Yeah and sometimes I get like a pain goes trap – my muscle pain down here

Doctor: Shooting pains?

Patient: And it's like goodness what the hell is happening

Doctor: Yeah it's pressure on the nerve basically unfortunately the treatment for that is painkillers and physiotherapy and osteopathy if you want to try it but *there's no magic wand for that one*

Patient: There's nothing

Doctor: 'fraid not

Patient: Okay

---

language is particularly useful in this context, as it allows a degree of vagueness, and the speaker can hide behind perceived shared meaning.

7.3.2 Implications for foreign language learning

As with clusters, we would argue that some of the earlier stated findings have relatively clear educational implications.

The first is that learners who are able to sustain discussion of a topic over at least a couple of utterances need to be able to try and close the topic in a diplomatic and smooth way. Even learners who are not at this level can benefit from trying to close down someone else's topic! If one aim of learning a language is to be able to avoid being beaten at every turn by native speakers, then the ability to refuse to change topic is also a desirable skill. To achieve these skills, learners need to figure out that an idiom, proverb or metaphor is not carrying much additional information, and is probably being used to request a topic change. They then need to be aware of the differential effect of agreeing versus picking up the metaphor, possibly creating a cluster, and continuing to talk about it. We noted with clusters that it is often not enough to just teach the rough outlines of a discourse skill, as real-life situations are rarely simple and are never context-free. Learners, even at the beginner stage, need to be able to control *some* of the fine-tuning devices available. The situation is exactly the same with topic transitions; learners need to practice controlling the degree of metaphor, in order to agree to or reject a request for change, or indeed to decide how strong a request they wish to make, as a speaker.

Although there are few examples in the foreign language teaching or research literature of attempts to train learners to write figurative boundary frames, or to understand their import when they read them, our second point is that writers can usefully be taught to use metaphor sparingly to create edge effects round essays, paragraphs and/or topics within paragraphs. Precisely how teachers achieve this is unclear, though the ability to think laterally and coin an overarching metaphor (more discussion in Section 7.3.3) might be practiced at the stage of text revision – rather than at the drafting stage – and collaboratively by readers of the draft text.

Third, advanced learners need to establish that a combination of metaphor and direct address may imply that they are being manipulated, or more positively, that the writer is taking pains to avoid some sort of face-threatening act.

7.3.3 Helping language learners to use figurative language and thought in topic transition

In this section we describe an activity, based on Klippel (1984), in which students try and draw a telephone conversation to a close, or change the topic of the conversation, by using a range of closing strategies. As a lead-in, they are given extracts, such as the one in Box 7.1, in which an idiom is used to signal a desire for topic change. They are told (or they work out) that a typical closing sequence consists of:

Speaker A: Closing summary
Speaker B: Agreement
Speaker A: Agreement/confirmation
Speaker A/B: Introduces next topic

and are asked to identify this sequence in the extracts. The learners are then given a list of expressions that speakers might use to request a topic change and asked to match each idiom with its meaning. Next, they are then given cue cards (such as those in Box 7.2) and asked to act out the ensuing dialogue. Each set of cards contains a potential clash of interests.

Box 7.2   Topic-change activity: sample cue cards

Student A (call)
You have just split up with your girlfriend/boyfriend. You ring your friend to tell them about it.
Student B (receive call)
You are in a hurry to get out as you are meeting a friend at the cinema. Just as you are going out of the door, the phone rings.

Box 7.3   Topic-change activity: extract from student dialogue

S1:   Hello
S2:   Hello
S1:   This is Francis
S2:   Oh, hello. How are you?
S1:   Ah, you know. Me and Margaret, yesterday. We watched a movie together.
       You know, we are going with for more than one year so we are very good in good relationship, but yesterday she told me that she had, she had already been out another boyfriend
S2:   Oh really? I'm sorry.
S1:   I can't believe it, so I need someone to talk with about it.
S2:   But, Francis, *it'll iron itself out eventually*
S1:   Oh yeah
S2:   So you can find another girl
S1:   No, I can't! OK, OK, thank you.
S2:   Anyway, I'm in a hurry because I want to watch a film
S1:   Sorry
S2:   I'll call you back later
S1:   Thank you, see you
S2:   See you. Bye.

We piloted this activity with a group of advanced Japanese learners of English, and an extract from one of the dialogues that they produced is given in Box 7.3.

In this extract, student 2 uses the idiom *it'll iron itself out eventually* in an attempt to initiate topic change. The extract reveals a number of shortcomings with the activity. The main one is that the student comes across as sounding very harsh and uncaring. This is partly due to the nature of the task. The topic is perhaps a little too serious to be dismissed with an idiom, and this is the fault of the teacher who assigned the role cards. On the other hand, the idiom might have sounded more appropriate if it had been embedded in more sympathetic sounding language, such as 'I can understand, you must be feeling terrible, but I'm sure it'll iron itself eventually'. Moreover, when she changed the topic to the film, it would perhaps have been better if she had softened the blow by saying something along the lines of 'look, I'm really sorry, but ...' or if she had deflected the blame away from herself by focussing on the person having to wait for her outside the cinema. All of this indicates that the teaching of effective figurative language production involves much more than simply drawing attention to the move structure and a relevant idiom. This highlights a serious problem with the 'here's a list of idioms, now have a go at using them' approach. It suggests that a much more subtle approach, involving plenty of exposure to authentic usage, is needed. However, as we noted earlier, many teachers are unlikely to have the time to devote to this sort of activity. One way round this problem might be to make use of an online corpus, where students themselves carry out searches for idioms that they think they would like to use in their spoken or written discourse, and where they have the facility to expand the concordance lines to identify the broader contexts in which they are used. Another approach might be for the students to listen to extracts of native speakers carrying out the activity before they do it for themselves. This would also give them the opportunity to hear how native speakers often signal their use of figurative idioms by employing distinctive intonation contours (Vanlancker-Sidtis, 2003).

7.4   Overarching metaphor and metonymy

We turn now to the broad topic of constructing and interpreting discourses, interactions and texts as whole entities. It may be that a single figurative expression can suggest the speaker's or writer's stance towards an entire text or interaction. When this happens, the receiver may feel impelled to go back and reinterpret previous words in a new way. More commonly, there is some sort of textual recurrence of the linguistic expression or of the underlying figure, which can act as a trigger to alert the receiver that a particular interpretation is intended and perhaps that it is felt to be important. The recurrence often involves clusters, but it does not need to.

The producer may just be organising the workflow. Examples would be the recurrent journey expressions in one of the lectures described by Corts and Pollio (1999: p. 95) – 'We'll come back to that again a little bit later' or 'Another topic that comes up' – or the creation by book reviewers of hypothetical reading teams who journey together, for part of the review text, through the book being reviewed (Low, in press b):

> Sergio Grinstein and colleagues *take us through* the process of
>   phagocytosis. The chapter provides a comprehensive *guide* to
>   the dynamic nature of the process
> We are *given a tour of proteins*
> The final chapter *takes us into the nucleus*

> Cockcroft (2004: p. 481)

Where a metaphor has an extended scope and applies more 'globally' to whole sections of an oral or written discourse (Lukeš, 2005), we will follow Allbritton *et al.* (1995) and others by referring to it as 'overarching'. What overarches may be linguistic or conceptual, or a mixture of the two (like Cameron's LAVA IS TREACLE and LAVA IS RUNNY BUTTER which appeared repeatedly in the primary teacher's talk, but also served conceptually to structure stretches of explanatory and discovery text). An overarching metaphor may serve a range of purposes, from making playful asides, to hinting at the author's stance, establishing how the listener/ reader should 'work', or explicitly offering a new or important conceptualisation of the topic under discussion (as with the clustered metaphors in Corts and Meyers' (2002) sermons). Clearly the language learner as listener or reader needs to do three things: (a) establish whether a word or expression *is* signalling a broader scope, and if it is, (b) try and work out what that scope might be (and whether the text changes course) and (c) establish its importance to the argument.

While we accept the fact that an overarching metaphor may occasionally have no overt surface clue or marker at all, as with some types of allegory, we remain sceptical of approaches such as the semiotic method reported by Labbo (1996) where it is assumed in advance that all behaviour and discourse must be metaphoric, that overarching metaphor must be there to be found, irrespective of textual evidence.

The role of overarching conceptual metaphors in providing schematic structure within texts has been studied in depth by Allbritton *et al.* (1995). In a series of experiments, they presented respondents with a number of texts in their native language, some of which were structured around overarching conceptual metaphors, and some of which were not. They then showed the respondents sets of words and phrases from the texts and asked them whether they recognised them. Before the respondents saw the words from the texts, however, they were shown another word or sentence, (a 'prime'). Some of the primes were related to the same overarching conceptual metaphor as the target, but others were not. The researchers found that the respondents were significantly more likely to recognise words and phrases that had been preceded by a word or phrase from the same overarching conceptual metaphor. They were also more likely to recognise words and phrases that had originally been presented in texts that had been structured around overarching conceptual metaphors. These findings suggest that readers are better able to recognise words and expressions which correspond to a metaphorical schema set up in a text than words and expressions that do not. This in turn suggests that consistent metaphorical schemata enhance the reader's ability to link elements of text representations. Allbritton *et al.* argue that this is because readers look for and expect to find metaphor-based schemata in texts, and that they then use these schemata to help them understand the texts.

This contention is supported by a study by Robins and Mayer (2000) that demonstrated that the presence of consistent metaphor schemata in texts can influence the way in which readers respond to dilemmas that are presented in those texts. They found, for example, that people who had just read a text in which international trade was discussed in terms of the overarching metaphor TRADE IS A TWO WAY STREET were likely to argue that tariffs are a bad idea. On the other hand, people who had just read a text in which international trade was discussed in terms of the overarching metaphor TRADE IS WAR were more likely to argue that tariffs are a bad idea. This finding suggests that overarching conceptual metaphors not only structure texts, but that they also have the ability to influence people who read those texts.

7.4.1 Implications for foreign language learning

First, learners need to recognise how they themselves are going to organise their discourse and, if they are to give oral presentations or write relatively long texts, how to use metaphor (in particular the journey metaphor) appropriately. Teaching this lends itself very easily to figurative thinking discussions and collaborative teamwork about where you might want to add in journeys. This work also fits neatly into teaching writing as a process. Second, learners need to locate recurrent metaphor and establish whether it is being used stylistically, or whether a substantive point is intended. Third, they need to establish if a speaker (or writer) evaluates, limits or even changes an overarching metaphor. It, as it is crucial to understand how the author positions themselves and the reader with respect to it. Fourth, conversation may well involve a rather different use of structuring devices from lectures, with a greater emphasis on networks that participants need to keep track of and actively develop. When listening to a lecture or sermon, learners need to distinguish workflow organisers and listen for repeated single overarching metaphors. Fifth, a high degree of associative fluency may also be a key skill in helping receivers keep up with producers in both formal and informal contexts.

One contribution that an ability to deal with overarching metaphor might make to language learning, particularly for students of English for Academic Purposes (EAP), is in the area of critical thinking. It has been suggested that international students at English-speaking universities sometimes need to be trained to respond critically to the information with which they are presented (Flowerdew and Peacock, 2001). It has been observed that they can be reluctant to question the views of lecturers and authors in their subject fields, and to put forward their own views. This is often attributed to cross-cultural differences in academic traditions and argumentation patterns (Flowerdew and Miller, 1995). However, in the context of academic listening, it has been shown that an inability to interpret the lecturer's stance in the first place may be largely to blame (King, 1994). Littlemore (2001b) showed that lecturers may present the evaluative components of their lectures through the use of metaphors, and that international students often misinterpret such stances precisely because they misinterpret the metaphors.

7.4.2   Helping learners with overarching metaphor

In this section, we describe a study (Littlemore, 2004c) that investigated critical *reading* ability. International students' critical reading skills were successfully developed through a process in which they were encouraged to identify and criticise the conceptual metaphors that underlie argumentative text.

The participants in the study were thirty advanced EAP students, studying for an MBA in Public Service Administration in an International Development department at a British university. They were divided into an experimental group (N = 15) and a control group (N = 15). Both groups participated in a general critical thinking session. The experimental group was also given a metaphoric awareness-raising session, whereas the control group was given no such session. The aim of the study was to investigate whether or not the metaphoric awareness-raising session had any lasting effect on the critical reading abilities of the students in the experimental group. The metaphoric awareness-raising session took place at the beginning of the academic year, whereas the test of its effectiveness took place, just after the general critical thinking session, five months later. In this way, it was possible to test the long-term effectiveness of the training session.

In the metaphoric awareness-raising session, which lasted approximately 90 minutes, the students were introduced to the notion of conceptual metaphors. As an example, they were asked to identify the metaphor (SOCIETY IS A BODY) which is thought to underlie the expressions in Box 7.4.

The students then discussed the political implications of conceptualising society as a body. They asked to think of other metaphors that could be

---

Box 7.4   Overarching metaphor study: preliminary exercise

Society is a ...?
– society is making great strides
– the head of state
– China finally stood up and was counted
– The backbone of society
– The bowels of society
– Spies are the eyes and ears of society
– The voice of *America*

---

used to describe society, and to comment on their political implications. Next, they were asked to consider the implications of metaphorically construing the British Civil Service as a machine, a company and a living organism. Finally, they examined a number of conceptual metaphors in context. The students were split into small groups, and each group was given a short text containing an underlying conceptual metaphor. Their task was to identify the metaphor and perceive its strengths and limitations. They were fianlly asked to think up alternatives to the metaphor, and to discuss their ideas with the rest of the group.

Five months later, the students in both the experimental group and the control group were asked to complete a test of critical thinking. They were given a short management text entitled 'The Ecological Niche' (from Hicks and Gullet, 1975). This text contains the conceptual metaphor COMPANIES ARE TREES, and much of the argument rests on the entailment that companies must adapt to fit their local environment. The students were asked to write a critical evaluation of the argument presented, introducing further arguments that they judged to be relevant. They were told that their evaluations should show that they were clear about the structure of the argument (e.g., which claims were *reasons, conclusions* and *assumptions*) and that they recognised the argument's strengths and weaknesses.

Of the fifteen students who had attended the metaphoric awareness-raising session, seven made explicit references to the underlying metaphor and used these references to support their critical evaluations. Interestingly, in accordance with the hypothesis, none of the students in the control group made any reference to the underlying metaphor. The three examples which follow serve to illustrate some of the ways in which students in the experimental group used their metaphoric awareness in order to critically evaluate the text. The language in these examples has not been corrected. The italics simply highlight expressions of interest.

Example 1

It might have been more helpful to *specifically (not metaphorically)* identify those organizational factors or environmental factors which can interact with and support each other.

Example 2

The use of an ecological system as an *analogy* cleverly illustrates the interdependency of an organization and its environment, but *what the authors fail to do is to fully explain what a niche actually is*. If they are using it to *include markets*, then their argument is a strong one ... however, if 'niche' is meant to be a *physical locality*, then their argument is weak. This is particularly so in the modern day global economy or environment.

Example 3

Some organizations, particularly Governmental ones, have much more power than their citizens. When this is the case, *the metaphor doesn't work as well*. The organization is often *imposed from above*, demands taxes, and the people have no choice.

In the first example, the student drew attention to the fact that a metaphor was being used to make a generalisation, and to avoid discussing specific organisational factors, as not all of these would support the argument. She showed an awareness of how metaphors can be used to present half-truths.

In the second example, the student was able to appreciate that the metaphor of an 'ecological niche' can be read on two different levels. It can either be interpreted in a rather abstract way, to include markets, or it can be interpreted in a much more concrete way, to refer to a physical locality. This student was able to see that the strength of the argument depends, to a large extent, on the way in which one interprets the metaphor.

In the third example, the student was able to identify the *limitations* of the metaphor. She pointed out that when the organisation is a governmental organisation, the metaphor does not work.

Although this study is not empirically rigorous, these examples do suggest that the metaphoric awareness of each of these students may have enhanced their critical thinking in a different way. The first student was able to point out how the authors' use of metaphor enabled them to generalise, and possibly to over-simplify the issue, the second student was able to read the metaphor in two different ways, and the third student was able to perceive its limitations. These findings suggest that in some circumstances, metaphoric awareness-raising can help students improve their critical thinking skills, though it must be noted that these were advanced EAP students studying texts from their own discipline. The approach may not be as successful with lower-level students, or with students on general English programmes.

7.5 Conclusion

In this chapter we began by noting that learning to produce metaphor and learning to understand it in a foreign language are very different activities. We also noted that there is minimal empirical research beyond the level of individual experience and anecdote about learning to do either in a textual or discourse context. We therefore attempted to summarise some of the ways in which metaphor has been found to manifest itself in clusters, to mark transitions and to structure large stretches of discourse. From these we drew a number of conclusions about what learners need to attend to. We then hypothesised ways in which figurative thinking might aid them in acquiring discourse skills, with the aim of encouraging future teaching and particularly research.

8
Figurative Thinking and Lexico-Grammatical Competence

8.1 Introductory comments

So far, we have focussed mainly on functional and textual aspects of communicative language ability. In this chapter, we turn to an area of language learning whose relationship to figurative thinking may be less obvious, namely that of grammar. Grammatical competence refers to a language learner's knowledge of, and ability to use the grammatical system of the target language. Of all Bachman's categories, this is the one that we might expect to be least related to metaphoric competence. However, with recent developments in the field of conceptual metaphor and cognitive linguistics, it is clear that many of the phenomena that language educators regularly treat as grammatical have a strong metaphoric or metonymic component, though one often needs to look within the lexical item (of, say, phrasal verbs) to find it.

A number of cognitive linguists (e.g., Langacker 1987; 1991) make the strong claim that language is inseparable from other types of interaction with our environment. For them, most grammar is not arbitrary, but meaningful, and it is wrong to separate syntax from semantics. In order to follow the reasoning of cognitive linguists, it is often necessary to employ metaphor. For example, the abstract use of 'on top of' in 'I think everything's just got *on top of* him' is metaphorically related to the physical sense of 'on top of'.

Although cognitive linguists would argue that most grammar reflects meaningful cognitive organisation, and that the current most frequent sense of a grammatical word can reflect an earlier and more concrete sense, the complex nature of the grammaticalisation process (Hopper and Traugott, 1993; Bybee *et al.*, 1994) means that the relationship often becomes somewhat opaque. In order to be useful to language learners, we would argue that it must still be possible to see a relationship.

We begin this chapter by examining five areas of grammar where the relationship between concrete and abstract senses of grammatical words remains relatively easy to perceive, if one employs metaphor. These are demonstratives, prepositions, phrasal verbs, aspect and modality. We then go on to discuss the notion of 'grammatical metaphor' (Halliday, 1985; 1994) and end with some comments on the implications of restricted collocations.

8.2 Demonstratives

The terms 'this/these' and 'that/those' in English form part of a minimal closed set, where the two sets of items contrast with each other and sometimes with 'it' or 'the'. The basic sense of 'this' (as in 'You see this pencil I'm using?' or 'John, Ssh. Can't you see I'm talking to this man?') involves an entity which is physically close, and thus clearly in existence here and now, of considerable current relevance, highly visible and potentially tangible. On the other hand, 'I'm trying to talk to that guy over there, but it's not easy!' positions the listener as more distant, less visible (indeed, so small as to become invisible and seemingly non-existent, if the distance is great enough). In many cases, such as 'I'm worried about *these* wasps, not *those* over there!', 'that/those' also reflects a lower degree of threat, or something of less current relevance, which needs less attending to and is less knowable. In these examples, it is fairly easy to see how the basic senses of *these* and *those* are involved.

On the other hand, sentences such as the following nine are not easily explained in terms of this basic sense, unless metaphor is invoked.

(1) After eating: '*That* was really good!'
(2) Oh *that* (awful) woman/man!
(3) Joke opening: 'There was *this* Englishman. ...'
(4) Phone: Hello! Is *that* John? No, *it's* Peter.
(5) Noise downstairs at night: Who's *that*?
(6) Social introduction: 'Peter, *this* is John!'
(7) We could hear *this* dreadful drumming all night!
(8) *This* is no longer the case.
(9) *That* was a dreadful thing to say!

The physical separation implied by 'that' flags the non-existence ('finished and gone') of food in (1). The complaint (2) uses physical separation to signal psychological rejection, while the joke introduction (3) uses it to force a sense of familiarity on the listener. In the phone response (4) and the cry in the dark (5), there is actual physical distance, but more importantly, there is also a strong sense of the unknown, the psychologically unfamiliar. In the social introduction (6), 'this is ...' does indicate familiarity, but it also acts as a performative, to *create* social acceptance (or in effect, social existence within the conversation group). The 'this' in the report of a past event in (7) serves both to intensify the awfulness of the drumming and to emphasise its current importance to the report. The 'this' in (8), serves a summarising, cohesive function, pulling ideas together, and can be contrasted with the somewhat dismissive, and negatively evaluated, 'that' in the rebuke (9).

In sum, if metaphor is allowed to play a role in explaining grammatical words, all the above examples can be accounted for in a very straightforward manner in terms of metaphorical distancing. The mechanisms invoked in all the stated examples are, in our experience at least, extremely easy for a teacher to teach, or a learner to comprehend, and can frequently be acted out physically and humorously in the classroom. Metaphor is thus not only relevant, but its use permits a 'human-sized' account of an otherwise highly abstract or arbitrary system (Low, 1992).

As well as metaphor, 'part for whole' metonymy (synecdoche) also underlies some uses of 'this' and 'that'. For example, in the question:

(10) Have you got *this* dress in blue?

a specific dress is used to stand synecdochally for a set of dresses or even a general type of dress. Metaphor (distancing oneself) and metonymy (reference to a general phenomenon) can also combine, leading to the hint of distaste in,

(11) It's got *that* awful 'pebble dashing' all over the front of it.

Given the earlier discussion about figurative thinking, it might be felt that native speakers do not 'think' much when choosing or using these terms and that 'thought' is restricted to a teacher offering an explanation to learners. However, it will be noted that variations on all the above examples are perfectly possible (e.g., 'There was *that* Englishman ...'; 'Oh, *this* man ... !') and the listener needs to establish quickly whether the speaker is indicating an evaluation, or whether the use of the demonstrative alters the illocutionary function of the utterance. However, while Low (1992) has argued that explanations like the above would be useful as a teaching device, we know of no empirical research on whether they are effective.

8.3   Prepositions and particles

Prepositions and particles represent a traditional and recurring nightmare for all learners of English. Inasmuch as prepositions represent a closed set and generally act as the dependent item in phrases ('*at* school', '*on* average'), it is reasonable to treat them (as most EFL coursebooks do) as essentially grammatical phenomena. On the other hand, there has been much research in the last twenty years into the extent to which the different senses of prepositions and particles are orderable, in a straight-forward manner, away from one or more prototypical senses (e.g., Lindner, 1981; Brugman, 1981, Lindstromberg, 1998; Tylcr and Evans, 2003). For present purposes, 'prototypical sense' can be read as roughly the same as basic sense. The movement from sense to sense can often be accounted for in terms of simple location/ position extensions (e.g., 'eat up', where 'up' implies vertically filling a container), or of application of the same conventional metaphors that underlie much English vocabulary.

We will begin by using 'on' as a fairly typical example. Lindstromberg (1998) distinguishes two basic senses of 'on': on = contact ('*on* top of') and on = continuation, which tends to be realised as a particle in phrasal verbs like 'move on'. We will just consider his 'on = contact' sense here and apply a similar sort of argument to it as we did to 'this/that' earlier.

> If the cat is 'on top of' the TV, it is next to it, vertically above it and touching it. This in turn typically implies that:
>
> The cat exists;
> The cat is close to the TV;
> The cat is visible (even salient);
> 'on-ness' is not temporary (the cat is not moving);
> The cat is located with respect to the TV (i.e., the focus is on the cat).

This interacts with several common conceptual metaphors:

1. UP, TOUCHING, OR CLOSE IS ALIVE, ACTIVE, HEALTHY, GOOD, IMPORTANT, OR RELEVANT   The result of turning a television 'on' is that the TV comes 'on' and stays 'on', till you turn it 'off'. Again, if you are 'on heroin' it is actively affecting you and/or you habitually take it. Both examples seem to conflate the senses of contact and continuation.

2. PSYCHOLOGICAL STATES (AND RELATIONS) ARE PHYSICAL STATES (OR RELATIONS)   In English, one can be 'on' as well as 'in' a par-ticular state. Examples of 'on' are 'on edge', 'on top of the world' or by a further extension from (1) given earlier, 'turned on'. If we agree to a bet then 'You're on for £10'. Conversely, if you feel ill you might say, 'I'm feel-ing a bit off' and if you dislike someone then, 'She's rather stand off-ish'.

3. SOCIAL ACCEPTABILITY/STATUS IS A PHYSICAL STATE OR (RELATION)   If you are working, you are 'on the job' or 'on standby', but if you are sick, not working and at home, you are 'off' or 'off work'. In the latter case, 'off' implies both social incapacity and a distance from the 'relevant' (work) location. On the other hand, if an activity, place or person is *not* permitted, it is outside the 'space' and 'off limits' or 'off bounds'.

The notion of 'socially active', 'socially ongoing' and possibly even 'socially acceptable' can also be seen in the big conceptual metaphor complexes such as LIFE IS A JOURNEY, with its notion of a pathway that the traveller follows; if things are going well or as planned, we are 'on track', 'on course' and 'on our way'. If we get lost, however, we are 'off course' or have 'lost our way'.

As well as metaphor, metonymy is also involved in some 'on' expressions; in the non-contact use of '*on* top', for example ('Which bunk do you want?' 'I'll sleep *on* top'), the beds may not be touching, but there is still relative physical closeness. Similarly in the (admittedly particle rather than preposition) 'X is far off', a lack of contact is used to mark considerable but genuine physical distance.

Several attempts have been made to apply a conceptual approach to teaching prepositions and particles, though, as with the studies in Chapter 2, the focus has been consistently on metaphor rather than metonymy. Boers and Demecheleer (1998), for example, developed Lindstromberg's (1998) ideas by investigating the effectiveness of a cognitive semantic approach to teaching figurative senses of 'behind' and 'beyond'. They introduced 131 French-speaking EFL learners of different levels (beginners to advanced) to the causal sense of 'behind' ('Who's *behind* the strike?') and the inaccessibility sense of 'beyond' ('It's *beyond* me'). They found that students who had received cognitive semantic definitions of the prepositions performed significantly better than students who had received traditional definitions. They suggested that in addition to sequencing teaching from the literal to the extended, teachers could usefully employ clines of three or four sentences, like (12–15). The clines could however be queried and discussed by the learners, the teacher, or by both together.

(12)   You can't see Snowdon from here, it's over there, *beyond* those hills.

(13)   We cannot buy this house: it's *beyond* our means.

(14) His recent behaviour is *beyond* my understanding.
(15) The use of English prepositions is *beyond* me.

Cognitive linguists explain the relationship between expressions such as these in terms of *image schemata*. Essentially an image schema is a simple state or relationship, like 'containment', but which appears to underlie behaviour, beliefs or linguistic expressions. Image schemata are also held to be psychologically real, to some extent 'imageable', and developed by individuals as a result of ongoing bodily experiences, though there is some controversy surrounding the precise mechanism by which virtual identity is achieved despite different experiences. Nevertheless, young children are thought to be developing an image schema for *containment* when they repeatedly put objects in and out of boxes. By doing this, they develop prototypical senses of 'in' and 'out'. They then start to extend the concept of containment into different domains, as in the following examples (Kawakami, 1996):

(16) My brother is *in* high school   (social domain)
(17) My brother is *in* love   (emotional domain)
(18) My brother is *in* trouble   (abstract domain)

The implicit claim is that one reason why teaching basic (or protypical) senses of prepositions first is effective is that it replicates the first language learning process.

Tyler and Evans (2004), though not reporting empirical research, do provide a conceptually-based lesson plan for teaching 'over'. It is essentially teacher-led, starting with an explicit presentation involving pictures and image schemata, followed by active engagement in the form of physical action. The teacher starts by showing pictures of a cat jumping over a wall and pointing out that (1) the wall represents an obstacle and (2) 'over' can relate to the cat in mid-jump or having completed the jump. The teacher emphasises the fact that 'over' has developed an additional meaning in English, of 'finished' or 'completed', which can be reinforced with examples such as 'the lesson is over' or 'the war is over'. Learners throw a ball to one another in order to learn the transfer sense of 'over'. The physical activity is reinforced by considering the transfer involved in prepositional verbs like 'sign over', 'hand over', and 'win over'. The findings of the studies reported in Chapter 2, plus Lindstromberg and Boers's (2005) successful use of Total Physical Response techniques might suggest that teachers could usefully begin by throwing a ball, then adding an obstacle, and use pictures to reinforce 'jumped over X', 'flew over X', 'walked over X' or 'ran over X'.

We argued in Chapter 2 that, in the case of idioms, L1 patterns have been shown to affect learners' expectations of the L2, and the same is true for prepositions. Lowie and Verspoor (2004) showed that L1 (Dutch) patterns of prepositional usage significantly affect the way learners use them in the L2, but that, as one might expect, the relationship becomes weaker as students become more proficient in the target language. Total Physical Response techniques may also help students who are learning a language which expresses manner of movement in a different way from their own language (Slobin, 2000; see also Chapter 4, Section 4.3.4).

8.4 Phrasal (and prepositional) verbs

If cognitive semantic approaches are effective in the teaching of prepositions, then it ought to follow that they are applicable to the teaching of phrasal and prepositional verbs, as these frequently exploit the more metaphorical and less transparent extensions of prepositional senses. We will use 'phrasal verb' as a cover label for both types.[1] As with prepositions and particles, it has been argued that the etymological evolution of phrasal verbs generally involves metaphorical or metonymic processes. For example, 'she brushed the crumbs off the table' can be extended metaphorically to form expressions such as 'she gave him the brush off' (Dirven, 2001).

One of the first to apply cognitive linguistics to the teaching of phrasal verbs was Rudzka-Ostyn (1988), who argued that it is beneficial to teach the metaphorical or extended meanings of phrasal verbs alongside their basic meanings. Learners were accordingly invited to draw parallels between expressions such as 'the paint has worn off' and 'her enthusiasm has worn off'. Dirven (2001) developed Rudzka-Ostyn's ideas for language learning by taking her examples of 'across', and fitting them into a 'logical semantic network' (see Figure 8.1). He argued that these examples show 'an almost perfect semantic gradation on the continuum from literal to figurative meanings of phrasal verbs' (ibid, p. 19).

In Dirven's diagram, senses 1, 2 and 3 are metaphorically and metonymically related to the basic sense, which should be taught first. Extended senses should then be taught explicitly as an expanding network.

As regards teaching phrasal verbs, studies reported earlier like Li (2002), Vespoor and Lowie (2003), Skoufaki (2005b) and the various studies by Boers *et al.* all contain occasional phrasal verbs, but phrasal

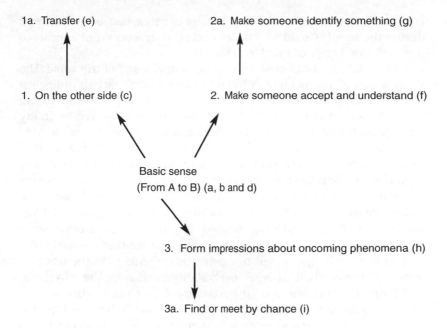

1a. Transfer (e)

2a. Make someone identify something (g)

1. On the other side (c)

2. Make someone accept and understand (f)

Basic sense
(From A to B) (a, b and d)

3. Form impressions about oncoming phenomena (h)

3a. Find or meet by chance (i)

a. The children ran *across* the road without looking.
b. He's the first man to have walked *across* the mountains.
c. She was sitting *across* the table from me.
d. There will soon be a bridge *across* the river.
e. The teachers always see their pupils *across* the busy street.
f. He does not know how to get his ideas *across* to his pupils.
g. Marketing is about putting *across* to the customers the qualities of the product.
h. She came *across* as a very intelligent person.
i. I came *across* an old friend during my holiday.

Figure 8.1 Dirven's (2001) semantic network of phrasal verbs involving 'across'

verb results are not reported separately. One or two recent studies have focussed specifically on using cognitive semantic approaches to the teaching of phrasal verbs, but their findings are mixed. For example, when he revisited the result of Kövecses and Szabó (1996), Kövecses (2001), found that students who had been introduced to conceptual metaphors underlying phrasal verbs containing 'up' and 'down' (as a teacher-led explanation and without much active engagement by the learners) nevertheless performed significantly better on a subsequent phrasal verb test than students who had simply been given translations of the verbs. Interestingly, five of the phrasal verbs in the test had not been introduced during the training session. The students had thus continued to use the conceptual metaphors that had been discussed during the training session. The conceptual instruction thus appears to have led to a degree of incidental learning.

Kurtyka (2001) conducted a much less formal study of this topic. The study involved asking eight Polish secondary school teachers of English to use a cognitive semantic approach to teach phrasal verbs involving 'in' and 'out' to their 16–19 year-old students, who ranged in ability from pre-intermediate to advanced. The teachers themselves decided that the materials would not be appropriate for the pre-intermediate students, and therefore only used them with the intermediate and advanced students. They found (like Li, 2002) that the students generally enjoyed the technique, and improved their knowledge of the phrasal verbs studied – though no statistical evidence is provided. Most importantly, they noted (like Skoufaki, 2005b) that the improvements were not uniform across learners. Kurtyka suggested this reflected variation in cognitive style. Cognitive semantic approaches to the teaching of phrasal verbs rely heavily on one's ability to visualise the movement and positions represented by the prepositions or particles. However, as we saw in Chapter 3, individuals are known to vary in both their preference for and capacity to engage in mental imagery, so learners who process information in images may be more likely to appreciate and benefit from a cognitive semantic approach than students who engage in more verbal processing.

In order to investigate some of these issues, we carried out a very small, exploratory study, in which we attempted to teach a number of phrasal and prepositional verbs containing 'up' and 'down' to a group of nine English for Academic Purposes university students in the United Kingdom, by referring to conceptual metaphor theory. Before and after the training, the students completed a short test of their existing knowledge of phrasal and prepositional verbs containing 'up' and 'down'. They also completed a short questionnaire about the usefulness of verbal imagery in completing the exercise and the test. The sample is too small to draw conclusions about learning, but it did illustrate graphically two problems that can occur with a cognitive semantic approach.

First, some of the students mistakenly assumed that the first conceptual metaphor MORE IS UP / LESS IS DOWN was a kind of overarching, superordinate metaphor, which subsumed all the others. These students found it hard to work with multiple examples and derive a set of underlying relationships in their heads which differed yet were interrelated. Second, several students found it difficult to deal with the apparent contradictions between the conceptual metaphors. Thus they found it difficult to reconcile MORE IS UP with DISAPPEARING IS UP, arguing that if something disappears, then there is *less* of it than there was at the beginning. From a pedagogical perspective, a better approach might be to introduce the students to one conceptual metaphor at a time. Teachers could then allow their students plenty of time to understand each conceptual metaphor and work with its instantiations, before moving on to the next.

Research does suggest that learners tend to be motivated by conceptual approaches. Robbins (2004), for example, compared two approaches to the learning of phrasal verbs: knowledge of conceptual metaphors, and simple memorisation of the phrasal verbs. She found that the students ranked the conceptual metaphor approach significantly more highly in terms of how interesting, useful and motivating they found it. This result agrees closely with the feedback results obtained by Li (2002).

What the empirical studies do not, unfortunately, show is whether much is to be gained pedagogically by decoupling the verb and particle in a phrasal verb and treating each as separately meaningful. Prepositions and particles vary markedly in the extent to which they retain their basic or protypical meanings (Quirk and Greenbaum, 1973: p. 348) – 'he moved out' does, he 'turned up' does not. On the slim research evidence available, we suggest that if you can find a meaning or explanation for a preposition or particle, then little harm is done by teaching it, though you might also want to retain other teaching techniques. If a meaning cannot easily be found, then the most obvious technique is simply to learn the expression directly as a multiword formula, through repeated exposure. Classroom management expressions ('Go through the exercise', 'quieten down') are obvious candidates for this approach. Another way, that is less communicative, but does actively involve learners, is to present learners with examples of 'real' language from corpora (like Box 8.1 from the Bank of English) and to ask them whether they fit Dirven's categories. Willis (1996) raises the important point that this sort of language focus activity is at its most effective when it involves learners in the study of language items that they have recently encountered, either in a text or during a particular task.

Research does not yet show whether younger or less proficient learners would find conceptually-based notions more problematic than advanced learners, but the potential for drawing and acting out the relationships suggests that it is reasonable for teachers to include metaphor in their instruction, and in order to do so, they may find Lindstromberg's (1998) *'English Prepositions Explained'* a useful, comprehensive resource.

Box 8.1 Selected Bank of Engilsh concordance lines demonstrating various phrasal and prepositional verbs containing *across*

as a person too as he always **came across as** such a likeable fellow. Occasionally one **comes across** a garden centre which, unlike so the aim was simply to **cut across** barriers and explore new endemic in the workplace, **cutting across** all industries, health campaigns to **get the message across**. The dominions **lie almost directly across** the Indiamen's route he will be **sitting across** the table from Palestinian a way of **getting across to** the Africans that ... the fist shot and managed to **get across** the goal to save were they able to **put across** any arguments?

8.5 Tense / aspect

There are at least three points where metaphor or metonymy offer straightforward accounts of English tense/aspect. Whether it is peda-gogically effective to teach them this way is unknown; we have found occasional anecdotal reports (e.g., Holme, 2004), but no systematic empirical studies.

Point one is the use of the present tense by academic writers to suggest that certain past studies will be treated as important, relevant to the current argument and unchallenged (19, see following extract). The findings are in all probability being rejected in (20).

(19) The findings from Low's (2001) study *suggest* that metaphor *is* often used to convey evaluation.

(20) The findings from Low's (2001) study *suggested* that metaphor *was* often used to convey evaluation

Past and present tenses thus function much like 'this' and 'that' (see earlier), by suggesting that things exist, and are more relevant and important in the 'here and now'. The classic study by Tarone *et al.* (1981) also demonstrated that writers use active and passive forms ('Smith claims' versus 'It has been claimed by Smith') for a similar purpose.

Point two also involves the use of the past tense to denote psychological distance, but this time to mark politeness in requests. Politeness involves a lack of intrusion into a person's individual psychological space, and this is facilitated in reality by restricting touching, or actually moving away from the affected person. The relationship LACK OF INVOLVEMENT IS PHYSICAL DISTANCE thus combines both metaphor and metonymy (Taylor, 1989, in Kövecses, 2002). This is realised in practice along with the general maxim MORE X IS MORE Y, so one can be increasingly polite by accumulating past tenses and indeed other markers of 'distant' relationships:

(21) Can you help me?
(22) Could you help me?
(23) I wonder if you could help me?
(24) Do you think you could help me?
(25) I was wondering if you could help me.
(26) I was wondering if you could possibly help me?

Our third point relates to the English future aspect markers 'will' and 'going to'. It is frequently very hard to establish how sentences like (27) and (28) differ in meaning (Littlemore and Low, in 2006):

(27) If we invest in this project, *we'll lose* all our money.
(28) If we invest in this project, *we're going* to lose all our money.

The original sense of movement towards something remains the basic meaning of 'going to', as in 'What are you doing? I'm going to the bathroom'. The future aspect, 'I'm going to go', can be treated as metaphorical, employing the same image schematic notion of a path leading to a goal. The goal is now the future and 'I' am moving towards it, as in expressions like 'We're approaching Easter'. 'Will' is more complicated than 'going to', as it has several senses, starting historically with 'want/desire' and extending metaphorically through 'willingness' and 'expectation', to its most recent meaning of 'command/instruction' (Tyler and Evans, 2001).

'We're *going to* lose all our money' in (28) positions 'us' metaphorically on a path that currently exists, on a trajectory towards future bankruptcy. The implication is that the metaphorical 'downward path' is already happening – or at least the future signs are already visible. The 'will' in 'we'll lose all our money' involves no such positioning, however. It simply involves an expectation, or prediction, that bankruptcy will definitely occur. The chances are that a speaker would only say (28) if they were already somewhat committed to the investment (and had already gone some way down the path) and were perhaps more emotionally aware of the implications. 'Will' is thus preferable where one wishes to show more clinical objectivity.

Our argument is therefore that, irrelevant of whether the metaphor matches the exact historical grammaticalisation pathway (Hopper and Traugott, 1993), metaphorical senses of 'will' and 'going to' are probably worth establishing for language teaching, because they allow learners to establish the meaning of pairs of sentences that are otherwise very hard to differentiate.

8.6   Modality

Modal verbs are another aspect of grammar that could be taught through the use of metaphor. Modal verbs are usually classified into 'deontic', denoting some kind of real-world obligation, permission or ability, and 'epistemic', denoting necessity, probability or possibility (Sweetser, 1990: p. 49). It is often argued that deontic meanings are chronologically earlier and semantically more basic. Deontic obligation prototypically reflects social pressure external to the speaker, whilst epistemic necessity or probability could be argued to reflect a reality internal to the speaker.[2] The two senses can be illustrated in the case of 'must' as follows:

(29)   (I told them that) John must be home by ten.
(30)   (I conclude that) John must be home already.

According to Sweetser (1990), both types of modality involve metaphor. Given this, it becomes possible to conceptualise the internal in terms of the external. She uses Talmy's (1988) notions of forces and barriers to explain deontic modality. 'Can' (as in 'You can go now') represents a potential, but absent barrier; 'must' is a compelling force directing the subject towards the act. 'Ought to', 'have to' and 'need to' also reflect obligation but the differences are that 'ought to' has strong moral overtones, 'have to' has a meaning of being obliged by an extrinsically imposed authority, and 'need to' is an internally imposed obligation.

After having analysed deontic modality in terms of sociophysical forces, barriers and paths, Sweetser goes on to argue that epistemic modality constitutes a metaphorical extension, in the sense that our internal intellectual and physiological states are metaphorically construed in terms of our external experiences.

To illustrate, the use of *may* in the phrase 'it may be the case that' indicates that there is no barrier to the speaker's process of reasoning from the available premises to whatever conclusion is expressed (Sweetser, 1990: p. 59). This ties in with the idea that our reasoning processes are often metaphorically construed as a journey through space. Sweetser gives all the other modal verbs a similar treatment. For example, she explains the deontic use of 'must' in 'you must come home by ten' in terms of a direct force compelling someone to be home by ten. The epistemic use of must in 'You must have been home last night', on the other hand, means that 'the direct available evidence compels me to the conclusion that you were home' (ibid., p. 61).

Although Sweetser's theory is able to account for many aspects of the relationship between deontic and epistemic modality, it is not completely watertight. For example, the *deontic* 'You can go' often implies not just that you are able to go, but that you *should* do so. This involves a metonymic addition to the ability subcomponent of 'can', indicating that deontic modality is *not* always more straightforward than epistemic modality.

To the best of our knowledge, no studies have yet investigated the applicability of Sweetser's approach to language teaching, but it does meet Shortall's (2002) claim that learners should be introduced to prototypical ('basic') grammatical constructions before extensions. Under Shortall's approach, deontic modality would be taught at initial level and epistemic modality at intermediate level, leaving authentic texts that mix them to advanced level. However, we remain cautious of adopting such a step-by-step approach to teaching modality for two reasons. First, even lower level learners will at times encounter authentic texts containing both types of modality, and they need to be able to deal with them. Second, in many cases they will simply be able to transfer the two types of modality from their L1. Research suggests that the relationship between deontic and epistemic modality described by Sweetser is fairly robust across languages (Traugott and Dasher, 2002), so at the beginning and intermediate stages it would be more of a matter of awareness raising. Only at advanced levels would learners be made aware of the subtle ways in which the epistemic modals in the target language differ from those in their own language. An example would be French-speaking students of English saying 'you must know that' to mean 'it's important to be aware of the fact that'.

8.7 Grammatical metaphor (and metonymy?)

Another example of the role that metaphoric thinking can play in clarifying the link between grammar and cognition is that of Halliday's

(1994) theory of 'ideational metaphor'. Ideational metaphor is part of a broader theory of 'grammatical metaphor'[3] and occurs when concepts are viewed as a different type of process or entity from what we might expect (in Halliday's terms, they are not 'congruent' with the original, or with our expectations). A process, for example, is treated as an object, or an inanimate entity is treated as a person, as in (32) where Saturday is treated as a participant in the launch,

> (31)   The project was launched on Saturday (congruent mode)
> (32)   Saturday saw the launch of the project (metaphorical mode)

One of the most common types of ideational metaphor is 'nominalization', in which dynamic processes (as in 33) are metaphorically treated as stable states (as in 34).

> (33)   The train leaves at midday (congruent mode)
> (34)   The train's midday departure (metaphorical mode)

A key characteristic of nominalisation is the fact that it permits writers to condense a series of sentences or propositions into a shorter form. It is thus a textual form of the psychological chunking that listeners use to make sense of complex arguments and serves to stop the reader actively processing information that is old and can be assumed, or which is back-grounded at a particular point in the argument. To illustrate this, Martin (2001) cited part of a speech by Nelson Mandela:

> I was not born with a hunger to be free. I was born free – free in every way that I could know. Free to run in the fields near my mother's hut, free to swim in the clear stream that ran through my village, free to roast meals under the stars and ride the broad backs of slow moving bulls.
>
> [...]
>
> It was *this desire for freedom of my people to live their lives with great dignity and self-respect* that animated my life, that transformed a frightened young man into a bold one, that drove a law-abiding attorney to become a criminal, that turned a family-loving man to live like a monk. (Mandela (1995))

The initial sentences emotionally evoking Mandela's childhood are syntactically simple. In the later paragraph, the tone changes to something more serious and highbrow and the first paragraph is condensed into a long noun phrase, based round the abstract 'this desire'. Not only does the nominalisation serve to shift the level of the argument, and to 'package', as Halliday puts it, the sentences, but it also becomes something 'known' and 'given'. As such, and particularly when used as the opening (Halliday's 'theme') of a sentence that goes on to add 'new' information, it becomes unchallengeable. There are two factors that account for this emergent unchallengeability. First, nouns prototypically refer to objects and objects are more stable than processes – nominalisation creates 'an event frozen in time' (Butt *et al.*, 2000: p. 75). Second, it is easy to say that a proposition or a sentence is not true, but hard to say the same of a noun.

The ability to condense and background sets of ideas as one develops an argument matches perfectly the incremental and hierarchical way in which scientific and mathematical argumentation proceeds, using short cover labels for whole sets of previously demonstrated reasoning. Indeed, Halliday (1994: p. 353) saw scientific discourse as the origin of 'this kind of nominalizing metaphor'. A process may be mentioned at length at the beginning of an academic article, and then nominalised as a state or entity employing shorter and shorter phrases. *Guillen-Galve* (1998) cites a medical journal article, where the clause 'should a nerve fascicle become accidentally impaled ...' later becomes 'accidental nerve fascicle penetration ...'. then 'penetration', then 'ANFP' and finally, 'it'.

Language learners need to pay particular attention to nominalisation pathways because writers often omit to give full, unpacked versions of the noun phrase. Guillen-Galve found this with his medical article, and Mandela (see earlier) makes no mention of 'desire' in the first paragraph. The reader must create coherence by inferring – and in the process demetaphorising the grammatical metaphor. Writers also rely at times on not being challenged by the reader, and, as backgrounding is rarely taught in foreign language courses (Low, 1999d), teachers could usefully help their earners to develop querying routines to check whether the original 'process' is still valid.

There is some psychological grounding for the way nominalisations impart a sense of seriousness or formality (or simply confuse the reader). Abstract nouns take longer to process than both verbs and concrete nouns (Tyler *et al.*, 2002) and complex noun phrases increase the cognitive processing load even further, as readers need to hold a substantial amount of information in their head before finally reaching the verb.

To sum up, in order to understand complex nominalisations in a text, readers need to query

- 'What does this noun X connect back to?' (i.e. making judgements that 'X is roughly the same concept');
- 'Has this expanded notion actually been agreed/ settled?' (i.e. making judgements about 'Why am I being told this?), and
- 'Is the writer trying to sound more serious?'

When producing a text, one also needs to ask 'Have I shortened expressions progressively?'. This is all rather different from the routines suggested earlier and involves few of the skills discussed in Chapter 3, apart from noticing and differentiating.

Although a great deal has been said about grammatical *metaphor*, there has been less interest in the role of *metonymy* in changing word class and conveying different viewpoints. One could argue for instance that the use of short phrases to stand for longer expressions involves metonymy rather than metaphor (Radden, 2005: p. 17). However, to keep things simple, we will only suggest here that while nominalisation is a type of grammatical metaphor, many types of verbalisation involve metonymy. For example, 'I'll pencil it in', 'he shoveled down his food' and 'he legged it' all involve a process whereby a noun stands metonymically for an action associated with that noun, and thus takes on 'verb' status. As with nominalisation, the process of verbalisation can result in more incongruent forms of expression that can serve a particular rhetorical function. For instance, we recently overheard the following comment made by one American tourist to another.

(35)   If you wanna know the truth, I'm kinda *churched out*.

Here, the expression *churched out*, stands metonymically for the fact that this person has visited too many churches and would like to do something different. Verbalising the word 'church' endows it with a certain amount of instrumentality allowing it to be construed as the agent responsible for the speaker's tiredness or *ennui*. 'Churched out' thus condenses 'tired out' and 'by visiting churches', but the visiting needs to be inferred (what we might call inferential demetonymising). One could usefully treat expressions like this as both a conceptual and a grammatical blend. We will return to the notion of grammatical blends in Section 8.8.

Another interesting parallel that might be drawn is that whereas nominalisation often results in more formal-sounding language, grammatical *metonymy* often leads to an informal conversational style (as in the examples given earlier).

In order to understand and appreciate the metonymic changes in grammatical class in the aforementioned examples, it is necessary to identify the metonymic links between a pencil, a shovel, a leg, a church and the contexts in which they are used (querying 'What do they do?' 'What are they used for?'). In *writing* for 'pencil', and *running* for 'leg' the functions are fairly prototypical, but for *quickly disposing of a large amount of substance* for 'shovel' and *visiting churches* for 'church', less central features of the entity are being referred to. In the first of these examples, image formation may help a language learner work out the meaning, whereas the second two rely almost entirely on contextual clues. These examples highlight the ways in which different metonymic expressions may trigger different types of processing strategy. A number of researchers (e.g., Radden (2005) and Ruiz de Mendoza and Otal Campo (2003)) have explored the role of metonymy in several areas of grammar, though to date there have been no metonymically focussed teaching intervention studies with respect to grammar. We hope that such studies will now start to be conducted.

8.8 Phraseological patterning and collocation

The fact that words tend to co-occur, resulting in collocations and phraseological patterns, illustrates the close relationship between grammar and lexis. Patterns are grammatical constructions involving clear restrictions on word choice. For example, when we 'get down to' something, it is usually something serious and/or detailed, such as 'business', 'work' or 'the specifics'. The choice of words that can follow 'get down to' is therefore restricted. Metaphoric and metonymic expressions exhibit a particularly strong tendency to develop such fixed patterning (Deignan and Potter, 2004). It is crucial that language learners respond to and produce this patterning, yet it often appears to pose a serious problem, and knowledge of it frequently lags far behind vocabulary knowledge (Bahns and Eldaw, 1993; Howarth, 1996). Moreover, when learners realise that they need to use collocations, they have repeatedly been found to avoid them (Philip, 2005), or create elaborate paraphrases (Gabrys-Biskup, 1992). Patterns tend to be treated as unimportant by cognitive linguists and have so far not formed part of the empirical studies of figurative language learning we have examined. Above and beyond methods found useful with vocabulary learning in general, we thus have very little idea of what is pedagogically effective.

There are occasions where the literal and the figurative senses of a word seem to be associated with fairly fixed distinct grammatical patterns:

Literal	The light reflected off the roof
	The crystal reflected the light
Figurative	She reflected (calmly) for a moment
	He reflected (on life or the fact that life was miserable)
	He reflected ruefully that he should have resigned.

In many other cases, the situation is more complicated. Table 8.1 illustrates a number of literal and figurative examples of 'leak' taken from the *Bank of English*. These examples show that figurative 'leak' shares some constructions with literal 'leak', but that it has some constructions resembling those of a verb like 'tell' (or better, 'communicate' or 'divulge').[4] This sort of partial sharing is not rare. It recurs with, for example, 'reveal', where you can literally 'reveal a leg' or figuratively 'reveal a secret' (in both an agentive and non-agentive sense), but you can only 'reveal that X' figuratively. As 'leak' or 'reveal' are transferred figuratively to mean 'communicate', they transfer not only some of their meanings and implications, but also some of their grammatical structure. However, since they also take on structure associated with 'communicate', the result would appear to be a grammatical, as well as a semantic or conceptual, blend from which new features emerge (see Chapter 3). This does not dovetail neatly with the idea of conceptual metaphor, where the actual words employed do not matter, so given the current state of our knowledge, perhaps teachers should teach conceptual and linguistic blending as analogous processes.

Table 8.1   Literal and figurative 'leak'

Literal	Figurative
A leak from an underground petrol tank	A leak from the Pentagon
Hydrogen fuel has leaked out	The secret has leaked out
A leak-proof package	A leak-proof guarantee
It leaked oil all over the place.	–
–	Washington leaked the fact that
–	A widely leaked email
–	The news was leaked by employees
–	When word leaked out that

Table 8.2 Seeing and looking over

Verb	Noun	Sense
oversee	–	Be in charge of
overlook	oversight	Forget to do something
look over	overview	Have a general idea

Another problem for conceptual explanations is restrictions on word class. Table 8.2 represents a compound problem that university students crucially need to master. The rows give semantic not grammatical matches. First, there is no English verb to 'view over' or 'to overview'. Second, there is a semantic mismatch between all the verbs and all the nouns. In our experience, even advanced learners remain confused. Exploring the basic senses of, and relations involved in, 'see', 'over' and 'oversee' will generate relevant concepts, but will not help the learner resolve the problem of what form has what meaning. The only pedagogic solution would seem to be to prioritise the forms most likely to be needed (so academic assignments mostly need 'to overlook' and offer 'an overview') and to teach them directly in context, with support from pictures and corpus lines.

There are also restrictions concerning the types of metonymy that different languages allow. Panther and Thornburg (2003) noted that the RESULT FOR ACTION metonymy seems commoner in English than in German. Thus while English speakers use less agentive result verbs 'Have your documents ready' or (more arguably) 'Stand behind the yellow line', German speakers use more agentive forms (Halten Si Ihre Dokumente bereit', literally *'Hold* your documents', or 'Stellen Sie sich hinter die gelbe Linie', literally *'Put* yourself behind the line').

Cross-linguistic differences are thus important; indeed they add another layer of confusion to examples like 'leak'. French and Spanish speakers for example cannot use the same verbs for transitive and intransitive leaking. Nesselhauf's (2003) study of German learners of English found that, in general, learning problems arose where L1–L2 collocations were different, rather than when they were similar, suggesting that collocations are (a) psychologically real, (b) below the level of consciousness in many cases and (c) transferred to the L2 by language learners. Nesselhauf also considers cross-linguistic sense differentiation, and cites a German student who wrote 'draw a picture from [a tree]' – German 'von' means 'from' or 'of'. In this case, a conceptual explanation might help; Lindstromberg (1998) argues that in English 'of' consistently highlights a connection between two things, while 'from' highlights their separation. This explanation seems reasonably valid for

English, and does explain why you can say 'made from paper' or 'made of paper', but 'this is made from old paper by a process of compression' would sound odd with 'of'.

8.9   Conclusion

Though educators like Holme (2001; 2004) have suggested using schemata of journeys and spaces to teach English tense/aspect via direct bodily experience, empirical studies of figurative learning have thus far tended to ignore grammatical phenomena. It is, however, clear that metaphor and metonymy *are* involved in a range of grammatical phenomena which learners of English need to be able to understand and use. In some cases a motivated, conceptual account can be given, which can serve to reduce the apparent arbitrariness of the grammar and, on the evidence of the phrasal verb studies, increase learner motivation. In other cases, where collocation and patterning are involved, a few generalisations are possible (e.g., 'Verb + that ...' structures tend to imply mental events or communicating), but teaching needs to retain a phraseological focus. Ultimately, the conceptual and the linguistic both need to be acquired and to that end we proposed the notion of grammatical blending as a parallel to conceptual blending.

9
Strategic Competence

9.1 Introductory comments

So far, we have discussed the contribution that figurative thinking might make to the various components of what Bachman refers to as 'language competence'. The second major dimension of the Bachman model and the final area where figurative thinking may play a role is 'strategic competence'. In very general terms, strategic competence refers simply to a student's ability to use language interactively. This is a very broad notion, and recent reformulations of the Bachman model (see, for example, Douglas, 2000) have extended it even further to include a number of very general, non-linguistic skills, such as evaluating a situation, deciding whether to respond, planning what is needed to achieve an adequate response and organising the 'elements of language knowledge' to do it. Concepts such as 'evaluating' and 'planning' are too general for a meaningful discussion about how language users handle metaphor to achieve their intentions, so we will focus instead on the earlier formulation, in terms of 'communication strategies'.

There are two principal approaches to the study of communication strategies: the 'interactional' approach and the 'psycholinguistic' approach. Proponents of the interactional approach focus more on the ability of two interlocutors to manipulate the conversation and to negotiate shared meaning (see, for example, McNamara, 1995).

Proponents of the psycholinguistic approach, on the other hand, tend to define strategic competence as a speaker's ability to use strategies to compensate for gaps in their knowledge of the target language, in order, for example, to keep a conversation going (see, for example Poulisse, 1990). These strategies are generally referred to as 'compensation strategies' (Tarone, 1983: p. 62).

Strategic competence overlaps with some of the components in the 'language competence' component of Bachman's model, particularly those that appear under the heading 'illocutionary competence'. Illocutionary competence is all about using language strategically to build relationships, manipulate and persuade people of our viewpoints, and therefore, by its very nature, constitutes a large interactional aspect of strategic competence. We have already dealt with these in the preceding chapters (Chapter 6 in particular), so there is no need to cover this ground again. On the other hand, we have not yet touched on the role of figurative thinking in the use of *compensation* strategies, so these will be the main focus of this chapter.

9.2   What are compensation strategies?

As we saw earlier, 'compensation strategies' is a catch-all term designed to cover the range of attempts that learners make to communicate their ideas when faced with gaps in their knowledge of the target language. The three main types of strategy in this category are *word coinage, circumlocution*, and *transfer from the L1*. *Word coinage* involves making up an entirely new word out of existing words, for example, if a learner did not know the word *scissors*, he or she might refer to 'cutters'. *Circumlocution* involves giving lengthy descriptions as a substitute for unknown vocabulary items. For instance, if a learner did not know the word for a chessboard, he or she might say something like 'it is used for playing a game; it has black and white squares on it, and it is sometimes made of wood'. *Transfer from the L1* can involve the use of a word or expression from the speaker's native language, spoken with 'target language' pronunciation, or it can involve a direct translation of an L1 expression, resulting in an expression that may, or may not, exist in the target language. Before discussing the potential role of figurative thinking in the formulation of each of these three types of strategies, we will consider the extent to which compensation strategies contribute to foreign language learning in general.

9.3   Does the use of compensation strategies promote foreign language learning?

Compensation strategies form part of a broader area of research that is concerned with 'learning strategies', which are defined by Oxford (1993: p. 175) as 'specific actions, behaviours, steps, or techniques that students employ – often consciously – to improve their own progress in internalising, storing, retrieving, and using the second language'. According to Oxford (1990), compensation strategies constitute one of six categories of language learning strategies, the others being: memorisation; the use of mental processes; the organisation of emotions; management of learning; and learning with others.

Unfortunately, little is known about the long-term effectiveness of strategy training or about the best form that such training might take (Hassan *et al.*, 2005: p. 10). Moreover, the field of learning strategy research is currently undergoing a process of re-evaluation, and there is a move away from 'strategy identification' towards a wider, more qualitative focus on 'self regulatory behaviour'. Self-regulatory behaviour involves a much wider set of interrelated components, of which the use of appropriate learning strategies is only one (Dörnyei, 2005). According to Dörnyei, it is 'a multidimensional construct, including cognitive, metacognitive, motivational, behavioural, and environmental processes that learners can apply to enhance academic achievement' (ibid.: p. 191). Self-regulatory behaviour is thus not dissimilar to learner autonomy, which we discussed in Chapter 4, as it involves a capacity to engage with, and to exert a degree of control over, the learning process. However it appears to be a slightly wider construct, as it includes important attitudinal variables, such as motivation and self-efficacy. The relevance of self-regulatory behaviour to this chapter is that it puts some of the claims that we will make below into perspective: we will be claiming that figurative thinking can contribute to the formulation of a small number of compensation strategies. Given that compensation strategies are but one type of learning strategy, and that learning strategies are but one aspect of self-regulatory behaviour, it has to be admitted that the overall contribution of the suggestions made in this chapter to language learning *in general* is likely to be reasonably small.

We now turn to compensation strategies themselves, and consider their relationship with foreign language learning. Most of the foreign language learning research that we have been able to find regarding compensation strategies relates primarily to performance, and there has been very little research into their effect on learning, even in the short term. One exception to this is a study by LaPierre (1994, cited in Swain, 1995), who found that when pairs of students negotiated a solution to a gap in their target language knowledge, they were still using this solution up to a week later. This finding is promising, but needs to be consolidated by more research. Despite a lack of research in the area, one would expect compensation strategies to make some sort of contribution to learning as they increase language output. Swain (1995) argues that language output serves three important language learning functions: it enables learners to notice gaps in their knowledge of the target language; it helps them to test out hypotheses; and it provides opportunities for metalinguistic reflection. One would expect compensation strategies to contribute to the first two of these: first, they are a response to perceived gaps in one's target language knowledge and by judging their effectiveness learners will become more aware of the seriousness of these gaps; and second, compensation strategies provide opportunities for hypothesis testing and are one way of triggering feedback from one's interlocutor concerning the appropriateness of one's utterances. Moreover, research with Japanese learners of English (Nakatani, 2002) suggests that repeatedly putting them in a situation where they have to use compensation strategies makes them more likely to use them, and improves their overall levels of communicative competence, at least in the medium term. Against this, researchers, such as Skehan (1998), have suggested that excessive use of compensation strategies can lead to fossilisation, as learners can rely on the use of strategies, rather than learning new expressions. On balance, it is probably safe to say that learners can usefully be made aware of the learning potential of compensation strategies, but that more research is needed before we can make explicit statements about their relationship with foreign language learning. We now look at the type of contribution that figurative thinking can make to three types of compensation strategy: word coinage, circumlocution and transfer.

9.4   The role of figurative thinking in word coinage strategies

The strategy of *word coinage* involves making up new words or expressions to get one's meaning across. No language has exact words for every possible concept its speakers might want to talk about. As a result, speakers are often forced to use the words that are available to them in original or innovative ways in order to express the concepts they want. Word coinage is therefore a naturally occurring process that takes place in the L1 as well as in the L2. In order to coin new words, speakers need to adapt or combine words that are available to them in innovative ways in order to express the concepts they want. This process often relies on figurative thinking, as it involves the ability to stretch the conventional boundaries of word meaning using metaphor and metonymy. Indeed, the use of metaphoric and metonymic extension processes to fill lexical gaps created by new semantic fields, such as computing and telcommunications, has been central to change and development in language (Rudzka-Ostyn, forthcoming).

For example, Dirven (1985) gives an interesting historical account of ways in which the sense of the word 'cup' have been extended by native speakers over the years: this extension has involved both metaphorical and metonymic processes. The first recording of the word *cup* to denote a *drinking vessel* dates back to 1000, its first recorded use to denote a *part of an acorn* is in 1545, its first recorded use to denote a *hip joint* is in 1615, its first recorded use to denote a beverage is in 1773, its first recorded use to denote a *hollow* is in 1868, and its most recent recorded use is to denote a *part of a bra* (date unknown). This process of extension is not limited to nouns, as Dirven demonstrates by means of a historical account of the various meanings of the adjective *sweet*. The use of the word *sweet* to mean sugary derives from the Latin use of the word *suadus*. It is first recorded as meaning *friendly* in 825, it is first recorded as meaning *melodious* in 900, and it is recorded as meaning *not corrosive* in 1577. Recent word coinages in English include 'ring-fenced budgets', 'beacon schools' and 'computer mouse'. Each of these new expressions retains a metaphorical or metonymic relationship with the basic senses of its constituents: ring-fenced budgets remain enclosed and protected; beacon schools metaphorically shine (therefore radiating good practice) and guide people; and computer mice still bear a slight physical resemblance to real mice in terms of their size and shape.

Many of the meaning extensions that have developed over time also involve changes in word class and, as we saw in Chapter 8, these word class changes can sometimes involve metaphor or metonymy. For example, the derivation of the verb 'to weather' from the noun 'weather' involves a metonymic focus on a type of change that can result from particular types of weather. The use of productive derivational suffixes, such as '–y' and '–er' also involves metonymic processing. For example: 'a towny' and 'a villager' involve a metonymic focus on location; 'wife-beater' and 'church-goer' involve a metonymic focus on habitual activity; and 'sight-seer', 'murderer' and 'voter' all involve a metonymic focus on a temporary or context-dependent action (Panther and Thornburg, 2001). As we saw in Chapter 4, when figurative word coinages such as these have taken place, their phraseology tends to fix and fossilise, especially if they have involved changes in the part of speech.

All of the examples cited above involve words or expressions that have become accepted as mainstream in the English language, but the process of word coinage can also take place on a much less formal, *ad hoc* basis, as speakers adapt existing words to express concepts for which they cannot recall the exact word. The words that are coined on such occasions will not necessarily become incorporated into the language. The relatively high frequency with which native speakers create *ad hoc* word coinages in this way has been well documented, particularly amongst children (Clark, 1981; 1982). For example, Clark (1981) cites cases where children have used words such as *sleeper* for *bed*, *darking* for *colouring in* and so on. In an examination of the characteristics of children's lexical innovations, Clark (1982) highlights the fact that they are polysemic, that they rely heavily on the context, and that they demand cooperation between the speaker and the listener. Many of the word coinages that are created by children involve the combination of existing morphemes. For example, Elbers (1988) cites expressions such as *moon-nuts* (for *cashew nuts*) and *car-milk* (for *petrol*), which involve metaphoric or metonymic extensions of the meanings of the words 'moon' and 'milk'.

Both Clark's and Elber's studies focus on word coinages produced by children, and it is uncertain whether adults employ this strategy to the same extent. Cameron and Low (1999a: p. 84) comment that 'the use of metaphor-like utterances to fill lexical gaps decreases with age ... although since such catachresis is found across language use, it may just become more adult-like and less noticeable'. On the other hand, Gerrig and Gibbs (1988) believe that adults are at least as creative as children because their greater range of experiences heightens the mismatch between the meanings they wish to convey and those that are held in common by the community. There is some evidence for this in Carter and McCarthy's (1995: pp. 310–311) study of the CANCODE corpus of spoken English, where they found a number of examples of word coinage, including utterances, such as 'I don't want a romantic a *mewsy* pub' or 'We're *greenly* challenged, so sorry about that'. Although more research is needed in this area, it seems reasonably safe to conclude that the metaphorical or metonymic extension of word meaning in order to coin new words is a reasonably widespread practice among native speakers.

In many ways, the lexical innovations that are made by native speakers are similar to the compensation strategies used by foreign language learners when faced with gaps in their knowledge of the L2. One particularly productive area for word coinage is the possibility that the English language offers for noun compounds. These are often (but not always) metaphoric; Tarone (1978), for example, cites an instance of an L2 word coinage strategy where the word 'airball' was used to approximate the word 'balloon'. The students in Tarone's study were able to convey their intended meaning, so the strategy of word coinage (whether it involves transfer from the L1 or not) does appear to be a useful way of maintaining the flow of communication, thus ensuring that the input continues. Strategies such as these are also likely to lend themselves to hypothesis testing, allowing learners to 'stretch their interlanguage to meet communicative goals' (Swain, 1995: p. 127), and may serve to trigger useful feedback from interlocutors and teachers. Teachers could usefully point out to their students the preferences that particular languages have for different types of word coinage and the phraseology that typically accompanies them. For example, Spanish makes little use of compounding expressions (such as 'ill car') and Spanish speakers are more likely to say 'rooms for sleep' (for bedrooms) and ' shoes for skiing' (for ski boots) (Butterworth and Hatch, 1978, cited in Horst, 1996). Spanish learners of English may therefore need to be made aware, for example, of the compounding option in English. Other word coinage possibilities that appear to vary from language to language include the use of derivational suffixes, such as '–y' and '–er' in English (see above), and the use of diminutives, such as '–ito' and '–ita' in Spanish.

Clark (1981) makes an important distinction between the *momentary* lexical gaps (temporary difficulties retrieving the right word from memory) which are often experienced by both adults and children to the same extent, and *chronic* lexical gaps (where the speaker is unaware of any word form that is conventionally used to express that particular meaning) which are also experienced by both adults and children but to differing extents. She maintains that chronic gaps, rather than momentary gaps, provide excellent opportunities for the kind of creative lexical innovations mentioned earlier. This distinction is relevant to foreign language learning because one would expect foreign language learners to be faced with far more *chronic* gaps than native speakers and, therefore, to employ more word coinage strategies.

It is unclear whether foreign language students can and should be explicitly trained to employ word coinage strategies such as these. There is some evidence to suggest that the decision to use word coinage strategies is mostly a matter of the student's personality. For instance, Ridley and Singleton (1995) encountered an English-speaking student of German who made extensive use of word coinages, consistently producing the highest number of innovations in her group. Her preference for innovation was also found to manifest itself in French, where she was an advanced student, so her strategy preference appears not to have been related to her level of proficiency. Ridley and Singleton noted that 'lexical creativity is for her often a first line of attack rather than a last resort' (ibid.: p. 145). Of particular interest are the student's comments that 'it's tough luck' if the message is not always understood, because that she 'can always point at something or get by' when communicating orally (1995: p. 145), and Ridley and Singleton's observation that 'she displays a certain risk-taking attitude'. Their study suggests that, at least for this student, the strategy of coining new words is a matter of personal style, and that it may be related to the student's general risk-taking tendency. This means that it migth be harder difficult to foster the strategy amongst other, more cautious students. More worryingly, Ridley and Singleton found this student to be poor in relation to her peers in terms of overall lexical proficiency. This implies that a certain amount of fossilisation had set in (as Skehan would predict), due to the fact that she could always 'get by' with her word coinages.

On the other hand, Littlemore (2003b) found the frequent use of word coinage to be significantly related to the perceived 'level' of a student's output in the target language ($p < 0.05$). This result was part of a study (reported in Littlemore, 1998; 2001c; 2003b), in which 82 intermediate French-speaking students of English were shown photographs of plants or animals. The participants were asked to look at the photographs one by one and to make clear in English what object they saw, either by naming it, or in any other way. They were asked to do this in such a way that an English speaker, who would later listen to the recordings of the session, would be able to identify the objects. During this activity, the students had no access to a dictionary, nor were they under any time pressure. The students were recorded and the recordings transcribed. The strategies used by the students were then identified, coded and counted. The recordings were then played to two native speakers who were asked to rate each student's performance in terms of ease of comprehension, the stylishness of the language used and the 'perceived level of the student'. The native speakers perceived the level of the students who used more word coinage strategies to be significantly higher then that of the students who avoided these types of strategies, although in reality, all students were at the same level. We must be careful not to over-interpret the findings made in this study, as there were actually very few instances of word coinage in the data (0.04%). The safest conclusion we can draw at this point is that students should be made aware of the possibilities presented by word coinage strategies, but that they also need to know about the pitfalls they involve, and to be shown how to signal their word coinages clearly and appropriately. 'Word coinages' should be seen primarily as an opportunity for learners to develop their inter-language and to trigger feedback from native speakers and teachers that will help them approximate to native speaker norms with respect to conventional usages and phraseological issues (all of which presupposes, of course, that the student's aim is to sound like a native speaker).

9.5 The role of figurative thinking in circumlocution strategies

As we saw earlier, *circumlocution* involves offering lengthy descriptions as a substitute for unknown vocabulary items. Circumlocution features prominently in Poulisse's (1990) taxonomy of communication strategies. This taxonomy includes a category called 'conceptual' strategies, which consists of 'analytic conceptual strategies', where the student lists some of the target object's properties (such as, for example, the fact that it has four legs or that it is round) and 'holistic conceptual strategies', where the student refers to a related concept that shares some of the principal features of the target item (such as, for example, the fact that it looks like an owl, or that it is a kind of bird). Within the holistic conceptual strategy category, a large place is given to the use of analogy, which is of particular interest here. Whereas many analogies are likely to be fairly literal (e.g., saying 'it's like a snail' to refer to a slug), some are likely to involve metaphorical or metonymic processing, but one would not expect such strategies to be used in great quantities. Indeed, in a study designed to elicit comparison-based compensation strategies, Littlemore (1998; 2003b) found that only 2 per cent of the total number of strategies produced in the study consisted of original metaphorical analogies, and that 2.8 per cent consisted of metaphorical analogies that were conventional in the target language (English). Examples of metaphorical analogies produced by the students that are fairly novel in English, included:

(1) 'it has like a chicken on its head' (target item = seahorse)
(2) 'its head is like a punk' (target item = seahorse)
(3) 'a pipe for smoking' (target item = acorn)
(4) 'chewing gum' (target item = slug)
(5) 'like a lit candle' (target item = squid)
(6) 'like a helicopter' (target item = dragonfly)

Metaphorical analogies, produced by the students, that are more conventional in English, included:

(7) 'it has eyes on its back' (target item = peacock)
(8) 'it's shaped like a ball' (target item = radish)
(8) 'it's like a little horse that lives in the sea'
    (target item = seahorse)

Box 9.1 Extract from a student's response to the communication strategies elicitation task (author's own italics)

Er the next animal is a very elegant animal it's er a bird which has like a *bride* you know he has really beautiful, a really beautiful erm er skin and er he have feather and on those feather there are many *eyes*, like *eyes* and it's a very colourful animal and yeah that's all.

These analogies are all 'metaphorical' in that they feature an incongruous relationship between the vehicle term, and the context in which it occurs. Let us look, for example, at the following extract (Box 9.1), in which one of the students attempts to describe a peacock.

In this example, the student sets the scene by telling us that it is an animal, or to be more precise, a bird. She then introduces the incongruous idea of a bride, requiring the hearer to carry out a certain amount of restructuring in order to make sense of the utterance (presumably, the tail of a peacock looks something like the train on a wedding dress). A listener is highly likely to treat this utterance as they would a novel metaphor. The student then makes another incongruous utterance, by saying that 'there are many *eyes*' (presumably referring to the dots on the peacock's back). Most native speakers of English would probably be aware of this conventional comparison, and would process it very much as they would process a conventional metaphor. In other words, the understanding would be virtually automatic and there may be very little processing work to be done, but they would still recognise the fact that some sort of comparison was being made.

In order to assess the communicative effectiveness of novel versus conventional analogies, such as these, Littlemore (2003b) compared the quality evaluations given by the native speakers with the percentage of novel and conventional metaphoric comparison strategies that were employed by the students. She found that the percentage of *conventional* metaphoric analogies that the students used was significantly related to ease of comprehension ($p < 0.01$), stylishness of language ($p < 0.01$) and the perceived level of the student ($p < 0.01$). However, the use of *novel* metaphoric analogies was related to none of these ratings. These findings suggest that, although the students produced very few conventional metaphoric analogies, when they did, it had a significant and positive effect on the way in which native speakers perceived their language performance. On the other hand, the use of novel metaphoric analogies did not have this effect. It may therefore be useful for language teachers to encourage their students to produce metaphoric analogies that are conventional in the target language, but not novel ones. Unfortunately, this is easier said than done, as it is very difficult for a language learner to gauge whether a particular metaphorical analogy is conventional or novel in the target language. One way round this problem might be for students to draw on their L1 knowledge. All three of the conventional metaphorical comparisons listed earlier exist in French as well as in English. This reflects the likelihood of there being some degree of transferability, at least between languages that are reasonably close to one another. For languages that are not close to one another, it may be useful to encourage students to preface their metaphorical comparisons with appropriate signalling expressions, such as 'we say in my language that it looks a bit like a ...'. Further research is needed to investigate the effectiveness of such an approach but we are able at this point to explore the issue of transfer in a little more depth.

9.6   The role of figurative thinking in transfer strategies

As we saw before, transfer from the L1 can involve the use of a word or expression from the speaker's native language, or a direct translation of an L1 expression, resulting in an expression that may, or may not, exist in the target language. Although the vast majority of transfer is unlikely to involve figurative thinking, one possible exception to this is *creative transfer strategies* (Kumaravadivelu, 1988). Kumaravadivelu defines 'creative transfer' as:

> the process in which a language learner attributes to a lexical item of the target language all the functions – referential and conceptual meaning, connotation, collocability, register restriction – of its assumed first language translation equivalent. (1988: p. 316)

He refers to it as 'a complex process by which learners translate a language-specific idiomatic usage and produce highly creative ... usages' (ibid.: p. 316). Some good examples of this type of strategy are given by Nemser (1991) who observed the production, by German learners of English, of 'ill car' to mean 'ambulance' and 'side jump' to mean 'extramarital affair'. Despite their apparent creativity, these examples turn out to be a result of transfer from the L1. 'Ill car' is a direct translation of 'Krankenwagen', meaning ambulance, and 'sidejump' is a direct translation of the 'Seitensprung', meaning extramarital affair.

For Kumaravadivelu, the apparent 'creativity' in this types of transfer results from the fact that conventional idioms transferred directly from the L1 can sound 'exotic and original' if they do not happen to be conventional in the L2. To us, the accidental production of creative-sounding utterances as a result of straightforward transfer from the L1 does not sound like a particularly creative process in itself. The creativity is more likely to lie in the hypothesis-making process that the student needs to engage in, in order to decide which idiomatic usages are likely to be acceptable in the target language culture, and which are not.

Kumaravadivelu's position is supported by Paribakht (1985), who found that even her advanced Persian ESL students still relied to some extent on the creative transfer strategies of *transliteration of L1 idioms and proverbs* (i.e., attempting to translate an L1 idiom or proverb directly into the target language) and *idiomatic transfer* (i.e., assuming that words have the same metaphorical properties in the target language as they do in the native language). She concluded that idiomatic and cultural aspects of the L1 are often the last things to be abandoned.

A more detailed study of L2 students' tendencies to transfer L1 idioms into the L2 was conducted by Irujo (1993). Irujo was interested in discovering whether, given an L1–L2 translation task containing idioms, advanced learners of English would attempt to use English idioms, or whether they would avoid them, and use non-idiomatic synonyms or paraphrases instead. She hypothesised that participants would: be prepared to use their knowledge of the target language to produce large numbers of idioms; produce more idioms that were common to both languages; and use more high frequency, semantically transparent idioms. Her results supported the first two hypotheses, but not the third. This indicates that advanced students are inclined to use existence in the L1 as the principal criterion on which they decide whether or not to employ idioms in the L2. They appear not to consider the individual properties of the idioms themselves.

Kellerman (1987a; 1987b) found that language learners tend to be suspicious of idioms in the L2 that look too much like idioms in the L1 and, when presented with such idioms, claim that they would not use them. This can be contrasted with Danesi's (1992a) finding that they tend to rely on L1 metaphors when writing in the L2. Paribakht's and Irujo's findings appear to lend support to Danesi's position, indicating that what learners *think* about the target language may not always resemble what they actually *do* with it when under pressure to produce it.

The findings from the research into creative transfer thus appear to suggest that although learners may claim to be suspicious of L2 idioms that resemble idioms in the L1, when they are faced with a task where they have to produce the L2, they occasionally fall back on translations of

L1 idioms. The role of the teacher is therefore to alert students to the similarities and differences between L1 and L2 idioms, and to encourage them to conduct their own detective work in this area. Teachers need to help their students to develop the necessary confidence to decide when it is appropriate to transfer an idiomatic expression, and when it is not. In order to do so, they might draw on Boer's and colleagues' work on idioms that we referred to in Chapter 2, as it suggests paying attention to the source domains, and assessing whether these source domains are (or were once) salient in the target language culture. If so, then the idiom may well be transferable, if not then it is perhaps better to avoid it. This process may involve analogical reasoning, as 'the defining characteristic of analogical reasoning is the identification of the correspondences between two systems and the transfer of relational information from one system to the other' (Vosniadou, 1995: p. 300). The teacher may then need to provide additional phraseological information about the idiom in the target language.

Although for the researchers mentioned earlier, creative transfer refers explicitly to the transfer of idioms, the term could apply equally well to the transfer of figuratively extended word senses. For example, we saw earlier that the word 'cup' in English can be used to refer, amongst other things, to a sporting competition, a part of a bra, a part of an acorn, and a hip joint. None of these senses exist for the word 'tasse' in French and an English speaker learning French would not get very far by translating them directly into French. The same applies for metonymically extended senses, such as the use of the word 'table' in French, which refers to a style or quality of cooking, a sense which it does not have in English. If a learner was interested in discovering whether or how these figurative extensions exist in the target language, s/he could say something along the lines of: 'in English, we say it has the shape of a *cup*'; or 'in French, we say that it has a famous *table*', accompanied with an appropriate gesture, followed by the question 'how do you say this in French/English?' in order to elicit the appropriate French or English expression. This communication strategy would serve as a powerful learning strategy as it could be used to elicit feedback and provide valuable opportunities for learning (Bialystok, 1983).

9.7 The promotion of figurative compensation strategies in the language classroom

We have shown in the preceding sections that some compensation strategies are likely to involve a degree of figurative thinking, and that figurative thinking may therefore contribute, at least in part, to strategic competence. But to what extent is it worth training students in the use of figurative compensation strategies in the language classroom? As we saw in Section 9.3, the link between the use of compensation strategies and language learning is by no means clear, and research into the effectiveness of communication strategy training in general has produced mixed results. In this section we suggest a number of activities designed to place students in situations where they are obliged to use figurative word coinage, circumlocution and creative transfer strategies, but we urge caution in this area, as we do not yet know exactly how useful such activities are likely to be.

One way to encourage students to use *word coinage strategies* might be to put them in a position where they have to convey ideas for which there may not even be a widely known word in the target language. For example, they could be shown a series of visual instructions from a furniture shop, on how to put together a complicated bookcase, and asked to put these instructions into words. Alternatively, they could be asked to describe abstract shapes or pictures to other students in the group, who have to draw the shapes. They could then be played recordings, or shown transcripts, of native speakers doing the same activity (see Willis, 1996), in order to give them idea of how native speakers coin new words, and how they signal their usage of word coinages. Another important feature of word coinages (as we saw in Chapter 5) is that the tendency to coin new words and phrases often reflects a desire to be in or out of a particular speech community, and can even be involved in creating the speech community itself. In some language teaching contexts, it may therefore be beneficial for the teacher to look at the language used, past and present, by the speech community in question, and to explore, with the students, how it has evolved.

Another point that is worthy of development is the issue of cross-cultural variation in the kind of word coinage strategies that different languages allow. For instance, in Section 9.4, we referred to the verb 'to weather' as in 'it weathers well', which is metonymically derived from the noun 'weather'. This metonymic verbalisation process (which we also mentioned in Chapter 8) should lend itself to useful teaching exercises, as the process works with some, but not all, nouns. For example, in English we can talk about '*mushrooming* costs', 'hot *desking*', and '*papering* the walls', but we cannot use the verbs 'windowing' or 'bookshelving' (although we do talk about '*booking* tickets' and '*shelving* plans'). More importantly, the capacity to verbalise in this way varies wildly from language to language.

Other languages have the potential to employ metonymy in the verbalisation process, but they do it differently, and with different words. For instance, in French the noun 'béton' (concrete) can be metonymically verbalised to form the verb 'bétonner' (to concrete, to build using concrete), and the noun 'noyau' (the pit or stone of a fruit) can be metonymically verbalised to form the verb 'denoyauter', which means to take the stone out of a fruit, and metaphorically extended to form the verb 'noyauter', which means 'to infiltrate' (to get to the core). Of the three English examples mentioned above, the only one that works in French is (wall) paper and to paper the walls. The noun 'tapisserie' (one meaning being 'wallpaper') and the verb 'tapisser' (to wallpaper) are both used. Spanish is similar to French in that of the three English examples, the only one that properly translates is 'papering', as in 'empapelar una habitación (a room)' from 'papel' (paper). Interestingly, 'empapelar' can be metaphorically extended in Spanish to form the informal, and slightly aggressive 'empapelar a alguien' (to paper someone), which means 'to make things very difficult for them'. None of the three English examples mentioned here work in Japanese, but unlike in English, it *is* possible to say 'to curtain' in Japanese, which means 'to draw the curtains'. Given this considerable variation between languages, it may well be worthwhile for language teachers to discuss with their students the types of words that can be coined in the target language, and to encourage them to compare this with the word coinage patterns in their own language.

One way to encourage students to use *circumlocution strategies* might be to adapt the techniques used by some of the researchers to investigate the effectiveness of these strategies. In these studies, participants are usually put in situations where they have to convey a set of ideas or meanings, for which they lack the adequate target language resources, and they are therefore obliged to use circumlocution strategies. For instance, students might be shown pictures of vocabulary items for which they do not know the word in the target language, and asked to convey what these items are in the target language; or they might be asked to translate texts containing difficult vocabulary items into the target language without using a dictionary. Again, they could be played recordings, or shown transcripts of native speakers performing the same activity to expose them to authentic-sounding signalling devices. It should be borne in mind that, unlike the other two types of compensation strategies discussed in this chapter, circumlocution strategies will only rarely involve figurative thinking.

The use of *creative transfer* strategies, where students assess the extent to which idiomatic expressions can be transferred from the L1 to the

L2 are best encouraged in the context of native–non-native speaker interaction. The easiest way for most language teachers to organise contact between their students and native speakers of the target language is to set up an intercultural email exchange project where, for example, English learners of French are paired with French learners of English, and encouraged to engage in email correspondence for a particular purpose (Ushioda, 2000). The English-speaking students write in French, and the French-speaking students write in English, and they provide feedback on each other's writing. Such projects have often been praised as they involve learners in a type of learning that is based on constructivist learning theory, which holds that learners learn best not through explicit instruction, but through interacting with others, thereby testing out their hypotheses and adapting what they know and understand (O'Dowd, 2004).

Intercultural email exchanges apparently work best when the teacher provides a tangible reason for correspondence, for example, English-speaking students of French might be asked to prepare a presentation on French eating habits, based on information provided by their correspondents, who are French-speaking students of English (Dudeney, 2000). The use of creative transfer strategies could be built into such an activity in the following way: The students could each be asked to think of three, difficult-to-translate, idiomatic expressions that they use in their own language to talk about eating habits, and which they might want to use in their presentation. They might come up with expressions such as: 'pig out'; 'throw something together'; or 'get a take-away'. Their task would then be to find out, in the course of their email correspondence, how these expressions translate into French. They could do so by giving their correspondent the English version, along with a literal translation into French, and asking them how to say it in more authentic-sounding French. The French correspondent would then be expected to provide an appropriate rendering, along with some guidance on how the expression is used in French. The English-speaking student of French would then be expected to recycle this expression by using it in their presentation. Any mistakes in usage could be picked up the teacher in the type of post-task language focus session that Willis (1996) recommends, where the learners and teachers identify, process and practice specific language features that have arisen in the task. The learning outcomes would be that the English student had learned several new French idiomatic expressions, and the French student had learned several new English ones, and that each would have some idea of how the expression is used in the target language. Although some advocates of task-based learning approaches may argue against front-loading the language focus in this way, such an activity is likely to encourage the students to *negotiate for meaning*, which, according to Foster (1998), 'is not a strategy that language learners are predisposed to employ' (ibid.: p. 1). One important caveat is that this activity requires quite a high degree of L1 literacy and awareness, and may not work equally well with all types of learners.

The effectiveness of these techniques remains to be tested, as does the communicative effectiveness of the many of strategies themselves. We hope that research will continue in the area, and that the effectiveness and reliability of some of the techniques will be put to the test with students of various levels from a variety of backgrounds.

9.8 Conclusion

In this chapter we have looked at how figurative thinking might be used by language learners to compensate for gaps in their knowledge of the target language. We have seen how it might contribute to the formulation of word coinage, creative transfer and, to a lesser extent, circumlocution strategies. In order to get a fuller picture of the contribution that figurative thinking might make to strategic competence, we need to consider these claims together with those made in previous chapters, where it was argued that figurative thinking is likely to contribute to a range of more interactive communication strategies, such as using language to inform, persuade and influence, educate and entertain, and perhaps most importantly to form relationships. In other words, it can be used for both transactional and relationship-building goals. We develop our discussion of the role of figurative thinking in a variety of learning and communication goals in Chapter 10.

Part III
Conclusions

of metaphors, idioms and proverbs in discourse tasks like changing topic are also subject to 'rules', or at least expectations (Chapter 7). When learners are forced to operate within these parameters, the play becomes more 'ludus'-like. The problem for language learners, teachers and researchers alike is that, to a large extent, we do not know what the rules of the game actually are! The limitations of metaphor and metonymy as well as the types of phraseological patterning often come across as being largely arbitrary, although some of the research outlined in Chapter 8 is beginning to reveal a degree of systematicity in some areas. For the time being, given this less than perfect situation, the best that we can do as teachers is to give learners some guidance as to how they might use the context of an utterance or a text to decide how much figurative decoding is necessary, and when to stop. In terms of production, the challenge is to help learners to determine the likely acceptability of an utterance by drawing on their knowledge of the figurative language usage patterns in L2 system, its culturally determined limitations, and the differences that they are already aware of between figurative patterning in their language and the target language. The only way to do this is by exposing them to both conventional and creative figurative language, and helping them to develop their skills in the areas of noticing, relevant schema activation, analogical reasoning, associative fluency and image formation, which contribute in different ways to metaphor interpretation and production. Learners need opportunities to be creative, and to experiment with the figurative potential of the target language, but they also need feedback on whether or not the figurative language that they have produced is conventional in the target language (Low, 1988).

From a research perspective, much more work needs to be done in order to investigate the ways in which metaphor and metonymy are conventionally exploited in different languages, and to account for the phraseological restrictions that different languages impose. Researchers in the fields of cognitive linguistics (and to a lesser extent in corpus linguistics) have begun to identify a few patterns in these areas, but a great deal more needs to be done. Such research would be of considerable benefit to language teachers, course designers, and of course foreign language learners.

10.3 How do language play and task-based learning fit together in the teaching of figurative language?

Bachman's framework has served to demonstrate the numerous functional aspects of figurative language. One of the most effective ways to help

10
Promoting Figurative Language Competence in the Foreign Language Classroom

10.1 Introductory comments

In this book, we have tried to examine the role of figurative thinking in foreign language learning, focussing on all five areas of competence in Bachman's (1990) model, namely sociolinguistic, illocutionary, textual, lexico-grammatical, and strategic. It will hopefully be apparent from the previous chapters that there is some variation in the exact nature of its contribution to each of these different areas, and that teachers will therefore need to deal with it in different ways. Generally speaking, in the areas of sociolinguistic and lexico-grammatical competence, the main issue seems to be one making learners aware of the presence of figurative language, and of the ways in which figurative mechanisms operate differently across languages. In contrast to this, in the areas of illocutionary, textual and strategic competence, figurative language takes on a much more functional role, so, in addition to recognising how it reflects stance, increases coherence and cohesion, and contributes to an argument, learners need to know how to use it for maximum effect. This variation is reflected in the types of teaching activities that we have suggested in the different chapters.

The majority of the activities that we have outlined in this book have some sort of *consciousness-raising* function (see Willis and Willis, 1996) in that they are designed to draw the learners' attention to metaphorical or metonymic aspects of the target language. Activities, such as the hyperlinked vocabulary learning activity outlined in Chapter 2 are designed to demonstrate the links between the figurative and the more 'basic' senses of a word. Corpus-based approaches, such as those outlined in Chapters 5 and 8 are designed to sensitise learners to the different, yet related senses that words have, and to the phraseological patterns that accompany these different senses. The activities based on conceptual metaphor, such as the 'ecological niche' text in Chapter 6 are designed to raise learners' awareness of underlying conceptual metaphors in discourse, and the persuasive function that they can sometimes perform, and to help learners critically evaluate the arguments that these metaphors are being used to support, in the texts that they read. Some of the activities that we have suggested involve the learners in close language analysis. For example, we have suggested that the close analysis of poems, advertisements and cartoons may help learners gain deeper access to the target culture. We also suggest that learners be encouraged to *play* with the forms of conventional idioms, and *experiment* with the figurative potential of words and phrases with which they are familiar.

On the other hand, other activities in this book are more prototypically *task-based,* in that they involve the learners in well-defined language-learning tasks, with specific sets of goals, and followed by language focus sessions (Willis, 1996). For example, in Chapter 6, we mentioned two activities involving conceptual metaphors: a debate over government intervention in the economy and a presentation of the learners' own organisations. Both of these activities constitute specific tasks with well-defined end-goals. Although Willis does not normally include role-plays in her definition of 'task', the role-play activity outlined in Chapter 7, where learners were encouraged to employ idioms to signal their desire for a topic change, has a clear functional focus and specified outcome, as well as providing opportunities for language analysis, and is therefore very 'task-like'.[1]

The varied nature of these activities underlines our strong belief that when it comes to the teaching of figurative language it is important to allow learners the opportunity to play with the target language, to try things out and test hypotheses, without losing sight of the functions that the language is being used to perform, and the phraseology that is conventionally used. What is interesting, therefore, about many of these activities is that they bring together aspects of both *language play* (Cook, 1997b; Cook, 2000; Low, 1988) and *task-based learning* (e.g., Willis, 1996), which have often been seen as opposing principles in foreign language acquisition. We will thus look in a little more detail at the roles played by language play and task-based learning in figurative language learning, and at the ways in which they need to interact in order to facilitate this learning.

10.2   Teaching figurative language and the issue of 'Language Play'

We have seen in this book that many words and expressions can have their senses extended to mean slightly different things, and that these extension processes often involve metaphor or metonymy. We have also seen that figurative uses of language can serve to perform important communicative functions, such as explication, persuasion, and relationship building. It is therefore important for language learners to have the necessary confidence to be able to develop and interpret figurative extensions of word meanings, and to form and test out their own hypotheses regarding potential figurative extensions of word senses. In order to develop this confidence, learners need to have the opportunity and the space to 'play' with the target language. Many of the activities outlined in this book are indeed designed to encourage a learner to play with the figurative potential of the target language. As such, they provide ways in which learners can destabilise their inter-language system, thus preventing fossilisation and allowing linguistic development to take place (Bell, 2005). Another important feature of language play is that people generally enjoy it, and enjoyment and humour are often instrumental to learning (Cook, 2000). As Taylor (2002: 92–93) puts it, 'delight in form-focussed activities is a facet of human cognition that shapes human language'.

In his book on language play, Cook (2000) draws attention to Caillois's (1961) distinction between 'conventionalised, rule-governed play' (ludus) and 'spontaneous, relatively free play' (paedia) and argues that both have a cognitive function in promoting creative thinking. It is relatively easy to see how the activities designed to help foreign language learners figuratively extend the uses of target language vocabulary and might involve paedia; a certain amount of free play is necessary when testing out hypotheses and pushing at the boundaries of acceptability. Examples of such apparent 'free play' activities mentioned in this book include playing around with possible figurative uses of known vocabulary, experimenting syntactically with conventional idioms, and extending existing conceptual metaphors and metonymies. On the other hand, as we saw in Chapter 2, the extended senses of words and phrases are never entirely arbitrary, as they are frequently governed by metaphorical and metonymic principles. Moreover, the restricted nature of much of the phraseology surrounding figuratively extended senses adds another set of rules, which can be much harder to identify or learn, as they are largely culturally determined (Chapters 4 and 5). Again, the use

learners understand and use figurative language to perform these functions is to engage them in authentic, well-defined tasks with specific functional goals. Indeed, many of the activities outlined in this book invite learners to focus on a particular function, and encourage them to use figurative language in order to perform this function. Willis (1996) argues that the best way to maximise the effectiveness of language learning tasks is to follow a three-stage task-based learning framework, consisting of a pre-task stage, a task cycle and a language focus. Let us look at how this cycle might apply to a task designed to encourage spoken figurative language production, say for example, the preparation of an advertising campaign for the learners' favourite ice-cream.

During the *pre-task stage*, when the teacher has outlined the task, stated its goals and explained its pedagogical purpose, the necessary figurative language resources would need to be activated. These could include relevant conceptual metaphors and metonymies, idioms or figurative expressions that might be useful. It might also be a good idea to follow Willis's suggestion of playing the learners a recording of native speakers performing a similar task before they perform it themselves, or showing them advertisements for other food products, which employ metaphor and metonymy.

It is during the *task cycle* where the real 'language play' is most likely to take place as the learners are relatively free to experiment with the target language and try things out for themselves. The best results are likely to be achieved if the learners are allowed to work in pairs or small groups, and then to report back to the class as a whole. The reason for this is that experimenting with figurative language is a potentially embarrassing and face-threatening activity. There is a strong likelihood of the learners producing expressions that are deemed to be 'wrong', and it is easier for them to experiment first in a smaller group. Moreover, spoken creativity is an 'emergent phenomenon' (Carter, 2004), and is therefore probably best nurtured in small groups that are not under the close scrutiny of the teacher or other learners.

It has been noted that in a language class, learners often engage in language play with each other during moments of 'off-task' behaviour as it creates 'time out' from classroom activities. This is not a bad thing, and should even at times be encouraged, as the sort of language play that learners engage in when they are 'off-task' can help them to engage, on a more personal level, with the language learning process. Cekaite and Aronsson (2005: p. 187) give a number of illustrations of how a group of 7–10 year-old language learners 'transformed a language teaching situation ... into a joking exploration of the aesthetic potential of language'. They noted that "language play is ... one of the crucial building blocks of peer run language lessons" (ibid.). If we want our learners to experiment playfully and spontaneously with figurative language, then we need to leave them to their own devices from time to time. This is also likely to promote a certain amount of co-operative learning, and strategy development. The teacher can always circulate, acting as a monitor, and encouraging the learners. If they overhear a markedly inappropriate utterance, they can comment on it individually to the learner in question, rather than in front of the whole group. When the learners report their ideas to the class, the teacher's role is to act mainly as a passive observer, making notes on instances of figurative language employed by the learners, and giving only brief feedback.

It is during the *language focus* stage, stage that the teacher can discuss the figurative language used by the learners, and comment on its level of appropriateness in the target language. Appropriate usages should be repeated and written on the board for reinforcement. Inappropriate usages should not be rejected out of hand, but alternative, more conventional forms could be suggested, and the teacher could focus on the types of devices generally used to signal novel figurative language use.

10.4   The role of figurative thinking in teaching the four skills

In Section 10.3, although we were focussing on spoken production, we did to some extent assume a sort of generic structure for the teaching of figurative language, applicable to the four skills of speaking, writing, speaking and listening. This is reasonable given that at least in terms of vocabulary, figurative thinking is likely to contribute in similar ways to each of the four skills. But, as we saw in Chapters 5 to 9, figurative language can be used to perform slightly different functions depending on whether we are reading, writing, speaking or listening to it, and these present learners with slightly different challenges. In this section, we look briefly at the functional aspects of figurative language that might be prioritised in the teaching of reading, writing, speaking and listening. These are in addition to the more general notions outlined earlier.

In the area of reading, we have found that learners can be helped to develop strategies to guess at the senses of words that have been figuratively extended to fit new contexts. They can also be taught to detect and evaluate underlying metaphors in order to critically analyse what they read. In addition to this, it may also be beneficial to teach learners to recognise figurative language clusters, and to identify the functions that are served by such clusters. When reading poetry or other types of literature, they are likely to benefit from having their attention drawn to the links between the language and culture, and to reflect on the universality of the figurative cultural references in the poetry.

In writing, learners are likely to benefit from being shown how to use figurative language creatively, appropriately and, at times, persuasively. We saw in Chapter 8 how the strategic use of tenses and grammatical metaphor can strengthen the rhetorical effect of academic writing. It may also be worth teaching learners how to control figurative language to provide overall structure and coherence to their writing.

In listening, learners may need to be helped to identify the types of signalling devices that are usually used to signal figurative language. This would include listening out for the types of intonation patterns that indicate the use of an idiom or a proverb. They may also need to be made aware of the wide range of functions that are performed by figurative language, and to realise that it is not there for decorative purposes alone. They may need to be helped to look for the evaluative component of ideas that are conveyed through figurative language. In conversation, they may benefit from being taught to listen out for a speaker's attempt to change the subject, or even close the conversation, which may be signalled by their use of idioms.

Finally, in speaking, we have shown that it is useful to encourage learners to structure their thoughts around one or two conceptual metaphors as this helps their debating skills as well as their ability to convey their ideas. It may also be worthwhile helping learners to use metaphor and metonymic communication strategies, and to signal their use of these strategies. Further research is needed to investigate the long-term effectiveness of these approaches, and to explore other areas of language learning where a focus on figurative language might be beneficial.

10.5 How is figurative language dealt with in published teaching materials?

In an influential article, which in many ways foreshadowed the things that we have been saying in this book, Carter and McCarthy (1995) stressed the need for creative language play to be incorporated into everyday language teaching materials. The thrust of their argument was that the ability to make and to understand the playful or creative use of language is an aspect of everyday language use, and that the teaching of creative language should not be confined to the realm of literature. They therefore established a continuity between language and literature teaching, proposing for example, that learners should be confronted with, and asked to explain, expressions such as 'a real angel', 'a closed book' or 'a gem' that are frequently used to describe people, or that they should be shown newspaper headings, such as 'giant waves down tunnel' or 'judge's speech ends in long sentences' (see too Alexander, 1983). This line of argument has been taken up and put even more forcefully in two recent book-length treatments of the subject by Carter (2004) and Cook (2000).

In this book we have extended the argument by offering an in-depth exploration of the teaching and learning of figurative language. We too would be unhappy to see the study of figurative language relegated to the domain of literature. We too would like to see the presence of more creative, 'language play' type activities in regular foreign language classrooms. We would be particularly keen to see more activities that offer learners the opportunity to explore the figurative potential of the target language, and to draw comparisons with their own L1 figurative language systems. We also believe that in order for language learners to see how native speakers use figurative language, it is important for them to be exposed to authentic, unadulterated examples of figurative language. These examples should be as 'undoctored' as possible, as many of the 'messy' parts of a script (the 'wells'; the 'ums', the pauses, etc.) may well provide vital clues to the ways in which the author intends the figurative language to be interpreted (see Grundy, 2004). We have shown in the preceding chapters how the production and interpretation processes involved in metaphor and metonymy are strongly affected by extralinguistic experiences and connotations, making these 'messy' parts of the script particularly important. Lessons on figurative language would also, in an ideal world, offer a way into the target language culture, as this may help learners to 'discover new, foreign connections between words and concepts, and therefore help them to internalise conceptualisations belonging to the foreign language' (Niemeier, 2004: p. 112).

How far have we come towards meeting these challenges? In what ways are learners being helped to developing their figurative thinking skills? What opportunities are they being given to identify relationships between language and culture? To what extent do they cross the boundary between language and literature in their lessons? In Section 10.4 we put forward a kind of 'wish-list' of things that 'ought to be done' with respect to the teaching of figurative language. We did not consider what is actually being done in the average language classroom. It is not feasible for us to get inside a representative sample of different types of language classrooms from around the world, so we have done the next best thing and analysed eleven popular EFL textbooks published after 1994 and one set of internet materials, in order to evaluate how they deal with figurative language.

The writers appear to have taken three broad approaches towards the teaching of figurative language. The first is 'present figurative language as something special'. This is the most traditional approach, and involves treating figurative language, or more usually some *aspect* of figurative language, as something exotic and unusual. It results in dedicated books on 'idioms' or 'phrasal verbs and idioms'. The second approach is 'present conceptual metaphor', where sets of lessons are structured around conceptual metaphors. The third approach is 'attempt to integrate figurative language into the textbook'. This is the most challenging approach to teaching figurative language. It involves raising the learner's awareness of the possibilities that are opened by conceptual metaphor, as well as the phraseological restrictions that are imposed on many types of linguistic metaphor. We now look briefly at some examples of the types of material that each of these approaches has produced.

10.5.1 The 'present figurative language as something special' approach

As we said earlier, the 'present figurative language as something special' approach has resulted in the publication of textbooks where certain aspects of figurative language (usually idioms or phrasal verbs) are given a privileged status. These include, for example, Flower's (2002) *Phrasal Verb Organiser*, Wright's (2002) *Idioms Organiser*, Workman's (1995) *Making Headway Phrasal Verbs and Idioms*, and McCarthy and O'Dell's (2002) *English Idioms in Use*. Although these books are an encouraging testimony to the importance that is starting to be attached to the teaching of figurative language, they are slightly problematic in that they risk perpetuating the myth that idioms somehow lie 'outside' everyday language use, and are not an intrinsic form of everyday communication. Moreover, two of the books (*Phrasal Verb Organiser* and *Idioms Organiser*) make heavy use of decontextualised multiple-choice activities, which appear to 'test' rather than to 'teach' the idioms in question. One good feature of *Phrasal Verb Organiser* is that it introduces the phrasal verbs first by preposition, and then by subject, thus encouraging the prototype-based figurative thinking we discussed in Chapter 8. However, in general, neither of these books offers much guidance as to how learners might actually learn the idioms and phrasal verbs, and it is generally the learners' responsibility to decide how they are going to proceed. *Making*

Headway Phrasal Verbs and Idioms, which is designed to be used in conjunction with *Headway Advanced*, is slightly better. It begins with a detailed coverage of multiword items, with a heavy focus on multiword verbs, rather than other types of idiom. Unfortunately, many of the exercises involve multiple choice, matching and meaning-guessing activities, so there are few opportunities for in depth learning. On the other hand, the book does contain some relatively authentic functional activities, in which the learners are encouraged to use idiomatic expressions, for example to discuss the merits of a play, or to write letters of complaint. There are a number of listening activities too, but the language in these is somewhat inauthentic, to allow for the inclusion of an unnaturally high density of multiword verbs.

English Idioms in Use provides more contextualised activities, and includes extensive coverage of the types of functions that idioms are used to perform, as well as suggesting follow-up activities that invite the learner to consider possible figurative extensions to core vocabulary items. It even includes a set of concordance lines for the word 'eye', and asks the reader to infer the metonymic uses. Activities such as these covertly provide the learner with subtle guidance in the use of a range of strategies designed to raise their figurative language awareness. It would be good to see more activities of this type.

One criticism that has been levelled at *English Idioms in Use*, which has also been made of other books designed to teach idioms, relates to its use of line diagrams to draw attention to the source domains of the idioms. MacArthur (2005) criticises the diagram used to illustrate the idiom 'flew off the handle' on page 91. This diagram features a small, inoffensive looking bird, sitting on a door handle, and as such, it does not convey any of the anger inherent in the idiom. MacArthur wonders why the illustrator did not choose to draw a more angry looking bird, or perhaps an axe-head flying dangerously off its handle, as this would serve as a more powerful mnemonic device. This is not a trivial point, as we saw in Chapter 2 that the use of more appropriate images leads to better learning. However, to be fair to McCarthy and O'Dell, this criticism cannot easily be made of many of the other, much more appropriate, diagrams used in the book. MacArthur also criticises Gude and Duckworth's (1998) *Proficiency Masterclass* for the same thing, and here the criticism seems much more justified. It uses a number of 'cute' line diagrams of animals, similar to those that might appear in children's storybooks, to illustrate idioms such as 'a snake in the grass' and 'a cold fish'. It would have been more appropriate to use a more dangerous looking snake (that is actually pictured in some grass) and perhaps a dead fish. Although not all illustrators are guilty of providing misleading diagrams MacArthur's message is an important one: if illustrations are intended to serve as mnemonic devices, then they should be well drawn, and convey the actual connotations of the idioms that they are supposed to represent.

10.5.2 The 'conceptual metaphor' approach

The second approach to the teaching of figurative language is to take Lakoff's theory of conceptual metaphor and apply it directly to materials production. We are aware of two attempts that have been made to do this. The first is Lazar's (2003) book *Meanings and Metaphors* and the second is a series of downloadable lessons (Clandfield, 2003). Both publications are similar in that they offer a series of photocopiable vocabulary lessons, each of which is structured round a conceptual metaphor, such as ANGER IS HEAT, or TIME IS MONEY. A positive feature of both these publications is that they embrace the idea of conceptual metaphors, thus emphasising the fact that metaphor underlies a great deal of everyday language. These materials reflect what Danesi (1995) describes as a 'conceptual' syllabus, in that they have designated units of study centred around conceptual domains (love, time, etc.). They should therefore, according to Danesi, enable language learners to go beyond grammatical and communicative proficiency, gain access to the target language community, and think like a native speaker. This all sounds very promising, but if we look more closely at the actual materials, it soon becomes apparent that they are unlikely to live up to this promise, because the language that they contain has a tendency to be somewhat artificial. *Meanings and Metaphors* in particular contains a number of texts that are artificially crammed full of metaphoric expressions, making them sound extremely unnatural. Moreover, apart from a couple of chapters on advertising in *Meanings and Metaphors*, emphasising the persuasive function of metaphor, little consideration is given to the functions that figurative language can serve, or to the ways in which different types of figurative language work together to perform these functions. Furthermore, little consideration is given to the phraseological aspects of linguistic metaphor, except for a number of decontextualised, dictionary-based examples in Clandfield. As we have seen throughout the previous chapters, figurative language can also operate as a surface-level phenomenon that is not easily explained by conceptual accounts, and these publications do not seem to take this into account.

10.5.3 The 'attempt to integrate figurative language into the textbook' approach

In some textbooks, a real attempt has been made to integrate figurative language throughout the book. For example Soars and Soars's (2003) *New Headway Advanced* contains a number of activities that involve figurative thinking. For example, learners are encouraged to make figurative extensions of word meaning (ibid.: p. 95), work out the meanings of proverbs (ibid.: p. 52) interpret poetry (ibid., p. 53) and work out the meaning of idioms (ibid.: p. 108). There is also a chapter entirely devoted to the teaching of 'metaphors and idioms, real and unreal tense usage, and hedging devices' (ibid.: pp 71–80), which begins with a discussion of the everyday nature of art and creativity. This could presumably be used to reinforce the message that metaphor is nothing special, and that it is no different from everyday language. One criticism of *New Headway Advanced* is that the figurative language activities usually occur in the context of some sort of 'language focus' activity at the end of a chapter, and there is not always adequate consideration of the functions that this type of language can serve.

This criticism cannot be made of McCarthy and O'Dell's (2002) *Advanced English Vocabulary in Use*, which foregrounds the importance of metaphor and cultural associations in the introductory chapters, and which then goes onto provide good coverage of linguistic metaphor, as well as making use of a number of conceptual metaphors in the subsequent chapters. For example, in the chapter on 'War and Peace' (ibid. p. 114), examples are given of a number of expressions involving the source domain of WAR. For example, they talk of the government *waging war on* drunken driving, and the Paparazzi *besieging the Princess's home*. Similar treatment is given in another chapter to the source domain of WEATHER, where learners are encouraged to guess the meaning of metaphorically extended weather terms, from a series of short contexts. The text switches smoothly between literal and metaphorical uses of the terms, thus imitating naturally occurring spoken discourse.

Another book that attempts to incorporate figurative language throughout is *Cambridge New Advanced English* (Jones, 1998). This book has a section at the end of each chapter on idioms, which sometimes covers phrasal verbs or collocations, and which corresponds to the theme of the unit. The structure of this section is the same for each unit. Learners are given a series of sentences containing an idiom, and a box containing the corresponding paraphrases for the idioms. They then have to match the idioms with the paraphrases. Whilst it is encouraging to see that these sections appear at the end of every chapter, there does not seem to be much evidence of recycling of the language that they contain. Many of the activities have a multiple-choice format, and some of the items are somewhat opaque, making it difficult in many cases for the learner to predict the right answer. For example, in one activity, the learners are asked to choose between the words 'keep', 'hold', 'stand' and 'turn' in order to complete sentences, such as: ' We were disappointed when they ... down our offer'; 'In an emergency, try to ... your head'; 'If you really want to do that, I won't ... in your way'; and 'He's feeling lonely and upset, will you be able to keep him company'. No guidance is given about how the senses of these words have been figuratively extended from their more basic senses. It is presumably up to the teacher to explain the relationship and to provide opportunities for more meaningful processing of the items. One way in which these activities could be improved would be to accompany them with the sorts of diagrams favoured by cognitive linguists (see Chapter 8), which show the extended meanings of the words 'keep', 'hold', 'stand' and 'turn'.

At first sight, our brief textbook survey is encouraging, as attempts are being made to introduce different kinds of figurative language, with some concern for phraseological, conceptual and functional issues. On the other hand, all of the publications mentioned in this section are *advanced* or *upper-intermediate* level textbooks. To the best of our knowledge, there is practically no coverage of figurative language at lower levels. This is a shame, as an ability to extend the vocabulary one has in a figurative way can bring a number of benefits even to low-level learners: first, it can allow them to talk about topics that they may previously have felt they lacked the vocabulary for; second, they can use it to perform a number of important communicative functions; and third, it gives them important insights into the target language culture. Taking these three advantages together, we might conclude that allowing learners to experiment with the figurative potential of the target language is likely to accelerate their learning. The challenge now is to produce a textbook for lower-level learners, which provides examples of authentic figurative language, as well as opportunities for figurative thinking, but which remains accessible to learners. This is a daunting task, but we are nevertheless throwing down the gauntlet.

10.6 Coverage of figurative language in learner dictionaries and reference materials

Writers of learner dictionaries have made efforts to incorporate recent metaphor research. For example, the *MacMillan English Dictionary for*

Advanced Learners includes a series of forty special features on conceptual metaphor. Positioned within entries for ordinary dictionary headwords, they consist of boxes containing examples of words and phrases that reflect certain conceptual metaphors. These examples are largely authentic and corpus-driven, and the conceptual metaphors themselves were selected for their productivity, accessibility and structural simplicity (Moon, 2004). This constitutes a radical departure from traditional lexicographical approaches to metaphor, and provides a good way of combining the best aspects of both conceptual and linguistic approaches to metaphor. Unfortunately, the explanations do not extend beyond the forty 'specially enhanced' entries, so a user would not know, for example, whether an economic boom was a metaphoric transfer from a sound boom.

A useful reference work on metaphor for learners of English is Deignan's (1995) *Collins Cobuild Guide to Metaphor*. This book is divided into twelve sections, each covering a broad domain, such as the human body, health and illness, and animals. Each of these sections contains a number of metaphoric expressions that contain vocabulary from these domains, and the examples are all taken from the Bank of English so they are relatively frequent in English, and bear authentic phraseology. One problem with Deignan's book is that it is difficult to see how it might be put to practical use, for example by a learner who has to write an essay on a given topic and would like to use some figurative language in their essay. The reason for this is that the expressions in the book are listed according to their source domain, rather than their target domain.[2] For example, the metaphorical expression 'the athlete was clearly in a bullish mood' appears under the subheading 'bull' in the chapter on animals, and 'a paralysed economy' appears under the subheading 'paralysed' in the chapter on physical disability. It would be useful to have a reference book where figurative expressions are grouped under target domains, rather than source domains, so that a learner who has been asked to write on a particular topic can easily access figurative expressions that are relevant to that topic. Three or four conceptual metaphors that tend to be associated with the particular target domain could be listed under each chapter, and expressions that reflect these conceptual metaphors could be grouped together. Such a book would be similar, in terms of format, to the *Longman Activator* (Summers, 1993), but would be more structured, as it would focus on a limited number of conceptual metaphors and metonymies per entry, and the figurative motivation of the expressions would be more apparent to the learner. Again, we are throwing down the gauntlet.

10.7 Conclusion

In this book, we have described figurative thinking, assessed the extent to which it is involved in foreign language learning and communicative language ability, and suggested ways in which it might be promoted in the language classroom by drawing on a number of different theories of foreign language learning. Our focus on the functions served by figurative language has obliged us to look at functional/pragmatic aspects of language learning. Our focus on grammar and on language learning strategies has meant looking at the more cognitive aspects, foregrounding the close relationship between language learning and our daily interactions with our environment. Finally, our focus on mediation and mediated learning, and the idea of learners working together to develop their understanding of figurative language, has involved looking at socio-cultural aspects of language learning. This eclecticism reflects the complex, multifaceted, and somewhat slippery, nature of figurative language. Teaching figurative language will never be easy, but we hope to have provided a few pointers in this book, and brought at least a little light into these rather murky waters.

Notes

1 What is 'figurative thinking'?

1. By learning, we mean the ability to recall the form and content across time, and/or the ability to interpret an utterance containing it and/or the ability to use it appropriately in an utterance. Learning may occur as a result of direct instruction. It may also occur when the teacher was in fact trying to teach something completely different, or as the result of more general exposure to the target language. When this is the case, we will talk about 'incidental learning'. Where a strategy or general skill is taught, the boundaries between 'learning' and 'incidental learning' are somewhat blurred.
2. 'Ergo figura sit arte aliqua novata forma dicendi' (Quintilian, IX, i, II).

2 Why is figurative thinking important for foreign language learners?

1. Our basic sense is roughly equivalent to Verspoor and Lowie's 'core' sense, as it allows for folk etymology to replace an original basic sense.
2. There was not full agreement about the nature of inferencing in the 1970s and 1980s; Ellis (1986: pp. 174–175), for example, restricted inferencing to two procedures, both *subconscious*.

4 Developing learner autonomy in figurative thinking

1. This is of course our shorthand for the probabilistic 'decide on balance that a certain expression is worth treating as figurative', as there is no guarantee that a native speaker or a linguist would see the expression as clearly figurative.
2. *Wuzhi* means five fingers in Chinese and the mountains resemble an outstretched hand with five fingers. Metaphorically, it means slapping someone's face, and possibly leaving a red mark.
3. This is a personality model which can be used to identify personality types along four continua: extravert/introvert; sensing/intuition; thinking/feeling; and judging/perceiving (see Ehrman, 1996 for more detail). It is not without its critics (e.g., Paul, 2004) who argue that it has not been extensively validated, and that it is based on a misinterpretation of Jungian psychology.

5 Figurative thinking and sociolinguistic competence

1. Here, we are using 'schemata' as it is generally understood in linguistics and mainstream psychology. This should not be confused with the cognitive semantic notion of 'image-schemata'.

2. We are excluding non-metaphorical cultural models, partly for reasons of relevance to the chapter and partly because their relationship with metaphorical models remains unclear (Emanatian, 1999: p. 205).
3. In the 1936 play written with Christopher Isherwood, 'The Ascent of F6'.
4. Register derives from systemic functional linguistics and is essentially a functional variety of language. Like a dialect it involves a group of participants (specialists) and is often associated with a specific mode (e.g., writing) and level of formality. Unlike a dialect, a register will normally have a topic and a purpose/function. The problem is that register can be interpreted very broadly, like 'the language of physical science' (Halliday, 1988) or very narrowly (Wales, 2001), like the language of physics journal editorials. This overlaps in a confusing way with the concept of genre. To Wales (2001) genres are 'groups of texts', to Martin (1998) they are social purposes and to Swales (1990) a genre is 'a class of communicative event' which has a form, constraints and a structure: an 'enacted discourse'. We follow Swales here.

7   Figurative thinking and textual competence

1. The Pragglejaz group is an informal group of metaphor researchers from various disciplines in linguistics, who are pursuing the reliable and valid identification of metaphor in natural discourse. See http://letlx.let.vu.nl/project/pragglejaz/
2. The italics here represent Cameron and Stelma's identification of metaphor vehicles. The terms in bold face are added by us to highlight relevant terms.
3. Technically, Corts and Pollio reported that gestural and figurative clusters (or 'bursts') overlapped.
4. The authors would like to thank Celia Roberts of Kings College, London and Director of the Patients with Limited English and Doctors in General Practice (PLEDGE) project, who kindly gave permission to use the data in this extract.

8   Figurative thinking and lexico-grammatical competence

1. Strictly speaking, 'He referred to John' is prepositional not phrasal, because you cannot move 'to' (* 'He referred John to') but you *can* add an adverb ('He referred repeatedly to John') (Quirk and Greenbaum, 1973: p. 348).
2. Some theorists postulate a third category, sometimes called 'dynamic modality', which is more subject-oriented. For example, 'Oscar can swim' refers to one of Oscar's abilities; it does not give information about the speaker's attitude. The exclusion of dynamic modality from Sweetser's theory limits its usefulness in the language classroom.
3. Grammatical metaphor also includes the more interpersonal 'metaphors of mood', but we do not discuss these here.
4. Our thanks to Susan Hunston for the example.

10   Promoting figurative language competence in the foreign language classroom

1. Other writers would probably classify role-play as a task of some sort. For example, Cameron (2001) would do so if the work was focused and had a goal, and Doughty and Long (2003) would treat it as a pedagogic task leading towards a more authentic 'target' task.
2. Rosamund Moon (personal communication).

References

Alexander, R. J. (1983) 'Metaphors, Connotations, Allusions: Thoughts on the Language-Culture Connexion in Learning English as a Foreign Language', L.A.U.T. Papers, Series B, No. 91 (Trier: University of Trier).

Allbritton, D., McKoon, G. and Gerrig, R. (1995) 'Metaphor-Based Schemas and Text Representations: Making Connections Through Conceptual Metaphors', *Journal of Experimental Psychology: Learning, Memory and Cognition*, 21 (3), 612–625.

Arleo, A. (2000) 'Life Cycles, Chaos and Zoom Lenses: A Comparative Analysis of some Conceptual Metaphors in the Discourse of Entrepreneurship Theory', *Anglais Specifique*, 27 (30), 19–31.

Athanasiadou, A. (2004) 'Teaching Temporal Connectors and Their Prototypical Non-Temporal Extensions', in M. Achard and S. Niemeier (eds), *Cognitive Linguistics and Foreign Language Teaching* (Berlin/New York: Mouton de Gruyter), pp. 195–210.

Atwood, M. (2003) *Negotiating with the Dead* (London: Virago).

Auden, W. H. (1936) 'Funeral Blues', published as 'Song IX' in *Twelve Songs* (Princeton, NJ: Princeton University Press).

Auden, W. H. and Isherwood, C. (1936) *The Ascent of F6: A Tragedy in Two Acts* (London: Faber and Faber).

BBC (2005) 'Word for Word 1', broadcast on BBC4, August 3.

Bachman, L. (1990) *Fundamental Considerations in Language Testing* (New York: Oxford University Press).

Bachman, L. F. and Palmer, A. (1996) *Language Testing in Practice* (New York: Oxford University Press).

Bahns, J. and Eldaw, M. (1993) 'Should We Teach EFL Students Collocations?', *System*, 21 (1), 101–114.

Barcelona, A. (2001) 'On the Systematic Contrastive Analysis of Conceptual Metaphors', in M. Putz, S. Niemeier and R. Dirven (eds), *Applied Cognitive Linguistics II: Language Pedagogy* (Berlin: Mouton de Gruyter), pp. 117–146.

Beebe L. M. (1983) 'Risk-Taking and the Language Learner', in H. Seliger and M. Long (eds), *Classroom Oriented Research in Second Language Acquisition* (Rowley, MA: Newbury House), pp. 39–66.

Bell, N. D. (2005) 'Exploring L2 Language Play as an Aid to SLL: A Case Study of Humour in NS-NNS Interaction', *Applied Linguistics*, 26 (2), 192–218.

Bialystok, E. (1983) 'Some Factors in the Selection and Implementation of Communication Strategies', in C. Faerch and G. Kasper (eds), *Strategies in Interlanguage Communication* (Harlow: Longman), pp. 100–118.

Black, M. (1962) 'Metaphor', in M. Black (ed.), *Models and Metaphors* (Ithaca, NY: Cornell University Press), pp. 25–47.

Black, M. (1979) 'More about Metaphor', in A. Ortony (ed.), *Metaphor and Thought*, 2nd edn (Cambridge: Cambridge University Press), pp. 19–41.

Bloomer, M. and Hodkinson, P. (2000), 'Learning Careers: Continuity and Change in Young People's Dispositions to Learning', *British Educational Research Journal*, 26, 583–597.

Boers, F. (1997) 'No Pain No Gain in a Free-Market Rhetoric: A Test for Cognitive Semantics?', *Metaphor and Symbol*, 12 (4), 231–241.

Boers, F. (1999) 'When a Bodily Source Domain Becomes Prominent. The Joy of Counting Metaphors in the Socio-Economic Domain', in R. W. Gibbs and G. J. Steen (eds), *Metaphor in Cognitive Linguistics* (Amsterdam: John Benjamins), pp. 47–56.

Boers, F. (2000a) 'Enhancing Metaphoric Awareness in Specialised Reading', *English for Specific Purposes*, 19, 137–147.

Boers, F. (2000b) 'Metaphor Awareness and Vocabulary Retention', *Applied Linguistics*, 21 (4), 553–571.

Boers, F. (2001) 'Remembering Figurative Idioms by Hypothesizing about their Origin', *Prospect*, 16 (3), 35–43.

Boers, F. (2004) 'Expanding Learners' Vocabulary Through Metaphor Awareness: What Expansion, What Learners, What Vocabulary?', in M. Achard and S. Niemeier (eds), *Cognitive Linguistics and Foreign Language Teaching* (Berlin/New York: Mouton de Gruyter), pp. 211–232.

Boers, F. and Demecheleer, M. (1995) 'Travellers, Patients and Warriors in English, Dutch and French Economic Discourse', *Revue Belge de Philosophie et d'Histoire*, 73, 673–691.

Boers, F. and Demecheleer, M. (1998) 'A Cognitive Semantic Approach to Teaching Prepositions', *English Language Teaching Journal*, 52 (3), 197–203.

Boers, F. and Demecheleer, M. (2001) 'Measuring the Impact of Cross-Cultural Differences on Learners' Comprehension of Imageable Idioms', *English Language Teaching Journal*, 55 (3), 255–262.

Boers, F. and Littlemore, J. (2000) 'Cognitive Style Variables in Participants' Explanations of Conceptual Metaphors', *Metaphor and Symbol*, 15 (3), 177–187.

Boers, F., Demecheleer, M. and Eyckmans, J. (2004a) 'Etymological Elaboration as a Strategy for Learning Figurative Idioms', in P. Bogaards and B. Laufer (eds), *Vocabulary in a Second Language: Selection, Acquisition and Testing* (Amsterdam/Philadelphia: John John Benjamins Press), pp. 53–78.

Boers, F., Demecheleer, M. and Eyckmans, J. (2004b) 'Cultural Variation as a Variable in Comprehending and Remembering Figurative Idioms', *European Journal of English Studies*, 8 (3), 375–388.

Boers, F., Eyckmans, J. and Stengers, H. (forthcoming) 'Presenting Figurative Idioms with a Touch of Etymology: More than Mnemonics?', *Language Teaching Research*.

Bortfeld, H. (2003) 'Comprehending Idioms Cross-Linguistically', *Experimental Psychology*, 50 (3), 217–230.

Bottini G., Corcoran R., Sterzi R., Schenone P., Scarpa, P., Frackowiak, R. S. J. and Frith, C. D. (1994) 'The Role of the Right Hemisphere in the Interpretation of Figurative Aspects of Language: A Positron Emission Tomography Activation Study', *Brain*, 117 (2), 1241–1250.

Briggs, C. L. (1986) *Learning How to Ask: A Sociolinguistic Appraisal of the Role of the Interview in Social Science Research* (Cambridge: Cambridge University Press).

Broner, M. (2001) 'Impact of Interlocutor and Task on First and Second Language Use in a Spanish Immersion Program', CARLA Working Paper 18 (Minneapolis, MN: Center for Advanced Research on Language Acquisition).

Brontë, C. (1853/1979) *Villette*, M. Lilly (ed.) (Harmondsworth: Penguin).

Brown R. (1958) *Words and Things* (Glencoe, Illinois: Free Press).

Brugman, C. (1981) *The Story of Over*, MA thesis (University of California: Berkeley).

Butt, D., Fahey, R., Feez, S., Spinks, S. and Yallop, C. (2000) *Using Functional Grammar: an Explorer's Guide* (Macquarie University: National Centre for English Language Teaching and Research).

Butterworth, G. and Hatch, E. (1978) 'A Spanish-Speaking Adolescent's Acquisition of English Syntax', in E. Hatch (ed.), *Second Language Acquisition: A Book of Readings* (Rowley, MA: Newbury House).

Bybee, J., Perkins, R. and Pagliuca, W. (1994) *The Evolution of Grammar: Tense, Aspect and Modality in the Languages of the World* (Chicago: University of Chicago Press).

Caillois, R. (1961) *Man, Play and Games* (Translated by M. Barash) (New York: Free Press of Glencoe).

Cameron, L. (2001) *Teaching Languages to Young Learners* (Cambridge: Cambridge University Press).

Cameron, L. (2002) 'Towards a Metaphor-Led Discourse', Workshop presented at the conference on 'Metaphor in Language and Thought' (October), Sao Paulo, Brazil.

Cameron, L. (2003) *Metaphor in Educational Discourse* (London: Continuum).

Cameron, L. and Deignan, A. (2003) 'Using Large and Small Corpora to Investigate Tuning Devices Around Metaphor in Spoken Discourse', *Metaphor and Symbol*, 18 (3), 149–160.

Cameron, L. and Low, G. D. (1999a) 'Metaphor. State of the Art Survey', *Language Teaching*, 32 (2), 77–96.

Cameron, L. and Low, G. D. (2004) 'Figurative Variation in Episodes of Educational Talk and Text', *European Journal of English Studies*, 8 (3), 355–374.

Cameron, L. and Stelma, J. (2005) 'Metaphor Clusters in Discourse: Methodological Issues', *Journal of Applied Linguistics*, 1 (2), 107–136.

Canale, M. (1983) 'From Communicative Competence to Communicative Language Teaching Pedagogy', in J. C. Richards and R. W. Schmidt (eds), *Language and Communication* (London: Longman).

Canale, M. and Swain, M. (1980) 'Theoretical Bases of Communicative Approaches to Second Language Teaching and Testing', *Applied Linguistics* 1 (1), 1–47.

Cano Mora, L. (2005) 'On the Verge of Impossibility: A Conversational and Discourse Approach to Hyperbole in Interaction', in Otal Campo, J. L., Ferrando, I. N. I. and Fortuño, B. B. (eds), *Cognitive and Discourse Approaches to Metaphor and Metonymy* (Castello de la Plana: Universitat Jaume I), pp. 175–186.

Carroll, J. B. (1993) *Human Cognitive Abilities. A Survey of Factor-Analytic Studies* (Cambridge: Cambridge University Press).

Carter, R. (2004) *Language and Creativity: The Art of Common Talk* (London: Routledge).

Carter, R. and McCarthy, M. (1995) 'Discourse and Creativity: Bridging the Gap Between Language and Literature', G. Cook and B. Seidlhofer (eds), *Principle and Practice in Applied Linguistics* (Oxford: Oxford University Press), pp. 303–320.

Carter, R. and McCarthy, M. (2004) 'Talking, Creating: Interactional Language, Creativity and Context', *Applied Linguistics*, 25 (1), 62–88.

Carton, A. (1971) 'Inferencing: A Process in Using and Learning Language', in P. Pimsleur and T. Quinn (eds), *The Psychology of Second Language Learning* (Cambridge: Cambridge University Press), pp. 45–58.

Cekaite, A. and Aronsson, K. (2005) 'Language Play, a Collaborative Resource in Children's L2 Learning', *Applied Linguistics*, 26 (2), pp. 169–191.

Channell, J. (1999) 'Corpus Analysis of Evaluative Lexis', in S. Hunston and G. Thompson (eds), *Evaluation in Text* (Oxford: Oxford University Press).

Charles, M. and Charles, D. (1999) 'Sales Negotiations: Bargaining Through Tactical Summaries', in M. Hewings and C. Nickerson (eds), *Business English: Research into Practice* (Harlow: Longman), pp. 72–83.

Charteris-Black, J. (2002) 'Second Language Figurative Proficiency: A Comparative Study of Malay and English', *Applied Linguistics*, 23, 104–133.

Charteris-Black, J. (2005) *Politicians & Rhetoric: The Persuasive Power of Metaphor* (London: Palgrave Macmillan).

Chiappe, D. L. and Kennedy, J. M. (2000) 'Are Metaphors Elliptical Similes?', *Journal of Psycholinguistic Research*, 29 (4), 371–398.

Chilton, P. (1994) ' "La Plaie qu'il Convient de Fermer ...": Les Métaphores du Discours Raciste', *Journal of Pragmatics*, 21 (6), 583–619.

Chilton, P. (1996) *Security Metaphors: Cold War Discourse from Containment to Common European Home* (Berne/New York: Peter Lang).

Clandfield, L. (2003) 'Vocabulary: Metaphor', available online at http://www.onestopenglish.com

Clark, E. V. (1981) 'Lexical Innovations: How Children Learn to Create New Words', in W. Deutsch (ed.), *The Child's Construction of Language* (London: Academic Press), pp. 299–328.

Clark, E. V. (1982) 'The Young Word Maker: A Case Study of Innovation in the Child's Lexicon', in E. Wanner and L. R. Gleitman (eds), *Language Acquisition: State of the Art* (Cambridge: Cambridge University Press), pp. 390–428.

Cook, G. (1997a) 'Schema', *ELT Journal*, 51 (1), 86.

Cook, G. (1997b) 'Language Play, Language Learning', *English Language Teaching Journal*, 51, 224–231.

Cook, G. (2000) *Language Play, Language Learning* (Oxford: Oxford University Press).

Corbett, E. P. J. (1990) *Classical Rhetoric for the Modern Student* (New York: Oxford University Press).

Corts, D. P. (1999) 'Spontaneous Production of Figurative Language and Gestures in College Lectures: A Comparison Across Disciplines', Unpublished PhD dissertation (Knoxville: University of Tennessee).

Corts, D. P. and Meyers, K. (2002) 'Conceptual Clusters in Figurative Language Production', *Journal of Psycholinguistic Research*, 31 (4), 391–408.

Corts, D. P. and Pollio, H. R. (1999) 'Spontaneous Production of Figurative Language and Gesture in College Lectures', *Metaphor and Symbol*, 14 (2), 81–100.

Cotterill, J. (2003) *Language and Power in Court: A Linguistic Analysis of the O. J. Simpson Trial* (London: Palgrave Macmillan).

Craik, F. I. M. and Lockhart, R. S. (1982) 'Levels of Processing: A Framework for Memory Research', *Journal of Verbal Learning and Verbal Behaviour*, 11, 671–684.

Dam, L. (1995) *Learner Autonomy 3: From Theory to Classroom Practice* (Dublin: Authentik Language Learning Resources).

Dam, L. (2000) 'Evaluating Autonomous Learning', in B. Sinclair, I. McGrath and T. Lamb (eds), *Learner Autonomy, Teacher Autonomy: Future Directions* (Harlow: Pearson Education), pp. 48–59.

Danesi, M. (1986) 'The Role of Metaphor in Second Language Pedagogy', *Rassegna Italiana di Linguistica Applicata*, 18 (3), 1–10.

Danesi, M. (1992a) 'Metaphorical Competence in Second Language Acquisition and Second Language Teaching: The Neglected Dimension', in J. E. Alatis (ed.), *Language Communication and Social Meaning* (Washington, DC: Georgetown University Round Table on Languages and Linguistics), pp. 489–500.

Danesi, M. (1992b) 'Metaphor and Classroom Second Language Learning', *Romance Language Annual*, 3, 73–86.

Danesi, M. (1995) 'Learning and Teaching Languages: The Role of 'Conceptual Fluency', *International Journal of Applied Linguistics*, 5 (1), 3–20.

Deignan, A. (1995) *Collins Cobuild English Guides 7: Metaphor* (London: Harper Collins).

Deignan, A. (1999a) 'Linguistic Metaphors and Collocation in Non-Literary Corpus Data', *Metaphor and Symbol*, 14 (1), 19–36.

Deignan, A. (1999b) 'Corpus-Based Research into Metaphor', in L. Cameron and G. D. Low (eds), *Researching and Applying Metaphor* (Cambridge: Cambridge University Press), pp. 177–199.

Deignan, A. (2003) 'Metaphorical Expressions and Culture: an Indirect Link', *Metaphor and Symbol*, 18 (4), 255–272.

Deignan, A. (2005) *Metaphor and Corpus Linguistics* (London: John Benjamins).

Deignan, A. and Potter, L. (2004) 'A Corpus Study of Metaphors and Metonyms in English and Italian', *Journal of Pragmatics*, 36, 1231–1252.

Deignan, A., Gabrys, D. and Solska, A. (1997) 'Teaching English Metaphors Using Cross-Linguistic Awareness-Raising Activities', *English Language Teaching Journal*, 51 (4), 352–360.

Dirven, R. (1994) *Metaphor and Nation: Metaphors Afrikaners Live By* (Frankfurt Am Mein: Peter Lang).

Dirven, R. (1985) 'Metaphor as a Basic Means for Extending the Lexicon', in D. Paprotte and R. Dirven (eds), *The Ubiquity of Metaphor* (Amsterdam: John Benjamins), pp. 85–119.

Dirven, R. (2001) 'English Phrasal Verbs: Theory and Didactic Application', in M. Putz, S. Niemeier and R. Dirven (eds), *Applied Cognitive Linguistics II: Language Pedagogy* (Berlin: Mouton de Gruyter), pp. 3–27.

Dörnyei, Z. (2005) *The Psychology of the Language Learner* (Hillsdale, NJ: Lawrence Erlbaum).

Doughty, C. and Long, M. H. (2003) 'Optimal Psycholinguistic Environments for Distance Foreign Language Learning', *Language Learning and Technology*, 7 (3), 50–80. Available online at http://llt.msu.edu/vol7num3/doughty/default.htm

Douglas, D. (2000) *Assessing Languages for Specific Purposes* (Cambridge: Cambridge University Press).

Drew, P. and Holt, E. (1988) 'Complainable Matters: The Use of Idiomatic Expressions in Making Complaints', *Social Problems*, 35 (4), 398–417.

Drew, P. and Holt, E. (1995) 'Idiomatic Expressions and their Role in the Organisation of Topic Transition in Conversation', in M. Everaert, E-J. van der Linden, A. Schenk and R. Schreuder (eds), *Idioms: Structural and Psychological Perspectives* (Hillsdale, NJ: Lawrence Erlbaum), pp. 117–132.

Drew, P. and Holt, E. (1998) 'Figures of Speech: Figurative Expressions and the Management of Topic Transition in Conversation', *Language and Society*, 27, 495–522.

Dudley-Evans, A. T. and Johns T. F. (1981) 'A Team Teaching Approach to Lecture Comprehension for Overseas Students', *The Teaching of Listening Comprehension (ELT Documents Special)* (London: British Council), pp. 30–46.

Dudeney, G. (2000) *The Internet and the Language Classroom: A Practical Guide for Teachers* (Cambridge: Cambridge University Press).

Eco, U. (1979) *The Role of the Reader* (Bloomington: Indiana University Press).

(The) Economist (1988) 'What the Squid Did', 11 June, p. 129.

Ehrman, M. (1996) *Understanding Second Language Learning Difficulties* (Thousand Oaks, CA: Sage).

Ehrman, M. and Dörnyei, Z. (1998) *Interpersonal Dynamics in Second Language Education. The Visible and Invisible Classroom* (London: Sage).

Elbers, L. (1988) 'New Names from Old Words: Related Aspects of Children's Metaphors and Word Compounds', *Journal of Child Language*, 15, 591–617.

Ellis, N. (1994) 'Implicit and Explicit Language Learning: an Overview', in N. Ellis (ed.), *Implicit and Explicit Learning of Languages* (London: Academic Press), pp. 1–32.

Ellis, R. (1986) *Understanding Second Language Acquisition* (Oxford: Oxford University Press).

Ely, C. (1986) 'An Analysis of Discomfort, Risk-Taking, Sociability and Motivation in the L2 Classroom', *Language Learning*, 36 (1), 1–25.

Ely, C. (1989) 'Tolerance of Ambiguity and Use of Second Language Strategies', *Foreign Language Annals*, 22 (5), 437–445.

Emanatian, M. (1999) 'Congruence by Degree: On the Relation between Metaphor and Cultural Models', in R. W. Gibbs and G. J. Steen (eds), *Metaphor in Cognitive Linguistics* (Amsterdam: John Benjamins), pp. 205–218.

Evans, R. and Evans, G. (1989) 'Cognitive Mechanisms in Learning from Metaphors', *Journal of Experimental Education*, 58 (1), 5–20.

Fainsilber, L. and Ortony, A. (1987) 'Metaphorical Uses of Language in the Expression of Emotions', *Metaphor and Symbolic Activity*, 2, 239–250.

Fauconnier, G. and Turner, M. (1998) 'Conceptual Integration Networks', *Cognitive Science*, 22 (2), 133–187.

Flower, J. (2002) *Phrasal Verb Organiser* (Boston, MA: Thomson Heinle).

Flowerdew, J. and Miller, L. (1995) 'On the Notion of Culture in L2 Lectures', *TESOL Quarterly*, 29 (2), 345–373.

Flowerdew, J. and Peacock, M. (2001) 'The EAP Curriculum, Issues, Methods and Challenges, in J. Flowerdew and M. Peacock (eds), *Research Perspectives on English for Academic Purposes*. (Cambridge: Cambridge University Press).

Forceville, C. (2005) 'Visual Representations of the Idealized Cognitive Model of Anger in the Asterix Album, La Zizanie', *Journal of Pragmatics*, 37, 69–88.

Foster, P. (1998) 'A Classroom Perspective on the Negotiation of Meaning', *Applied Linguistics*, 19 (1), 1–23.

Fussell, S. R. and Moss, M. M. (1998) 'Figurative Language in Emotional Communication', in S. R. Fussell and R. J. Kreuz (eds), *Social and Cognitive Approaches to Interpersonal Communication* (Mahwah, NJ: Lawrence Erlbaum), pp. 1–29.

Gabrys-Biskup, D. (1992) 'L1 Influences on Learners' Renderings of English Collocations: A Polish/German Empirical Study', in P. Arnaud and H. Bejoint (eds) *Vocabulary and Applied Linguistics* (London: Macmillan), pp. 145–189.

Gentner, D. (1988) 'Structure-Mapping in Analogical Development: The Relational Shift', *Child Development*, 59, 47–59.

Gentner, D. and Bowdle, B. F. (2001) 'Convention, Form, and Figurative Language Processing', *Metaphor and Symbol*, 16, 223–247.

Gernsbacher, M. A. (1990) *Language Comprehension as Structure Building* (Hillsdale, NJ: Lawrence Erlbaum).

Gerrig, R. J. and Gibbs, R. (1988) 'Beyond the Lexicon: Creativity in Language Production', *Metaphor and Symbolic Activity*, 3 (1), 1–19.

Ghosn, I. (2002) 'Four Good Reasons to Use Literature in Primary School ELT', *English Language Teaching Journal*, 56 (2), 172–179.

Gibbs, R. W. (1993) 'Process and Products in Making Sense of Tropes', in A. Ortony (ed.), *Metaphor and Thought*, 2nd edn (Cambridge: Cambridge University Press), pp. 252–276.

Gibbs, R. W. (1994) *The Poetics of Mind* (Cambridge: Cambridge University Press).

Gibbs, R. W. (1995) 'Idiomaticity and Human Cognition', in M. Everaert, E-J. van der Linden, A. Schenk and R. Schreuder (eds), *Idioms: Structural and Psychological Perspectives* (Hillsdale, NJ: Lawrence Erlbaum), pp. 97–116.

Gibbs, R. W. (2001) 'Evaluating Contemporary Models of Figurative Language Understanding', *Metaphor and Symbol*, 16 (3 and 4), 317–333.

Gibbs, R. W. (2005) *Embodiment and Cognitive Science* (Cambridge: Cambridge University Press).

Gibbs, R. W. and Bogdonovich, J. (1999) 'Mental Imagery in Interpreting Poetic Metaphor', *Metaphor and Symbol*, 14, 37–44.

Gibbs, R. W. and Nascimento, S. B. (1996) 'How We Talk When We Talk About Love: Metaphorical Concepts and Understanding Love Poetry', in R. J. Kreuz and M. S. MacNealy (eds), *Empirical Approaches to Literature and Aesthetics* (Norwood, NJ: Ablex), pp. 293–307.

Gibbs, R. W. and O'Brien, J. (1990) 'Idioms and Mental Imagery: The Metaphorical Motivation for Idiomatic Meaning', *Cognition*, 36, 35–68.

Gineste, M.-D., Indurkhya, B. and Scart, V. (2000) 'Emergence of Features in Metaphor Comprehension', *Metaphor and Symbol*, 15 (3), 117–135.

Giora, R. (1997) 'Understanding Figurative and Literal Language: The Graded Salience Hypothesis', *Cognitive Linguistics*, 7, 183–206.

Giora, R. (2003) *On Our Mind. Salience, Context, and Figurative Language* (Oxford: Oxford University Press).

Glucksberg, S., Newsome, M. R. and Goldvarg, Y. (2001) 'Inhibition of the Literal: Filtering Metaphor-Irrelevant Information During Metaphor Comprehension', *Metaphor and Symbol*, 16 (3 and 4), 277–293.

Goatly, A. (1997) *The Language of Metaphors* (London: Routledge).

Goddard, C. (2004) 'The Ethnopragmatics and Semantics of Metaphors', *Journal of Pragmatics*, 36, 1211–1230.

Goodman, K. S. (1967) 'Reading: A Psycholinguistic Guessing Game', *Journal of the Reading Specialist*, 4, 126–135.

Goosens, L. (1990) 'Metaphtonomy: The Interaction of Metaphor and Metonymy in Expressions of Linguistic Action', *Cognitive Linguistics*, 1, 323–340.

Grady, J. (1998) 'The Conduit Metaphor Revisited: A Reassessment of Metaphors for Communication', in J. P. Koenig (ed.), *Conceptual Structure, Discourse and Language* 2 (Stanford, CA: CSLI), pp. 205–218.

Grady, J. and Johnson, C. (2002) 'Converging Evidence for the Notions of *Subscene* and *Primary Scene*', in R. Dirven and R. Pörings (eds), *Metaphor and Metonymy in Comparison and Contrast* (Berlin: Mouton de Gruyter), pp. 533–554.

Graesser, A., Mio, J. and Millis, K. (1988) 'Metaphors in Persuasive Communication', in D. Meutsch and R. Viehoff (eds), *Comprehension of Literary Discourse: Results and Problems of Interdisciplinary Approaches* (Berlin: De Gruyter), pp. 131–154.

Grant, L. and Bauer, L. (2004) 'Criteria for Redefining Idioms: Are we Barking Up the Wrong Tree?', *Applied Linguistics*, 25 (1), 38–61.

Grice (1975) 'Logic and Conversation', in P. Cole and J. L. Morgan (eds), *Syntax and Semantics, 3: Speech Acts* (New York: Academic Press), pp. 41–58.

Grundy, P. (2004) 'The Figure/Ground Gestalt and Language Teaching Methodology', in M. Achard and S. Niemeier (eds), *Cognitive Linguistics and Foreign Language Teaching* (Berlin/New York: Mouton de Gruyter), pp. 119–142.

Gude, R. and Duckworth, M. (1998) *Proficiency Masterclass* (Oxford: Oxford University Press).

Guillen-Galve, I. (1998) 'The Textual Interplay of Grammatical Metaphor on the Nominalizations Occurring in Written Medical English', *Journal of Pragmatics*, 30, 363–385.

Gyori, G. (2000) 'Semantic Change as Linguistic Interpretation of the World', in S. Niemeier and R. Dirven (eds), *Evidence for Linguistic Relativity* (Amsterdam: John Benjamins), pp. 71–89.

Halliday, M. A. K. (1985) *Spoken and Written Language* (Geelong: Deakin University Press).

Halliday, M. A. K. (1988) 'On the Language of Physical Science', in M. Ghadessy (ed.), *Registers of Written English: Situational Factors and Linguistic Features* (London/New York: Pinter), pp. 162–178.

Halliday, M. A. K. (1994) *An Introduction to Functional Grammar*, 2nd edn (London: Arnold).

Harris, R. J., Lahey, M. A. and Marsalek, F. (1980) 'Metaphors and Images: Rating, Reporting and Remarking', in R. P. Honeck and R. R. Hoffman (eds), *Cognition and Figurative Language* (Hillsdale, NJ: Lawrence Erlbaum), pp. 163–181.

Hassan, X., Macaro, E., Mason, D., Nye, G., Smith, P. and Vanderplank, R. (2005) 'Strategy Training in Language Learning – A Systematic Review of Available Research', *Research Evidence in Education Library* (London: Eppi-Centre, Social Science Research Unit, Institute of Education).

Hicks, H. and Gullet, C. (1975) *Organizations: Theory and Behaviour* (Tokyo: McGraw-Hill).

Hoey, M. (1983) *On the Surface of Discourse* (London: Allen and Unwin).

Holme, R. (2001) 'Metaphor, Language Learning and Affect', *Humanising Language Learning*, 3 (6), available at http://www.hltmag.co.uk/prev.asp

Holme, R. (2004) *Mind, Metaphor and Language Teaching* (London: Palgrave Macmillan).

Holyoak, K. and Thagard, P. (1995) *Mental Leaps: Analogy in Creative Thought* (Cambridge, MA: MIT Press/Bradford Books).

Hopper, P. and Traugott, E. (1993) *Grammaticalization* (Cambridge: Cambridge University Press).

Horst, M. (1996) *Review of E. Clark* The Lexicon in Acquisition (Cambridge: Cambridge University Press, 1993), Vocabulary Acquisition Research Group

Virtual Library, available at http://www.swan.ac.uk/cals/calsres/vlibrary/mh96a.htm

Howarth, P. (1996) *Phraseology in English Academic Writing*, Lexicographica Series Major, 75 (Tubingen: Niemeyer).

Hulstijn, J. H. (2003) 'Incidential and Intentional Learning', in C. J. Doughty and M. H. Long (eds), *The Handbook of Second Language Acquisition* (Oxford: Blackwell), pp. 349–381.

Hymes, D. (1971) *On Communicative Competence* (Philadelphia: University of Pennsylvania Press).

Irujo, S. (1993) 'Steering Clear: Avoidance in the production of Idioms', *International Review Of Applied Linguistics*, 31 (3), 205–219.

Jackson, D. O. (2001) 'Language-Related Episodes', *English Language Teaching Journal*, 55 (3), 298–299.

Johnson, J. and Rosano, T. (1993) 'Relation of Cognitive Style to Metaphor Interpretation and Second Language Proficiency', *Applied Psycholinguistics*, 14, 159–175.

Jones, L. (1998) *Cambridge New Advanced English* (Cambridge: Cambridge University Press).

Katz, A. N. (1983) 'What Does it Mean to be a High Imager?', in J. C. Yuille (ed.), *Imagery, Memory and Cognition* (Hillsdale, NJ: Lawrence Erlbaum), pp. 39–63.

Katz, A. N., Paivio, A., Marschark, M. and Clark, J. M. (1988) 'Norms for 204 Literary and 260 Nonliterary Metaphors on 10 Psychological Dimensions', *Metaphor and Symbolic Activity*, 3 (4), 191–214.

Kawakami, S. (1996) *An Introduction to Cognitive Linguistics* (Tokyo: Kenkyusha).

Kecskes, I. (2000) 'A Cognitive-Pragmatic Approach to Situation-Bound Utterances', *Journal of Pragmatics*, 32, 605–625.

Kellerman, E. (1987a) 'An Eye for an Eye', in E. Kellerman, 'Aspects of Transferability in Second Language Acquisition. A Selection of Related Papers', Published PhD Dissertation (Nijmegen: University of Nijmegen Press), pp. 154–177.

Kellerman, E. (1987b) 'Towards a Characterisation of the Strategy of Transfer in Second Language Learning', in E. Kellerman, 'Aspects of Transferability in Second Language Acquisition. A Selection of Related Papers', Published PhD Dissertation (Nijmegen: University of Nijmegen Press), pp. 89–124.

Kimmel, M. (2004) 'Metaphor Variation in Cultural Context: Perspectives from Anthropology', *European Journal of English Studies*, 8 (3), 275–294.

King, P. (1994) 'Visual and Verbal Messages in the Engineering Lecture: Notetaking by Postgraduate L2 Students' in J. Flowerdew (ed.), *Academic Listening: Research Perspectives* (Cambridge: Cambridge University Press), pp. 219–238.

Kirkpatrick, E. M. and Schwarz, C. M. (1993) *The Wordsworth Dictionary of Idioms* (Ware: Wordsworth Publications).

Klippel, F. (1984) *Keep Talking. Communicative Fluency Activities for Language Teaching* (Cambridge: Cambridge University Press).

Knudsen, S. (1996) 'By the Grace of Gods – and Years and Years of Evolution. Analysis of the Development of Metaphors in Scientific Discourse', PhD thesis (University of Roskilde).

Knudsen, S. (2003) 'Scientific Metaphors Going Public', *Journal of Pragmatics*, 35, 1247–1263.

224   *References*

Koester, A. J. (2000) 'The Role of Idioms in Negotiating Workplace Encounters', in H. Trappes-Lomax (ed.), *Changes in Applied Linguistics* (BAAL/Clevedon: Multilingual Matters), pp. 169–183.

Kogan, N. (1983) 'Stylistic Variation in Childhood and Adolescence: Creativity, Metaphor and Cognitive Styles', in J. H. Flavell and E. M. Markman (eds), *A Handbook of Child Psychology*, 3 (4) (New York: Wiley), pp. 695–706.

Kövecses, Z. (1995) 'The "Container" Metaphor of Anger in English, Chinese, Japanese and Hungarian', in R. Zdravko (ed.), *From a Metaphorical Point of View: A Multidisciplinary Approach to the Cognitive Content of Metaphor* (Berlin/New York: Walter de Gruyter), pp. 117–147.

Kövecses, Z. (2001) 'A Cognitive Linguistic View of Learning Idioms in an FLT Context', in M. Putz, S. Niemeier and R. Dirven (eds), *Applied Cognitive Linguistics II: Language Pedagogy* (Berlin: Mouton de Gruyter), pp. 87–115.

Kövecses, Z. (2002) *Metaphor: A Practical Introduction* (Oxford: Oxford University Press).

Kövecses, Z. (2004) (ed.) 'Cultural Variation in Metaphor', Special edition of the *European Journal of English Studies*, 8 (3), 263–294.

Kövecses, Z. and Szabó, P. (1996) 'Idioms: A View from Cognitive Semantics', *Applied Linguistics*, 17 (3), 334–355.

Kövecses, Z. and Radden, G. (1998) 'Metonymy: Developing a Cognitive Linguistic View', *Cognitive Linguistics*, 9 (1), 37–77.

Kramsch, C. (1995) 'The Cultural Component of Language Teaching', *Language, Culture and Curriculum*, 8 (2), pp. 83–92.

Kumaravadivelu, B. (1988) 'Communication Strategies and Psychological Processes Underlying Lexical Simplification', *International Review of Applied Linguistics*, 26 (4), 309–319.

Kurtyka, A. (2001) 'Teaching Phrasal Verbs: A Cognitive Approach', in M. Putz, S. Niemeier and R. Dirven (eds), *Applied Cognitive Linguistics II: Language Pedagogy* (Berlin: Mouton de Gruyter), pp. 29–54.

Labbo, L. (1996) 'A Semiotic Analysis of Young Children's Symbol Making in a Classroom Computer Center', *Reading Research Quarterly*, 31 (4), 356–385.

Lakoff, G. (1987) *Women, Fire and Dangerous Things: What Categories Reveal About the Mind* (Chicago/London: University of Chicago Press).

Lakoff, G. (1993) 'The Contemporary Theory of Metaphor', in A. Ortony (ed.), *Metaphor and Thought*, 2nd edn (Cambridge: Cambridge University Press), pp. 202–251.

Lakoff, G. and Turner, M. (1989) *More Than Cool Reason: A Field Guide to Poetic Metaphor* (Chicago: Chicago University Press).

Lam, W. S. E. (2000) 'L2 Literacy and the Design of the Self: A Case Study of a Teenager Writing on the Internet', *TESOL Quarterly*, 34 (3), 457–480.

Langacker, R. W. (1987) *Foundations of Cognitive Grammar, Volume 1: Theoretical Prerequisites* (Stanford: Stanford University Press).

Langacker, R. W. (1991) *Foundations of Cognitive Grammar, Volume 2: Descriptive Application* (Stanford: Stanford University Press).

Langacker, R. (1993) 'Reference Point Constructions', *Cognitive Linguistics*, 4, 1–38.

Lantolf, J. P. (1999) 'Second Culture Acquisition: Cognitive Considerations', in E. Hinkel (ed.), *Culture in Second Language Teaching and Learning* (Cambridge: Cambridge University Press), pp. 28–49.

LaPierre, D. (1994) 'Language Output in a Cooperative Learning Setting: Determining its Effects on Second Language Learning', MA thesis (Toronto: University of Toronto, O.I.S.E.).

Lazar, G. (2003) *Meanings and Metaphors* (Cambridge: Cambridge University Press).

Legenhausen, L. (1999) 'Traditional and Autonomous Learners Compared; the Impact of Classroom Culture on Communicative Attitudes and Behaviour', in C. Edelhoff and R. Weskamp (eds), *Autonomes Lernen* (Ismaning: Hueber Verlag), pp. 166–182.

LePage, R. and Tabouret Keller, A. (1985) *Acts of Identity* (Cambridge: Cambridge University Press).

Levin, S. R. (1977) *The Semantics of Metaphor* (Baltimore: John Hopkins University).

Li, F. T. (2002) 'The Acquisition of Metaphorical Expressions, Idioms, and Proverbs by Chinese Learners of English: A Conceptual Metaphor and Image Schema-Based Approach', PhD thesis (Honk Kong: Chinese University of Hong Kong).

Lindner, S. (1981) 'A Lexico-Semantic Analysis of English Verb–Particle Constructions with Up and Out', PhD thesis (San Diego: University of California).

Lindstromberg, S. (1998) *English Prepositions Explained* (Amsterdam: John Benjamins).

Lindstromberg, S. and Boers, F. (2005) 'From Movement to Metaphor with Manner-of-Movement Verbs', *Applied Linguistics*, 26 (2), 241–261.

Little, D. (1991) *Learner Autonomy: Definitions, Issues and Problems* (Dublin: Authentik Language Learning Resources).

Littlemore, J. (1998) 'Individual Differences in Second Language Learning: Towards an Identification of the Strategy Preferences and Language Learning Strengths of L2 Students with Holistic and/or Imager Cognitive Styles', Unpublished PhD dissertation (UK: Thames Valley University).

Littlemore, J. (2001a) 'Metaphoric Competence: A Language Learning Strength of Students with a Holistic Cognitive Style?', *TESOL Quarterly*, 35 (3), 459–491.

Littlemore, J. (2001b) 'Metaphor as a Source of Misunderstanding for Overseas Students in Academic Lectures', *Teaching in Higher Education*, 6 (3), 333–351.

Littlemore, J. (2001c) 'An Empirical Study of the Relationship Between the Holistic/Analytic Cognitive Style Dimension and Second Language Learners' Communication Strategy Preferences', *Applied Linguistics*, 22 (2), 241–265.

Littlemore, J. (2002) 'Developing Metaphor Interpretation Strategies for Students of Economics: A Case Study', *Les Cahiers de l'APLIUT*, 22 (4), 40–60.

Littlemore, J. (2003a) 'The Effect of Cultural Background on Metaphor Interpretation', *Metaphor and Symbol*, 18 (4), 273–288.

Littlemore, J. (2003b) 'The Communicative Effectiveness of Different Types of Communication Strategy', *System*, 31 (3), 331–347.

Littlemore, J. (2004a) 'Interpreting Metaphors in the Language Classroom', *Les Cahiers de l'APLIUT*, 23 (2), 57–70.

Littlemore, J. (2004b) 'The Effect Of Cognitive Style On Vocabulary Learning Strategy Preferences', *Iberica*, 7, Revista de la Asociacion Europea de Lengaus Para Fines Especificados (AELFE), 5–31.

Littlemore, J. (2004c) 'What Kind of Training is Required to Help Language Students use Metaphor-Based Strategies to Work Out the Meaning of New Vocabulary?', *DELTA*, 20 (2), 265–280.

Littlemore, J. (2004d) 'Using Clipart and Concordancing to Teach Idiomatic Expressions', *Modern English Teacher*, 13 (1), 37–44.

Littlemore, J. (2004e) 'Conceptual Metaphor as a Vehicle for Promoting Critical Thinking Skills Amongst International Students', in L. Sheldon (ed.), *Directions for the Future: Directions in English for Academic Purposes* (Oxford: Peter Lang), pp. 43–50.

Littlemore, J. (2005) 'Figurative Thought and the Teaching of Languages for Specific Purposes', in E. Hernandez and L. Sierra (eds), *Lenguas Para Fines Especificos (VIII) Investigacion y Ensenanza* (Madrid: Universidad de Alcala), pp. 25–35.

Littlemore, J. (forthcoming) 'The Relationship Between Associative Thinking, Analogical Reasoning, Image Formation and Metaphoric Extension Strategies', in L. Cameron, M. Zanotto and M. Cavalcanti (eds), *Confronting Metaphor in Use: An Applied Linguistic Approach* (Amsterdam/Philadelphia: John Benjamins).

Littlemore, J. (submitted) 'The Misinterpretation of Metaphors by International Students at a British University: Examples, Implications, and Possible Remedies', *The Journal of English for Academic Purposes*.

Littlemore, J. and Low, G. (in press). 'Metaphoric Competence, Second Language Learning and Communicative Language Ability. *Applied Linguistics*.

Littlemore, J. (with Lindstromberg, S., Stengers, H. and Boers, F.) (in preparation) 'Dual Coding via Mental Pictures or via "Real" Ones: Does it Make a Difference and, if so, for Whom?', in F. Boers and S. Lindstromberg (eds), *Not So Arbitrary: Cognitive Linguistic Approaches to Teaching Vocabulary and Phraseology* (Amsterdam/ Philadelphia: John Benjamins).

Low, G. D. (1988) 'On Teaching Metaphor', *Applied Linguistics*, 9 (2), 95–115.

Low, G. D. (1992) 'Can Grammar be Humanised? And Can Cognitive Linguistics do it?', in J. Kohn and D. Wolff (eds), *New Tendencies in Curriculum Development* (Szombathely, Hungary: Szombathely Teacher Training College Publishing House), pp. 113–128.

Low, G. D. (1997) *Celebrations and SQUID Sandwiches: Figurative Language and the Manipulation of Academic Writing*, Unpublished project report (York, UK: University of York). Available at http://www.york.ac.uk/depts/educ/Staff/gdl_Celebration.pdf

Low, G. D. (1999a) ' "This paper thinks ..." Investigating the Acceptability of the Metaphor AN ESSAY IS A PERSON', in L. Cameron and G. D. Low (eds), *Researching and Applying Metaphor* (Cambridge: Cambridge University Press), pp. 221–248.

Low, G. D. (1999b) 'Validating Metaphor Research Projects', in L. Cameron and G. D. Low (eds), *Researching and Applying Metaphor* (Cambridge: Cambridge University Press), pp. 48–65.

Low, G. D. (1999c) 'Teaching Foregrounding Skills in Academic Text', in L. Kasanga (ed.), *Language(s) and the New Democracy: Participation, Rights and Responsibilities* (Pietersburg, South Africa: UNIN Printing Press).

Low, G. D. (2003) 'Validating Models in Applied Linguistics', *Metaphor and Symbol*, 18 (4), 239–254.

Low, G. D. (2005) 'Explaining Evolution: The Use of Animacy in an Example of Semi-Formal Science Writing', *Language and Literature*, 14 (2), 129–148.

Low, G. D. (forthcoming a) 'Metaphor and Education' in R. W. Gibbs (ed.), *The Cambridge Handbook of Metaphor and Thought* (Cambridge: Cambridge University Press).

Low, G. D. (forthcoming b) 'Metaphor and Positioning in Academic Book Reviews', in M. Zanotto, L. Cameron and M. Cavalcanti (eds), *Metaphor in Applied Linguistics: Research Perspectives* (Amsterdam: John Benjamins).

Lowie, W. and Verspoor, M. (2004) 'Input Versus Transfer? – The Role of Frequency and Similarity in the Acquisition of L2 Prepositions', in M. Achard and S. Niemeier (eds), *Cognitive Linguistics and Foreign Language Teaching* (Berlin/New York: Mouton de Gruyter), pp. 77–94.

Lukeš, D. (2005) 'Towards a Classification of Metaphor Use', in A. Wallington, J. Barnden, S. Glasbey, M. Lee and Z. Li (eds), *Proceedings of the Third Interdisciplinary Workshop on Corpus-Based Approaches to Figurative Language* (Birmingham: University of Birmingham, School of Computer Science), pp. 27–34.

MacArthur, F. (2005) 'Observations on the Visual Interpretation of Idioms in Two EFL Texts'. Paper presented at the XXIII Congreso de AESLA, Aprendizaje y uso del lenguaje en la sociedad de la Información y la Comunicación, Palma de mallorca, March.

Mandela, N. (1995) *Long Walk to Freedom* (USA: Time Warner Audio).

Martin, J. R. (1998) 'Practice into Theory: Catalysing Change', in S. Hunston (ed.), *Language at Work* (BAAL/Clevedon: Multilingual Matters), pp. 151–167.

Martin, J. (2001) 'Meaning Making: The Grammatical Politics of Symbolic Control', Presentation at the American Association for Applied Linguistics Annual Conference in St Louis, USA, March.

McCarthy, M. (1998) *Spoken Language and Applied Linguistics* (Cambridge: Cambridge University Press).

McCarthy, M. and O'Dell, F. (2002) *English Idioms in Use* (Cambridge: Cambridge University Press).

McDonough, J. and Shaw, C. (1993) *Materials and Methods in ELT: A Teacher's Guide* (Oxford, UK: Blackwell).

McGlone, M. and Bortfeld, H. (2003) 'The Implicit Influence of Idioms', Poster Presented at the 25th Annual Meeting of the Cognitive Science Society, Boston, USA, 31 July–2 August.

McIntyre, L. (2004) Review of 'Making Social Science Matter: Why Social Inquiry Fails and How it can Succeed Again', *Philosophy of Science*, 71, 418–421.

McNamara, T. R. (1995) 'Modelling Performance: Opening Pandora's Box', *Applied Linguistics*, 16 (2), 95–115.

Miller, A. (1987) 'Cognitive Styles: an Integrated Model', *Educational Psychology*, 7 (4), 251–268.

Mio, J. S. (1996) 'Metaphor, Politics and Persuasion', in J. S. Mio and A. N. Katz (eds), *Metaphor: Implications and Applications* (Hillsdale, NJ: Lawrence Erlbaum), pp. 127–146.

Moon, R. (1998) *Fixed Expressions and Idioms in English: A Corpus-Based Approach* (Oxford: Clarendon Press).

Moon, R. (2004) 'On Specifying Metaphor: An Idea and its Implementation', *International Journal of Lexicography*, 17 (2), 195–222.

Mori, Y. (2002) 'Individual Differences in the Integration of Information From Context and Word Parts in Interpreting Unknown Kanji Words', *Applied Psycholinguistics*, 23, 375–397.

Murphey, T. (1996) 'Near Peer Role Models', *Teacher Talking to Teacher: Newsletter of the Japan Association for Language Teaching, Teacher Training Special Interest Group*, 4 (3), 21–23.

Musolff, A. (2000) 'Political Imagery of Europe: A *House* Without *Exit Doors?*', *Journal of Multilingual and Multicultural Development*, 21 (3), 216–229.

Naiman, N., Frohlich, M., Stern, H. and Todesco, A. (1978) *The Good Language Learner*. Research in Education Series (Toronto: Ontario Institute for Studies in Education).

Nakatani, Y. (2002) 'Improving Oral Proficiency Through Strategy Training', Unpublished PhD Thesis (Birmingham: University of Birmingham).

Neaman, J. and Silver, C. (1991) *Kind Words: A Thesaurus of Euphemisms* (London: Angus and Robertson).

Nemser, W. (1991) 'Language Contact and Foreign Language Acquisition', in V. Ivir and D. Kalogjera (eds), *Languages in Contact and Contrast* (Berlin/ New York: Mouton de Gruyter).

Nesselhauf, N. (2003) 'The Use of Collocations by Advanced Learners of English and Some Implications for Teaching', *Applied Linguistics*, 24 (2), 223–242.

Niemeier, S. (2004) 'Linguistic and Cultural Relativity – Reconsidered for the Language Classroom', in M. Achard and S. Niemeier (eds), *Cognitive Linguistics and Foreign Language Teaching* (Berlin/New York: Mouton de Gruyter), pp. 95–118.

Norton R. W. (1975) 'Measurement of Ambiguity Tolerance', *Journal of Personality Assessment*, 39 (6), 607–619.

O'Dowd, R. (2004) 'Intercultural E-mail Exchanges in the Foreign Language Classroom', in A. Chambers, J. Conacher and J. Littlemore (eds), *ICT and Language Learning. Integrating Pedagogy and Practice* (Birmingham: Birmingham University Press).

Otal Campo, J. L., Ferrando, I. N. I. and Fortuno, B. B. (eds) (2005), Cognitive and Discourse Approaches to Metaphor and Metonymy (Castello de la Plana: Universitat Jaume I).

Oxford, R. L. (1990) *Language Learning Strategies: What Every Teacher Should Know* (Boston, MA: Heinle and Heinle).

Oxford, R. L. (1993) 'Research on Second Language Learning Strategies', *Annual Review of Applied Linguistics*, 13, 175–187.

Oxford, R. L. (1997) 'Cooperative Learning, Collaborative Learning, and Interaction: Three Communicative Strands in the Language Classroom', *The Modern Language Journal*, 81 (4), 443–456.

Oxford, R., Tomlinson, S., Barcelos, A., Harrington, C., Lavine, R. Z., Saleh, A. and Longhini, A. (1998) 'Clashing Metaphors about Classroom Teachers: Toward a Systematic Typology for the Language Teaching Field', *System*, 26, 3–50.

Paivio, A. (1983) 'The Empirical Case for Dual Coding', in J. C. Yuille (ed.), *Imagery, Memory and Cognition* (Hillsdale, NJ: Lawrence Erlbaum), pp. 307–332.

Paivio, A. and Harshman, R. (1983) 'Factor Analysis of a Questionnaire on Imagery and Verbal Habits and Skills', *Canadian Journal of Psychology*, 37 (4), 461–483.

Paivio, A. and Walsh, M. (1993) 'Psychological Processes in Metaphor Comprehension and Memory', in A. Ortony (ed.), *Metaphor and Thought*, 2nd edn (Cambridge: Cambridge University Press), pp. 307–308.

Panther, K.-U. and Thornburg, L. L. (1998) 'A Cognitive Approach to Inferencing in Conversation', *Journal of Pragmatics*, 30, 755–769.

Panther, K.-U. and Thornburg, L. L. (2001) 'A Conceptual Analysis of English – er Nominals', in M. Putz, S. Niemeier and R. Dirven (eds), *Applied Cognitive Linguistics II: Language Pedagogy* (Berlin: Mouton de Gruyter), pp. 149–200.

Panther, K.-U. and Thornburg, L. L. (2003) 'The EFFECT FOR CAUSE Metonymy in English Grammar', in A. Barcelona (ed.), *Metaphor and Metonymy at the Crossroads. A Cognitive Perspective* (Berlin: Mouton de Gruyter), pp. 215–232.

Paribakht, T. (1985) 'Strategic Competence and Language Proficiency', *Applied Linguistics*, 6 (2), 132–146.

Patten, B. (1988) 'Hair Today, No Her Tomorrow', *Storm Damage* (London: Flamingo Publishers).

Paul, A. (2004) *The Cult of Personality: How Personality Tests Are Leading Us to Miseducate Our Children, Mismanage Our Companies, and Misunderstand Ourselves* (London: Free Press).

Perez-Hernandez, L. and Ruiz de Mendoza, F. J. (2002) 'Grounding, Semantic Motivation, and Conceptual Interaction in Indirect Directive Speech Acts', *Journal of Pragmatics*, 34, 259–284.

Perrine, L. (1971) 'Psychological Forms of Metaphor', *College English*, 33, 125–138.

Peters, T. (1994) *The Tom Peters Seminar: Crazy Times Call for Crazy Orations.* (London: Macmillan).

Philip, G. (2005) 'From Concept to Wording and Back Again: Features of Learners' Production of Figurative Language', in A. Wallington, J. Barnden, S. Glasbey, M. Lee and Z. Li (eds), *Proceedings of the Third Interdisciplinary Workshop on Corpus-Based Approaches to Figurative Language* (Birmingham: University of Birmingham, School of Computer Science), pp. 46–53.

Picken, J. D. (2002) 'Helping FL Learners to Make Sense of Metaphor in Literature', Paper presented at the 36th Annual IATEFL Conference, York, 26 March.

Pickens, J. D. and Pollio, H. R. (1979) 'Patterns of Figurative Language Competence in Adult Speakers', *Psycholinguistic Research*, 40, 299–313.

Piquer Píriz, A. M. (2004) 'Young EFL Learners' Understanding of Some Semantic Extensions of the Lexemes "Hand", "Mouth" and "Head" '. European PhD thesis (Spain: University of Extremadura).

Pitts, M., Smith, M. and Pollio, H. (1982) 'An Evaluation of Three Different Theories of Metaphor Production Through the Use of an Intentional Category Mistake Procedure', *Journal of Psycholinguistic Research*, 11 (4), 347–368.

Pollio, H. R. and Burns, B. C. (1977) 'The Anomaly of Anomaly', *Journal of Psycholinguistic Research*, 6 (3), 247–260.

Pollio, H. R. and Smith, M. K. (1979) 'Sense and Nonsense in Thinking about Anomaly and Metaphor', *Bulletin of the Psychonomic Society*, 13 (5), 323–326.

Pollio, H. R. and Smith, M. K. (1980) 'Metaphoric Competence and Complex Human Problem Solving', in R. P. Honeck and R. R. Hoffman (eds), *Cognition and Figurative Language* (Hillsdale, NJ: Lawrence Erlbaum), pp. 365–392.

Pollio, H. R., Barlow, J. M., Fine, H. J. and Pollio, M. R. (1977) *Psychology and the Poetics of Growth* (Hillsdale, NJ: Lawrence Erlbaum).

Poulisse, N. (1990) *The Use of Compensatory Strategies by Dutch Learners of English* (Berlin: Mouton de Gruyter).

Prodromou, L. (2003) 'The Idiomatic Paradox and English as a Lingua Franca', *Modern English Teacher*, 12 (1), 22–29.

Qualls, C. D. (2003) 'Contributions of Abstract Reasoning and Working Memory to Metaphor Processing: an Aging Study', Poster presented at the 5th Conference on Researching and Applying Metaphor (RAAM5), Paris, 3–5 September.

Quintilian, M. F. (1st C. AD/1920) *Institutio Oratoria*, H. E. Butler (trans.), Loeb Classical Library (Cambridge MA: Harvard University Press).

Quirk, R. and Greenbaum, S. (1973) *A University Grammar of English* (London: Longman).

Radden, G. (2003) 'How Metonymic are Metaphors?', in A. Barcelona (ed.), *Metaphor and Metonymy at the Crossroads. A Cognitive Perspective* (Berlin: Mouton de Gruyter), pp. 92–108.

Radden, G. (2005) 'The Ubiquity of Metonymy', in J. L. Otal Campo, I. N. I. Ferrando and B. B. Fortuño (eds), *Cognitive and Discourse Approaches to Metaphor and Metonymy* (Castello de la Plana: Universitat Jaume I), pp. 11–28.

Radden, G. and Kövecses, Z. (1999) 'Towards a Theory of Metonymy', in K. Panther and G. Radden (eds), *Metonymy in Language and Thought* (Amsterdam: John Benjamins), pp. 17–60.

Radden, G. and Seto, K. I. (2003) 'Metonymic Construals of Shopping Requests in Have and Be-Languages', in K.-U. Panther and L. Thornburg (eds), *Metonymy and Pragmatic Inferencing* (Amsterdam: John Benjamins), pp. 223–239.

Rakova, M. (1999) 'Cross-Modal Transfers and Theories of Concepts', Paper presented at the 3rd conference on Researching and Applying Metaphor (RAAM3), Tilburg, September, 2003.

Rampton, B. (1995) 'Language Crossing and the Problematisation of Ethnicity and Socialisation', *Pragmatics*, 5 (4), 485–513.

Reichmann, P. and Coste, E. (1980) 'Mental Imagery and the Comprehension of Figurative Language. Is There a Relationship?', in R. P. Honeck and R. R. Hoffman (eds), *Cognition and Figurative Language* (Hillsdale, NJ: Lawrence Erlbaum), pp. 183–200.

Reyes, A. (1993) *The Fatal Bodice*, D. Watson (trans.) (London: Methuen).

Reynolds, R. E. and Schwartz, R. M. (1983) 'Relation of Metaphoric Processing to Comprehension and Memory, *Journal of Educational Psychology*, 75 (3), 450–459.

Richards, I. A. (1936) *The Philosophy of Rhetoric* (Oxford: Oxford University Press).

Riding R. J. and Cheema, I. (1991) 'Cognitive Styles – An Overview and Integration', *Educational Psychology*, 11 (3 and 4), 193–215.

Ridley, J. and Singleton, D. (1995) 'Strategic L2 Lexical Innovation: A Case Study of a University-Level Ab Initio Learner of German', *Second Language Research*, 11 (2), 137–148.

Ritchie, G. (2004) *The Linguistic Analysis of Jokes* (London: Routledge).

Robbins, J. (2004) 'A Cognitive Semantic Analysis of Phrasal Verbs With 'in' and 'out' and Implications for Second Language Teaching', MA Dissertation (Birmingham: The University of Birmingham).

Robins, S. and Mayar, R. (2000) 'The Metaphor Framing Effect: Metaphorical Reasoning About Text-Based Dilemmas', *Discourse Processes*, 31, 57–86.

Rohrer, T. (1995) 'The Metaphorical Logic of (Political) Rape: The New World Order, *Metaphor and Symbolic Activity*, 10 (2), 113–131.

Rubio Fernandez, P. (2004) *Pragmatic Processes and Cognitive Mechanisms in Lexical Interpretation: The On-line Construction of Concepts*, Unpublished PhD thesis (University of Cambridge, Research Centre for English and Applied Linguistics).

Rudska-Ostyn, B. (forthcoming) *English Phrasal Verbs: A Cognitive Approach*, Paul Ostyn (ed.), Unpublished Manuscript.

Rudzka-Ostyn, B. (ed.) (1988) *Topics in Cognitive Linguistics* (Amsterdam: John Benjamins).

Ruiz de Mendoza Ibáñez, F. J. and Otal Campo, J. L. (2003) *Metonymy, Grammar, and Communication* (Amsterdam: John Benjamins Publishers).

Sakuragi, T. and Fuller, J. W. (2003) 'Body-Part Metaphors: A Cross-Cultural Survey of the Perception of Translatability Among Americans and Japanese', *Journal of Psycholinguistic Research*, 32 (4), 381–395.

Samuda, V. (2001) 'Guiding Relationships Between Form and Meaning During Task Performance: The Role of the Teacher', in M. Bygate, P. Skehan and M. Swain (eds), *Researching Pedagogic Tasks: Second Language Learning, Teaching and Testing* (Harlow: Longman).

Sayce, R. A. (1953) *Style in French Prose* (Oxford: Clarendon Press).

Schmidt, R. (1990) 'The Role of Consciousness in Second Language Learning', *Applied Linguistics*, 11, 17–46.

Schäffner, C. (1996) 'Building a European House? Or at Two Speeds into a Dead End? Metaphors in the Debate on the United Europe', in A. Musolff, C. Schäffner and M. Townson (eds), *Conceiving of Europe – Unity in Diversity* (Aldershot: Dartmouth), pp. 31–59.

Schumann, J. (1999) *The Neurobiology of Affect in Language Learning* (Oxford: Oxford University Press).

Shen, Y. (1997) 'Cognitive Constraints on Poetic Figures', *Cognitive Linguistics*, 8, 33–71.

Shortall, T. (2002) 'Teaching Grammar', Developing Language Professionals in Higher Education Institutions (DELPHI) project, available online at http://www.delphi.bham.ac.uk/modules.htm

Sinclair, J. (ed.) (1990) *Collins Cobuild English Grammar* (London: Harper Collins).

Skeat, W. W. (1993) *The Concise Dictionary of English Etymology* (original 1884, Republished at Ware, UK: Wordsworth).

Skehan, P. (1998) *A Cognitive Approach to Language Learning* (Oxford: Oxford University Press).

Skehan, P. and Foster, P. (2001) 'Cognition and Tasks', in P. Robinson (ed.), *Cognition and Second Language Instruction* (Cambridge: Cambridge University Press), pp. 183–205.

Skoufaki, S. (2005a) 'Use of Conceptual Metaphors: A Strategy for the Guessing of an Idiom's Meaning?', in M. Mattheoudakis and A. Psaltou-Joycey (eds), *Selected Papers on Theoretical and Applied Linguistics from the 16th International Symposium, April 11–13, 2003* (Thessaloniki: Aristotle University of Thessaloniki), pp. 542–556.

Skoufaki, S. (2005b) 'Cognitive Linguistics and L2 Idiom Instruction', Paper presented at the First Annual Conference on Post-Cognitivist Psychology, Glasgow, 4–6 July.

Slobin, D. I. (2000) 'Verbalized Events. A Dynamic Approach to Linguistic Relativity and Determinism', in S. Niemeier and R. Dirven (eds), *Evidence for Linguistic Relativity* (Amsterdam: John Benjamins), pp. 108–138.

Soars, L. and Soars, J. (2003) *New Headway Advanced* (Oxford: Oxford University Press).

Spiro, R. T., Feltovich, P., Coulson, R. and Anderson, D. (1989) 'Multiple Analogies for Complex Concepts: Antidotes for Analogy-Induced Misconceptions in Advanced Knowledge Acquisition', in S. Vosniadou and

A. Ortony (eds), *Similarity and Analogical Reasoning* (Cambridge: Cambridge University Press), pp. 498–531.

Steen, G. (2004) 'Can Discourse Properties of Metaphor Affect Metaphor Recognition?', *Journal of Pragmatics*, 36, 1295–1313.

Steen, G. (2005) 'What Counts as a Metaphorically Used Word? The Pragglejaz experience', in S. Coulson and B. Lewandowska (eds), *The Literal-Nonliteral Distinction* (Berlin: Peter Lang), pp. 299–322.

Stengers, H., Boers, F. and Hoorelbeke, A. (in preparation) 'Harnessing an Imagistic Style in Remembering Idioms: From L2 to L3'.

Stevick, E. (1976) *Memory, Meaning and Method* (Rowley, MA: Newbury House).

Storch, N. (1998) 'A Classroom-Based Study: Insights From a Collaborative Text Reconstruction Task', *ELTJ*, 52 (4), 291–300.

Summers, D. (1993) *The Longman Activator* (Harlow: Longman).

Swain, M. and Lapkin, S. (1998) 'Interaction and Second Language Learning: Two Adolescent French Immersion Students Working Together', *Modern Language Journal*, 83, 320–337.

Swain, M. (1995) 'The Functions of Output in Second Language Learning', G. Cook and B. Seidlhofer (eds), *Principle and Practice in Applied Linguistics* (Oxford: Oxford University Press), pp. 125–144.

Swales, J. (1990) *Genre Analysis: English in Academic and Research Settings* (Cambridge: Cambridge University Press).

Sweetser, E. (1990) *From Etymology to Pragmatics: Metaphorical and Cultural Aspects of Semantic Structure* (Cambridge: Cambridge University Press).

Szalay, L. B. (1984) 'An In-depth Analysis of Cultural/Ideological Belief Systems', *Mankind Quarterly*, 25, 71–100.

Talmy, L. (1988) 'Force Dynamics in Language and Cognition', *Cognitive Science*, 2, 49–100.

Tarone, E. (1978) 'Conscious Communication Strategies In Interlanguage: A Progress Report', in G. Brown, S. Yorio and D. Crymes (eds), *On TESOL' 78: Teaching and Learning ESL* (Washington DC: TESOL), pp. 194–203.

Tarone, E. (1983) 'Some Thoughts on the Notion of Communication Strategy', in C. Faerch and G. Kasper (eds), *Strategies in Interlanguage Communication* (Harlow: Longman), pp. 61–78.

Tarone, E., Dwyer, S., Gillette, S. and Icke, V. (1981) 'On the Use of the Passive in Two Astrophysics Journal Papers', *ESP Journal*, 1 (2), 123–140.

Taylor, J. (1989) *Linguistic Categorization: Prototypes in Linguistic Theory*, 2nd edn (1995, Oxford: Clarendon Press).

Taylor, J. (2002) *Cognitive Grammar* (Oxford: Oxford University Press).

Thompson, S. V. (1990) 'Visual Imagery', *Educational Psychology*, 10 (2), 141–167.

Todd, Z. and Harrison, S. J. (2005) 'Metaphors in Reader Discussions', Presented at the Leeds–York Metaphor Research Group, 26 May.

Tomlinson, B. (ed.) (2003) *Developing Materials for Language Teaching* (London: Continuum Press).

Traugott, E. and Dasher, R. (2002) *Regularity in Semantic Change* (Cambridge: Cambridge University Press).

Trick, L. and Katz, A. N. (1986) 'The Domain Interaction Approach to Metaphor Processing: Relating Individual Differences and Metaphor Characteristics', *Metaphor and Symbolic Activity*, 1 (3), 185–213.

Trompenaars, F. (1993) *Riding the Waves of Culture. Understanding Cultural Diversity in Business* (London: Nicholas Brealey).

Tyler, A. and Evans, V. (2001) 'The Relation Between Experience, Conceptual Structure and Meaning: Non-Temporal Uses of Tense and Teaching', in Putz, M., Niemeier, S. and Dirven, R. (eds), *Applied Cognitive Linguistics II: Language Pedagogy* (Berlin: Mouton de Gruyter), pp. 63–108.

Tyler, A. and Evans, V. (2003) *The Semantics of English Prepositions: Spatial Scenes, Embodied Meaning and Cognition* (Cambridge: Cambridge University Press).

Tyler, A. and Evans, V. (2004) 'Applying Cognitive Linguistics to Pedagogical Grammar: The Case of Over', in Achard, M. and Niemeier, S. (eds), Cognitive Linguistics and Foreign Language Teaching (Berlin/New York: Mouton de Gruyter), pp. 257–280.

Tyler, L. K., Moss, H. E., Galpin, A. and Voice, J. K. (2002) 'Activating Meaning in Time: The Role of Imageability and Form Class', *Language and Cognitive Processes*, 17 (5), 471–502.

Underwood, G., Schmit, N. and Galpin, A. (2004) 'The Eyes Have It: An Eye-Movement Study Into The Processing of Formulaic Sequences', in N. Schmitt (ed.), *Formulaic Sequences* (Amsterdam/Philadelphia: John Benjamins Publishing Company).

Upton, C. (2005) Contribution to BBC (2005).

Ushioda, E. (2000) 'Tandem Language Learning via E-mail: From Motivation to Autonomy', *ReCALL*, 12 (2), 121–128.

Vanlancker-Sidtis, D. (2003) 'Auditory Recognition Of Idioms By Native And Nonnative Speakers Of English: It Takes One To Know One', *Applied Psycholinguistics*, 24, 45–57.

Vespoor, M. and Lowie, W. (2003) 'Making Sense of Polysemous Words', *Language Learning*, 53 (3), 547–586.

Vosniadou, S. (1995) 'Analogical Reasoning In Cognitive Development', *Metaphor and Symbolic Activity* 10 (4), 297–308.

Vygotsky, L. S. (1962) *Thought and Language* (Cambridge MA: MIT Press).

Waggoner J. E. and Palermo, D. S. (1989) 'Betty is a Bouncing Bubble: Children's Comprehension of Emotion-Descriptive Metaphors', *Developmental Psychology*, 25 (1), 152–163.

Wales, K. (2001) *A Dictionary of Stylistics* (Harlow: Pearson Education).

Walker, G. (2003) 'Ice Magic', *New Scientist*, 12 April, pp. 30–34.

Walter, C. (2004) 'Transfer Of Reading Comprehension Skills To L2 Is Linked To Mental Representations Of Text And To L2 Working Memory', *Applied Linguistics*, 25 (3), 315–339.

Williams-Whitney, D., Mio, J. S. and Whitney, P. (1992) 'Metaphor Production in Creative Writing', *Journal of Psycholinguistic Research*, 21, 497–509.

Willis, D. and Willis, J. (1996) 'Consciousness-Raising Activities in the Language Classroom', in J. Willis and D. Willis (eds), *Challenge and Change in Language Teaching* (Oxford: Heinemann), pp. 63–76.

Willis, J. (1996) *A Framework for Task-Based Learning* (Harlow: Longman).

Workman, G. (1995) *Phrasal Verbs and Idioms* (Oxford: Oxford University Press).

Wray, A. (1999) 'Formulaic Language in Learners and Native Speakers', *Language Teaching*, 32, 213–231.

Wray, A. (2000) 'Formulaic Sequences in Second Language Teaching: Principle and Practice, *Applied Linguistics*, 21 (4), 463–489.

Wright, J. (2002) *The Idioms Organiser* (Boston: Thomson Heinle).

Yu, N. (2004) 'The Eyes for Sight and Mind', *Journal of Pragmatics*, 36, 663–686.

Index